Necessity Is...

The early years of

Frank Zappa

&

the Mothers Of Invention

Necessity Is...

The early years of

Frank Zappa
&
the Mothers Of Invention

by Billy James

saf publishing

S·A·F

saf publishing

First published in 2001 by SAF Publishing Ltd.

SAF Publishing Ltd.
Unit 7, Shaftesbury Centre
85 Barlby Road
London. W10 6BN
ENGLAND

www.safpublishing.com

ISBN 0 946719 14 4

A CIP catalogue record for this book is available from the British Library.

Printed in England by The Cromwell Press, Trowbridge, Wiltshire.

Original illustration: Joel Levicke

acknowledgements

Love & thanks to Charlotte, Keith, my parents & family.

Thank you to: Bunk Gardner, Don Preston, Jimmy Carl Black, Euclid James Sherwood, Roy Estrada, Buzz Gardner, Ray Collins, Art Tripp, Ian Underwood, Richard Kunc, Cal Schenkel, Mark Volman, Howard Kaylan, Ruth Underwood, Bill Harkleroad, Pamela Des Barres, Alice Cooper, Michael Bruce, Neal Smith, Bill Wood, Patrick Neve, Guilia Di Nardo-Spies, Peter Banks, Jack Bruce, Mitch Mitchell, Don Brewer, Pete Radloff, Tom Cannon, George Scala, Wayne Langston, Andy Long, Carlo Vitale, Pat Ogelvie, Tom Brown, Joel Levicke, Jeff Levicke, Robert Gray, Michael Dawson, Daniel Coston, David Porter, Steve Propes, Co de Kloet, Thomas Roos, Mike Thompson, Patrick Neve, David Tedds, Alan Vorda, Mike Raab, Mick Fish, Dave Hallbery, Michael Grey, David Walley, Charles Ulrich, Arf Society, Debra Kedabra Magazine, Ptolemaic Terrascope magazine, Society Pages Magazine, Scott Renfroe, Bob & Suzannah Harris, Greg Lamastro, Daevid Allen, Rod Martin, Jeff Wolfe, Bob Beland, Roy Herman, Alan Mcbrayer, Lawrence Lerner, Bruce Cameron, Scott Sullivan, Phyllis Hammond, Mitch Myers, Scott Morrow, Essra Mohawk, Doug Tackett, Allessandro Pizzin, Bruce Benson, James Brown, Wayne Hunnicutt, Wolfman Jack Ent., George Anderson, Barb Dye, Ron Lamana, Sando Oliva, Brian Bukantis, Lawrence Lerner, Ronnie Newman, Andrew Greenaway, Skinny Naschka, Michael Dawson, Tom Brown, Bonnie Gardner, Tina Preston, Juha Romppanen, Tim Sundog, Jan Akkerman, George Stock, Peter John, Cor Gout, Peter Frohmader, Jeff Lynch, Chris Quinlan, Ed McCarthy, Gary Gold, Marcel Safier, Gary Brown, Jerry Kranitz, Wilhelm Murg, Kevin Julie, Artemiy Atemiev, Maureen Katagan, Phil McMullen, Fred Tomsett, Wolfhard Kutz.

Special thanks to Jos Schoone for being there from the beginning.
Thanks to Scott Savage, Peter Van Laarhoven and Paul Widger for proof reading.

A very special thanks to Bunk Gardner & Don Preston whose friendship and wisdom have remained an inspiration to me these past eight years – you guys are the greatest!

author's note

It should be noted that many of the interviews in this book were conducted at varyingly different times, some before the death of Frank Zappa. Inevitably some of the reminiscences are skewed by the mists of time and are on odd occasions contradictory. In this respect the old cliché comes to mind – "If you can remember the sixties then you weren't there." To avoid over-repetition some sections have been edited, but mostly the interview material in this book remains conversational and anecdotal and true to the spirit of the conversations and interviews from which they are taken.

The material taken from the interviews contained in this book are the opinions of musicians who, variously and collectively from 1964-1970, used to be in a band called the Mothers of Invention. Under no circumstances is this book intended to give the impression that any of these musicians still consider themselves to be operating under the name the Mothers of Invention. All references to subsequent musical work reflects these musicians recording and touring as a group simply called the Grandmothers. Nor should it be inferred that this book is an authorised history of the early years of the Mothers of Invention.

Billy James

foreword

Here is the story of a bunch of strange guys who used to be in a band called the Mothers of Invention. The tales of their exploits are memories of a rock 'n' roll family that existed from 1964 to 1970. In many ways this book is like a family album. Memories of a rock 'n' roll group that broke new ground, set new precedents and shook the fabric of the rock world as it existed then. We all have to pay homage to Mr Zappa for some of the brilliant songs he composed! But the group was more than just the music. The group was, as Frank put it, "a gestalt" – not in the therapy sense, but as in the short novel *More Than Human* by Theodore Sturgeon, where he suggests that an ESP experience can be achieved by band members who live and perform together for several years.

Here was a group of people who knew the others' needs and could function as a single person without outside communication. That was the Mothers who, when performing, never knew what they were going to play next. Frank would jump up in the air to signal the beginning of a new song and when he landed we were supposed to start playing even though we didn't know what the song was. We always came in with the right one as though we all had mental telepathy – and maybe some of us did.

The freak-out sections of some of the live albums still hold up as beautiful pieces of improvisation. Also some of the humor that appeared on the first few albums came out of the early band members. Some of the innovations brought about the legendary hand signals Zappa sometimes used to add some more order to the improvisational sections. Performing with odd time signatures – some pieces every bar was a different time signature. Also being disgusting – yes folks, we were the only ones who used this type of behaviour on stage, now everybody's doing it. Our appearance, whenever we went to restaurants (except New York), all the cooks would come out to see the weird freaks.

Equipment – all the woodwinds were electric and I had a home-made synthesizer (you couldn't buy one back then) along with truck springs, brass sculptures and drive shaft gongs – not your standard keyboard equipment. I remember evenings when we only played four songs during an entire two-and-a-half hour concert, the rest of the music being totally improvised. Although the band was called a rock 'n' roll group, we could and did perform a wide variety of material from "White Port Lemon Juice" an old r&b song to "L'Histoir Du Soldat" by Igor Stravinsky. From "Jelly Roll Gum Drop" to the "The Eric Dolphy Memorial Barbeque"; an atonal piece. Zappa himself was as profoundly in love with 50s r&b as he was with atonal and 12-tone orchestral music. The rest of the band came from all walks of musical life. When he joined the band Ray Collins was a r&b singer. Roy and Jim were your basic rock bass and drums. Bunk, Buzz and myself were jazz musicians with a long history of performing experimental music. Ian played an Ornette Coleman-kind of jazz in Europe and was an accomplished classical pianist. And Motorhead was in a class by himself. Even with all these diverse backgrounds, the group developed a comaraderie that survives to this day. It was a magic group at a magic time who were brought together by a magic force. Here is their story.

Don Preston

introduction

When a strange batch of musicians called the Mothers of Invention released their first LP *Freak Out!* a whole new musical language was born. Now often seen as being part of the West Coast psychedelic music scene, the original Mothers were always something much more than that. Led by musical genius Frank Zappa, the Mothers broke every rule in the book, then created some new rules and broke them. I would probably be safe in saying that the Mothers of Invention were, and probably always will be, one of the most bizarre and outrageous bands ever to surface in rock music. Freaky looks, intense improvisations, complex rhythms, hand signals, bizarre humor, stuffed giraffes and vegetables – you name it.

Pulling together elements of improvised jazz, 1950s doo-wop, classical avant-garde and wild rock music, the Mothers really were in a musical category of their own. They welded together a music which swooped from the highly composed and structured to the unbridled and improvised. Add to this lyrics which were often sociological, highly sexual, politically surreal and just plain bizarre, then you begin to get the idea.

Undoubtedly, the composing force behind the Mothers was the single-minded visionary Frank Zappa. Later on, Zappa's Mothers became synonymous with endless collections of session musicians that the maestro would hire and fire at will, often providing little more than a backing band for his innovative and pioneering ideas. However the nucleus of musicians that formed the basis of the Mothers group from 1964 to 1970 were far from being mere sidekicks. They were a touring and recording band whose total output was very much a sum of its parts.

As well as tracing the history of the early Mothers of Invention from conception to demise, this book also attempts to throw a little light on the contributions of the other members of the band; from Ray Collins' soulful voice, to Jimmy Carl

Black's solid drumming and droll Indian humor, to Bunk Gardner's intense solo-ing variations, to Don Preston's transformations, to Roy Estrada's pachucho fal-setto, to Motorhead just being Motorhead. This, coupled with the innovative compositional ideas and strict discipline of band leader Frank Zappa, produced one of the most original rock groups ever to surface in the history of music.

Undoubtedly and sadly, from the time Zappa disbanded the original Mothers to the time of his death, relations between some of the ex-members and their former bandleader soured to a point beyond reconciliation. It is not exactly a secret that Frank Zappa was quite often a difficult taskmaster to work with, a perfectionist driven by an obsessive workaholic zeal and an intense desire to deal with the world on his own terms. This meant that few musicians got that close to him.

This book concentrates mainly on a time when the Mothers were the freakiest band on the music scene, and their leader Frank Zappa was the leering, mous-tached, budding musical genius. There are also the many and varied musical con-tributions some of the members have made since 1970, including the formation of the Grandmothers and their subsequent touring and recording.

This is not a track-by-track analytical treatise (that has been done many times over with varying degrees of success), more pertinently this biography is punctu-ated by reminiscences, interviews and pictures, past and present, which tell the story of the early days of Frank Zappa and the Mothers of Invention. Hopefully, for the uninitiated, here are signposts for the discovery of a whole new musical universe. For the fan, there are reminders and valuable background information to some of the music they know and love.

In high school my all time favourite teenage rock 'n' roll record was *Uncle Meat*. In the early 1980s I began writing a textbook on rhythmic theory (the most com-prehensive written on the subject, yet it remains unpublished). Studying Zappa's music led me to the writing of subdivision charts (the mathematical breakdown of complex polyrhythmic figures) to help illustrate some of the text. Frank was always very encouraging of my pursuit of pushing the boundaries of the education of rhythm. One of Zappa's later band members told me about a desk where Frank kept a lot of his early charts/scores, some of which had been written when he was a teenager. In this desk was one of the subdivision charts that I had done for Frank. This was, and always will be a great honor to me! This book is dedicated to the late, great Frank Zappa – a true musical genius that the world will never see the like of again. Frank Zappa is, in every sense of the word, a legend.

Throughout the 1990s I've had the great fortune of having Bunk, Don, Jimmy, Roy and Motorhead record with me on several of my Ant-Bee albums – a dream come true. It has also allowed me to collect their thoughts and reminiscences into a single volume. Since then I have gotten to know each of my favourite Mothers – some of the most sincere and truly amazing people one could ever have befriended. This book is written for anyone who has ever been in, listened to or loved the Mothers Of Invention. Don't forget your Mothers!

Billy James

 the vault

(An unfinished cruddy little imaginary play by Don Preston)

PART I

Don, Jimmy Carl and Bunk visit Bunk's vault.

Don: Well, we're on our way to Bunk's vault.

Bunk: Make sure you get the candles.

Jimmy: Bunk, I understand you've saved a lotta stuff from the old days.

Bunk: Don't I save everything?

Don: He does.

Jimmy: You do.

Bunk: I have things that are relics, some thirty years at least.

Don: Well, let's go there. There's a secret entrance here in your studio.

Bunk: Yes, I discovered behind this was an entrance to some old catacomb.

Don: We gotta go down this stairway.

Jimmy: Ouch!... ooh man, this ceiling is too low.

Bunk: Here's the opening.

Jimmy: Wow! Look at those bats.

Bunk: Now we have to crawl through here.

Jimmy: It's pretty dark in here but there are those red panties of Jo-Annes that Artie used to wear on his head.

Bunk: (whispers) Don't tell him – I stole them.

Don: Over there – that's the green paint that he used to put on his moustache.

Jimmy:	Wow! And here is his green alligator shoes – look at those Bunk. Here's that hi-hat stand we used to use at the Garrick. We would put a glove on it and pump it up and down.
Don:	Look here in this locked glass case. The original recording we made of you and Peggy!
Jimmy:	(imitating Peggy) Right there Bunk! Right there!
Bunk:	I call her Edna now – now I wonder what's in this box?
Jimmy:	How long has it been since you been down here?
Don:	Oh my God!
Bunk:	What!?
Don:	There's my beaker from the Royal Festival Hall that I drank the vile foamy liquid from.
Jimmy:	Does it have any left in there?
Don:	I think there is a little left, might as well drink it... AAAARRRGGGHHH!!!!!
Bunk:	DON!!!!
Jimmy:	He's transforming!!!
Bunk:	Oh no, we won't be able to handle him down here!
Don:	Ugggghh – I'm OK now.
Jimmy:	Its lost its strength over the years. Look... is that Ray's baby doll arm he used to scratch his balls with?
Don:	Don't touch it!
Jimmy:	Hey man...there's my old high school sweater. The one Tom Wilson wore on *We're Only In It For The Money*.
Don :	There's the bicycle that I showed Frank how to play, which he then used on the Steve Allen show.
Bunk:	And right next to it is the bicycle seat that belonged to Peachy.
Jimmy:	The one you used to sniff... I wanted to!
Don:	Well, let's get out of here.
Jimmy:	Watch your head.

THE END?

one

Occasionally fate conspires to throw together a group of musicians whose instrumental interplay sparks off in all directions, where the ingredient parts make a compound that has an almost indefinably magical quality. Within the rock, jazz and classical worlds there are many obvious examples, but few more appropriate than the early incarnation of the Mothers of Invention. From their richly varying composite parts, this group could summon up an indefinable energy. At its best, the music could dazzle the listener with its speed and virtuosity, at other times it could make people laugh along with the verbal and musical puns. And at other times it could just plain 'freak you out'!

What many of the best sixties groups had in common was a synergy achieved by constant rehearsing, improvising and redefining the structures and boundaries of the music they were playing. Many started from basic blues and jazz and then expanded outward, while others were propelled by psychedelic drugs. All were fired by the feeling of excitement engendered by the relative newness of rock music as an art form. This increasing awareness allowed many musicians the freedom to explore uncharted musical territory, but the best were those who still retained a strongly defined sense of discipline thereby regulating the final output. In the case of the Mothers of Invention this discipline was provided by the catalyst and musical genius Frank Zappa.

But the band that made up the initial incarnation of the Mothers of Invention was not a collection of sidekicks and freaks that Zappa had collected together as is sometimes assumed, but a highly individual group of musicians from differing musical backgrounds. Like many great groups, the early Mothers were as like-minded as they were diverse. Certainly this was no ordinary rock group and those that couldn't stand the strict discipline imposed by Frank Zappa were unlikely to remain in the band for long. In the end, Zappa's musical vision went farther than the original Mothers could reach. But that is getting ahead of ourselves. To investigate the original nucleus of the group requires looking back to a time before a certain Frank Zappa turned up on the scene.

Jimmy Carl Black, a.k.a. Jimmy Inkinish Jr, was born on 1 February, 1938 in El Paso, Texas. His musical career started at the age of 12 playing trumpet. He was even solo first chair in the high school band. In 1958, in Kansas, when he was stationed there as a member of the US Air Force, he started playing the drums. His musical influences were mainly blues artists like Jimmy Reed, Muddy Waters and Howlin' Wolf. But his tastes were wide-ranging, liking anything from jazz to country music. His first love remained r&b and this was reflected in the music of the first band he formed in 1962 in Kansas called The Keys.

Like many of his generation, it wasn't long before Jimmy Carl Black felt the centrifugal pull of a city with a bigger musical orbit than Kansas could provide. Being serious about making music usually necessitated a move to the West Coast or New York. In Black's case it was Los Angeles. Just two weeks after moving to California Jimmy Carl Black met up with Roy Estrada.

Estrada, a native Californian/Mexican American, was born in the heart of the conservative Orange County on 17 April, 1943. His musical apprenticeship involved picking up whatever musical flotsam and jetsam he could garner from listening to a local orchestra that practised down the street where he lived in Santa Ana. Soon he had picked up some rudimentary bass, guitar and also sang a bit. Estrada honed his skills by jamming during the weekends with friends. These fledgling musicians all treasured their Barth guitars which they had purchased from a music store called Santa Ana Music. Eventually he and a close friend formed the core of a group called The Viscounts, which was more like a small orchestra playing standards like "April In Paris" as well as Latin music with its boleros, cha-chas and rumbas. They also played many of the top ten hits of the time like Little Richard tunes or "Wolly Bully". Many of the arrangements were supplied by the trumpet player Bill Cane, who later went on to work with the Righteous Brothers.

As a sign of the times The Viscounts soon drifted more and more toward becoming a blues band. For his part, Estrada would also take part in after-hours sessions at a club called The Garden Grove. The club would re-open at two in the morning and many of the local musicians would start showing up, often playing through the night. All sorts of strange types would hang out down at the Grove, as Roy Estrada remembers. "All these heavy players from the area would show up, mostly sax players. There was one guy I think his name was Sam Galpin, he could play a trombone and a keyboard at the same time. He could play stuff like Louis Prima, it was all very Vegas." (In fact Galpin later played keyboards at various Las Vegas casinos before joining Mallard on the recommendation of Elliot Ingber. Mallard was essentially formed in the mid-seventies from the remnants of Captain Beefheart's Magic Band.)

The Viscounts continued playing a mixture of blues and r&b standards, mostly at local beer bars. When their drummer upped and quit the band to get married, Estrada fortuitously ran into Jimmy Carl Black at the local music store and Black immediately offered his services as a drummer. They decided to team up as a rhythm section and as unlikely as it might sound they even got a gig backing Neil Diamond. Roy Estrada recalls: "I remember Jim and I did this gig in a club in San Jose. Neil Diamond had just started and wasn't known then. He was breaking in some new material, and he brought along his own music score. Isn't that weird? That was an odd scene. The Indian will remember that. There was this chick... You know how PR people come around, like whenever you go on tour there's always these people that kinda show you around, that's what she was doing. She was a big chick. And the Indian had a hard-on for her. (laughs)"

With Jimmy Carl Black on board, The Viscounts adopted the equally r&b-ish sounding name of the Soul Giants and started looking around for regular places to play. Black's brother-in-law got them an audition at a club called The Broadside in Inglewood. Roy Estrada remembers how, "It was a beer bar. The atmosphere inside was like the docks by the sea. You know, they had cork and a lot of fishing nets hanging on the side of the wall – it had some atmosphere to it. They had a fireplace in the middle. It was a nice club and it had a dancing area with a stage. So we got the job, and we opened the club."

Before their first appearance at the club, the owner suggested they needed a singer and recommended one of the carpenters who happened to be working on finishing the club's interior. The carpenter's name was Ray Collins. As it turned out Collins had a soulful voice that adapted well to the soul and r&b songs that the band used to cover. Roy Estrada again: "Yeh, the thing was, that's how we got the job. If we agreed to let him sing with us then we would get the job, and we did. So we started working the club and Ray started singing with us. He did some of the songs popular back then like 'Gloria'. At that time he hadn't said anything about Frank."

Ray Collins had already come across Frank Zappa having played with him in a previous band. He recalls that, "I was living in Pomona, Frank was raised in Lancaster I believe, and he moved to Ontario. But in Pomona, there was a bar called The Sportsman I used to frequent with my friends, and I was drinking there one night. Evidently, they hired a band, and Frank's band came in there, I don't know what they were called or if they had a name or not. I heard him playing r&b stuff, which I thought was pretty bizarre because they were playing pretty obscure things. They were a four piece – bass, drums, guitar, the basics – maybe two guitars, I guess. And so eventually I just walked in there one night and asked Frank if I could sing, and he said, 'Yeah, great!' And I was just drunk, and singing 'Work With Me, Annie' and whatever – 'Earth Angel' probably, and local r&b favourites. And we talked a little bit, and I told Frank that I had got this idea for a song called 'How's Yer Bird?' from the Steve Allen saying. So Frank said, 'Oh, great idea! I have access to a studio in Cucamonga. Maybe we'll get together and do it.' So he called me up a couple days later (we exchanged phone numbers obviously) and he said, 'I have written the song, "How's Yer Bird?"' So he said, 'Would you like to record it?' I said, 'Yeah, of course,' so we went up to Studio Z and we did 'How's Yer Bird?' with Dick Barber, 'Gnarler', on snorts and vocal noises. And on the other side was 'The World's Greatest Sinner,' which was a song written by Frank, having to do, I guess, with the movie *The World's Greatest Sinner*, which Frank scored. But it didn't make the film and ended up on the B-side. We were then apart for quite a few years. Then I got hooked up with the Soul Giants in Pomona, which actually was about two blocks from where Frank and I met in the original bar."

Back in Pomona again, Collins got a job doing menial work as a carpenter and drinking away his paycheck every week. "I came upon some guys that were building a place called The Broadside," Collins recalls. "A great club, a great concept for a club – the owner had other places and packed the people in. I used to go there. And they hired a band called the Soul Giants, featuring Roy Estrada on bass, Jim Black on drums, a horn player named Davy Coronado, a singer named Dave (I've forgotten his last name) and a guitar player named Ray Hunt. Another band that that used to play there was Three Days & A Night, featuring Henry Vestine on guitar – he was in the Mothers for a while later on. So I used to get up and sing with the Soul Giants, and the club owner, Skip, liked my singing better than he liked Dave's singing, so he told the Soul Giants they could stay, but Dave had to go. I always felt kind of bad about that, actually, but you know, I wanted to sing, so I got up and sang, and became part of the Soul Giants. And then Frank soon became part of the group."

The Soul Giants line-up was a fairly fluid one. Sax player Davey Coronado amazed everyone with his ability to play two saxophones at one time in harmony. Guitarist Ray Hunt had turned up at one of the after-hours sessions at the Garden Grove. Both Jimmy and Roy had already done their mandatory National Service, though it wasn't long before Ray Hunt was drafted, so for the moment the Soul Giants were left looking for another guitarist. At least that's one version. Other reports have it that Hunt left after he and Collins were involved a fight.

Ray Collins disagrees. "Absolutely not. I never touched Ray Hunt, I don't even remember shaking his hand. I never touched him in any matter, shape or form. But he didn't like me for some reason. And he used to play the wrong thing behind me – the wrong chord-changes or something – so finally I mentioned it to Roy and Jim, because Roy and I had gotten pretty close by then. And Roy said, 'Yeah, I noticed it too.' So it all came down to the fact that Ray Hunt didn't want to be part of the band, so we just got together after the show one night, and said, 'OK, Ray, you're not doing it right – so don't do it.' So he said, 'Great, so I'm leaving.' So I said (to the rest of the group), 'Don't worry about it, 'cause I know a guy that I worked with before from Ontario/Cucamonga and I think maybe he'd like to be in the band."

Roy Estrada takes up the story. "Ray said he knew a guy who played and that his name was Frank Zappa. Ray said, 'I'll have him come in. He just got out of jail.' Supposedly he had been there for making party tapes with this girlfriend of his."

Zappa had in fact spent ten days in jail in San Bernardino County for allegedly selling pornographic tapes to the vice squad. At the time he had his own little 5-track studio which he had acquired from an electronics wizard called Paul Buff. For a while the two called it Studio Cucamonga, but when Zappa bought it from Buff with money he had acquired from soundtrack recordings, it was rechristened Studio Z. Zappa's version of events was that he had been approached by a vice squad officer acting as a car salesman who asked him if he had any pornographic tapes. They said that they wanted such a tape for a party and if Zappa obliged them with such an item they would pay him $100.

As a result, Zappa and his then girlfriend Lorraine Belcher (described in one press report as his "buxom, red-haired companion") put together a mock sex tape. Once in the hands of the authorities, the tape was deemed to be obscene and Zappa was promptly thrown in jail and subsequently received a three-year probationary sentence as well as some coverage in the local press. However, the conviction just about financially destroyed his ambitions for Studio Z and it was closed down, only to be knocked down soon after by the city authorities in order to make way for a wider road.

The experience, if nothing else, meant that as a convicted felon, Zappa could avoid the draft. It may also have indicated that there was considerable notoriety to be gained from recordings of an explicitly sexual nature. In later interviews Zappa referred to the tape as being no worse than side four of *Freak Out!*

Jimmy Carl Black remembers. "Anyway, Frank came down and tried out with the band and he liked what we did, and we liked what he did, so he joined. A month later the saxophone player Davey Coronado left the band, leaving the position of leadership wide open. Frank took over as leader, and his very words were, 'If you will play my music, I will make you rich and famous.'"

Coronado had left apparently craving the sort of financial security that being in band couldn't deliver – his subsequent job in a bowling alley was certainly more secure if hardly as exciting. At the time the Soul Giants had mainly been covering r&b material like "Midnight Hour" and "Wolly Bully". Zappa himself described them as a pretty decent bar band. But it was clear from early on that Zappa's ambitions for the group were increasingly geared towards them playing his original material, as Roy Estrada recalls. "Once Frank joined we were playing the top ten even with him. He had short hair. After a while he said he had his own songs he wanted to try out. We said, 'Sure, we'll do that,' so we started doing that in the studio he had."

Having begun to try out Zappa's compositions, the Soul Giants no longer seemed like an appropriate name for the band – no doubt it smacked too much of a bar band that played cover versions. They started toying with other names, and for a brief period apparently reverted back to an old name The Blackouts (Zappa had previously used this for one of his high school bands in the '50s). For a while they even called themselves Captain Glasspack & The Magic Mufflers. "I think he [Zappa] was asking us for ideas for our name after a while," says Roy Estrada. "If memory serves, I suggested 'Muthas', and he said, 'Ahhh, I don't like that name.' (laughs) So we forgot all about it. Later on he said the Mothers was all right."

Zappa had actually worked in a three piece called the Muthers whilst he still had Studio Z, so it is arguable who to attribute the name to. Maybe Estrada had remembered the name from then and that was why he suggested it, and more pertinently perhaps that was why Zappa was reticent to use it again. In any event, legend has it that the group formally adopted their new name on Mothers Day, 1964. With a new name and some original material in their set they swiftly began to set up a number of gigs and garner some local attention. On the whole, they were met with looks of incredulity. Nonetheless news of the notoriety of the band was beginning to spread beyond Orange County due mainly to Zappa's attempts to get to know the right people in L.A.. As Roy Estrada puts it, "Frank used to drive back and forth to Hollywood. This was when we were still in Pomona. He used to drive to Hollywood to get into the scene, to get to know people."

The scene was actually based around a fairly select and far-out crowd that referred to themselves as 'freaks'. Just like the New York hip crowd, or San Francisco's hippies and flower people, this particular scene was based around a small contingent who hung out in various local clubs and coffee houses. The leader of the L.A. freaks was a guy called Vito who held court at a 24-hour place called Cantors Delicatessen on Fairfax Avenue. Vito generally instructed people, with the help of his main sidekick Carl Franzoni and his girlfriend Pamela Zarubica (later personified as Suzy Creamcheese) on how to become a freak. Zappa would eventually coin the phrase 'freak out' and describe the act as, "A process whereby an individual casts off outmoded and restricted standards of thinking, dress, and social etiquette in order to express creatively his relationship to his immediate environment and the social structure as a whole."

One of the people Zappa first got to know on these excursions into the world of the freaks was Herb Cohen, who swiftly offered his services as manager. Cohen had a lot of useful connections and introduced Zappa to Franzoni, who was trying to make it as an underground film-maker. He was interested in using the band in a film he was shooting and as a result the Mothers were lined up for an appearance in a film called *Mondo Hollywood*. Roy Estrada recalls the event. "It was supposed to be at a freaked-out party at a house. They filmed it at this big house and that was where we met Carl Franzoni. The guy had heights [platform shoes] and long hair, and also there was Vito. That was the first time we'd seen all freaked-out people. Carl was in his tights with his long beard, and long hair, and long tongue. Vito (then in his mid-fifties) was with this young girl – I liked it. I said, 'Geez, this is too much.' (laughs) It fit perfect – they fit to the music we were playing. We were playing 'I'm Not Satisfied', I think we started doing 'Suzy Creamcheese', it was our style back then. We'd just delve into elements of what was happening at the time. It so happens those people and the atmosphere at that party in that movie was perfect. We played the songs structurally, we kinda went 'out' sometimes in between songs. I think the film was shown at the time on underground TV. The long hair movement had just started then. We started letting our hair grow in Pomona. Frank heard that that's what was going on so we started to let it grow – but not like the Beatles. We just let it grow and we were one of the first to do that."

In fact, the final version of the film had the Mothers' performance removed from it. Cohen had tried to get the group some financial remuneration for their appearance but rather than succumbing to Cohen's request, the makers cut the sequence.

With Zappa fully installed at the helm as composer and Herb Cohen as manager, it was obvious that the Mothers had a chance of realising their potential as a group. The two men made a formidable team. Zappa was full of musical ideas and influences which ranged from *musique concrete* to the garage three-chord twang of "Louie Louie", whilst Cohen with his East Coast hard-headed attitude was full of business strategies. Cohen already had some experience in both band management and promoting, as he had managed Pete Seeger and also ran a club on the Sunset Strip called The Unicorn.

Cohen quickly set about trying to get record company interest in the band. It was an ideal way for an aspiring businessman to get into rock 'n' roll. He was sure that they had a certain something even if by his own admission he was a little unsure as to what it was. Understanding Zappa's complicated musical philosophy wasn't necessary to push the group forward. Don Preston, who would eventually become the Mothers keyboardist and electronics wizard, reiterates Herb Cohen's lack of understanding towards Zappa's complex work. "One of the things I remember was that he really didn't understand the music at all and often said as much to Frank. He didn't know what the fuck the Mothers were doing – especially the weird stuff. It was just way over his head because he was a businessman, and he didn't see how that could generate business. But he had faith in Zappa, so he just went along kind of for the ride and did as much as he could. Actually, he did quite a bit to get the band happening. Herb was always well diversified, if you will, he had other interests going for him. Through the years he was always investing in other ventures – like real estate and what-have-you. Herb's always been a shrewd businessman and knows how to use the connections available to him."

At any rate, the new music scene, although initially based around a small in-crowd, had the potential to be big business. On the West Coast, the germs of the bands that were to become the Doors, the Grateful Dead and the Jefferson Air-plane were beginning to stretch their musical muscles and broaden out from the staple r&b material that most bands churned out on a regular basis.

What began to make the Mothers stand out from these other bands was that their newly assumed leader was not solely rooted in the blues and r&b tradition, or even free jazz for that matter. Frank Zappa's two main musical passions in life were the late fifties vocal doo-wop groups and the avant-garde composer Edgar Varese. The latter was a musical pioneer who as early as the twenties had utilised tape collage techniques, noise and percussion into his music. His experiments were to be the starting point for many an avant-garde classical composer of the fifties and sixties, Zappa included.

However, making music which could match that of his mentor was only a twin-kling in Zappa's eye. For the moment, the Mothers contented themselves with playing mainly r&b-based material in new clubs like The Trip and the Whiskey-A-Go-Go on the Sunset Strip in Los Angeles. As the band began to find their feet, their set became increasingly extended and numbers could last for anything up to twenty minutes. As more and more groups started to appear, so music clubs started to crop up all over the West Coast. But in L.A. it was the Whiskey (inci-dentally in the building next door to Cohen's old club, The Unicorn) which was particularly important to any aspiring band. All the record executives would drop in, checking out if there was any talent amongst all this new weird music which was beginning to happen. The smarter executives were beginning to realize that there was now a potentially huge audience for this so-called hippie or freak music. As the Whiskey's notoriety grew, so celebrities of all sorts would start to hang out there.

Roy Estrada remembers. "We started playing at the Whiskey A-Go-Go, and also that other club managed by Elmer Valentine – they were both owned by the

Mafia at the time. When we first played the Whiskey, Johnny Rivers had just finished playing a long-term contract there. We were the group brought in to replace him, and to start off nobody had heard of us." Very soon word got around that there was an interesting new group playing a residency at the Whiskey. "One time Sonny and Cher came to see us," Estrada recalls. "Another time John Wayne came in all drunk."

By this time the Mothers line-up had settled down to Frank Zappa on guitar, Jimmy Carl Black on drums, Ray Collins on vocals, Roy Estrada on bass and Henry Vestine on second guitar. Vestine was one of a succession of guitar players that joined the band's ranks at that point.

"I don't know when he joined exactly," Roy Estrada recalls. "I think he joined us at The Broadside. This was before he went with the blues. What was cool about Henry was, at that time there was no wah-wahs or volume pedals at all, so he'd do it right there with his finger. He was one of the first guys I saw who would 'mmmyeow' (mimics wah-wah) and get that sound. There was no pedal, he did it with his hand."

However, it was just as the group was beginning to get interest from record companies that Henry Vestine left. Rumours have it that Vestine was unhappy with the contract that the group was being asked to sign. However it is highly possible that being mainly a blues player (he later joined Canned Heat) he was also uncomfortable trying to keep up with some of the weirder material. In any event Vestine was replaced by Elliot Ingber who had spent some time in the army, whilst also apparently doing some recording for an Elvis Presley movie. As a result, compared with the rest of the group, he had rather uncharacteristically short hair (a fact amply demonstrated on the sleeve to the first Mothers of Invention LP *Freak Out!*).

In the end, the Mothers signed for a $2,500 advance to MGM's jazz/r&b label Verve. They had impressed the record producer Tom Wilson who had seen the band playing their residency at the Whiskey-A-Go-Go. Legend has it that Wilson had only caught the ending to "Trouble Everyday" (the Watts riot song) which featured a bluesy guitar solo from Vestine. As a result, some have maintained that the record company initially intended to promote the group as an r&b act. However, Tom Wilson who was newly installed as MGM's chief A&R man, was an astute observer of musical trends – he had already produced both Dylan and John Coltrane – and it is difficult to imagine that he saw them purely as an r&b band. Wilson was, after all, no stranger to the weirder end of the musical spectrum, having signed the Velvet Underground to the same label at around the same time. Wilson must have noted a spark of creativity beyond the group's r&b beginnings, but even he was probably surprised at the extremely different music the Mothers would go on to record. At the time, neither the music nor the group with their scruffy longhaired looks could have been thought of as being hit material. In fact, Clive Davis of Columbia Records described the band at the time as having "no commercial potential". This was soon utilized by the group as a promotional ploy and the phrase quickly became the group's motto.

Although Verve were apparently happy to let the group take whatever musical direction they liked, they were not entirely happy with the name the Mothers which they considered sounded crude. Presumably they were concerned about its increasing use in popular vernacular as standing for 'Motherfuckers'. So, at their record company's suggestion, the group added the 'of Invention'.

However, MGM's confidence in the group must have been strong enough to financially support the band's decision to make their first musical recordings a double LP – albeit in the guise of a two-records-for-the-price-of-one special introductory package. (Nonetheless, many saw this as the first double album in the history of rock 'n' roll.) Recorded at TTG Studios in Los Angeles between November 1965 and January 1966, *Freak Out!* was released on an unsuspecting public in August of 1966. What people heard was arguably the first conceptual pop LP and way ahead of its time. Frank Zappa already had a clear vision of the mixture of music and satire that he wanted to put onto record. The LP's sleeve came complete with a letter from the fictitious Suzy Creemcheese of Salt Lake City, Utah. The letter implied just what Zappa wanted to get over about the group. With its talk of bearded weirdos who all smelled bad, it almost seemed to imply that the whole thing was an elaborate joke – which of course it wasn't. Zappa couldn't have been more serious about the music itself. However, he appeared to be smart enough to realise that the Mothers didn't stand a chance in hell of gaining success in the rock world with their type of music if they came across as serious musicians. Whilst the gatefold cover (again a first for a rock 'n' roll LP) was humorous, in the studio Frank Zappa was intensely serious. As Tom Wilson described it: "Frank gave it the full Toscanini and conducted their asses off."

Jimmy Carl Black describes the experience. "I have fond memories of that record. We recorded it at TTG studios, and I think we recorded the whole thing in three days, which shows how well-rehearsed the band was. Tom Wilson, the producer, had never really met the band and was quite shocked with the material we were playing. 'Who Are The Brain Police' and 'You're Probably Wondering Why I'm Here' were the type of songs that he wasn't exactly ready for. On the last night of recording we had $500 worth of rented percussion equipment, went into the studios and invited the freaks down to record with us. That's when we recorded sides three and four. Mac Rebannac, who later became Dr John, played keyboards on the album although he didn't get credited on the sleeve; Paul Butterfield came down and played with us; Kim Fowley sang 'Help I'm A Rock' – it was a fun trip."

Ray Collins has a different opinion. "I was kind of put out by the *Freak Out!* album when I got my first copy of it and saw it as a package. I went up to Frank's house, and he wasn't home, and I wrote him a note which said, 'The Mothers are on an uprising!' – he had it on his wall for a long time. And so we came back for a meeting. But one of the things that I didn't like about the album was the fact that he put Julian Herrera's (from the Tigers – one of Collins' first groups) name like in big letters, like it was a major part of my life, or a major part of anybody's life. But my association with the Tigers and Julian Herrera had absolutely nothing to do with Frank Zappa or the Mothers."

Ray Collins remembers how the track "Go Cry On Somebody Else's Shoulder" was written. "I think I was thinking about my ex-wife, if I remember right. So Frank and I were in Cucamonga, and so I told him I had this idea about, 'Don't bother me, Go away, Go cry on somebody else's shoulder.' He said, 'Great!' So I sat down at the piano and started playing it, and Frank joined in, and we created 'Go Cry On Somebody Else's Shoulder'. And then of course, the spoken part that's on the Mothers' album, is all just ad-libbed, right in the studio, about the khakis, and the Mexican input."

As is often the case with records that are ahead of their time, the LP initially did very little in commercial terms. Zappa himself commented, "After *Freak Out!* was released it sold terribly. In the first year, it didn't do shit. It cost so much money – $20,000 – an unheard-of amount of money for that day and age. An album in those days cost $8,000 and this was a double album! I didn't care if the record companies were ready for it. I knew there were people out there who would love it if they heard it. That's why I did it. Just because there's some bimbo at the record company who doesn't understand it, that is no reason not to try and push it through. Why should a guy in a middle management position be the ultimate arbiter of taste for the American public? What does he know? What does he care?"

Even if the LP didn't set the charts alight, it was a perfect statement of its time and captured the wacky lifestyle of L.A.'s freaks, a lifestyle that Zappa later claimed had nothing to do with drugs. It seems somewhat unlikely that the freak scene based around the coffee houses of L.A. wasn't buzzing with the same kind of drug activity that surrounded the hippies of Haight Ashbury.

It is well known that Frank Zappa remained completely against the use of drugs throughout his life and the following quote was typical of his standpoint. "I don't have any use for drugs myself. I've only smoked marijuana a few times and it made me tired and gave me a sore throat. I never could understand why people liked to do that. I've never taken LSD and as far as drinking is concerned, I like wine, but I'm not going to go out of my way to be drunk all the time. I'm having a good time just like this."

In keeping with the LP's title, the group's fans now also started to call themselves freaks and the LP became an underground hit – after all, it stood little chance of being played on the radio. The whole idea of a counter culture was now spontaneously combusting up the West Coast, the epicentre being Bill Graham's newly opened Fillmore West in San Francisco. Appropriately, the Mothers were one of the first groups to play this new venue, sharing a bill which also featured Lenny Bruce who died shortly after.

Bunk Gardner, who was just about to enter the group's ranks, remembers the comic genius. "I met Lenny in 1964 at a jam session for jazz musicians. A good friend from my hometown (Ray Graziano) took me to the session along with Joe Mani, another great musician and a very funny guy. Lenny loved to hang out with jazz musicians, and talked like one. He used all the slang in those days that jazz musicians used like 'man', 'blowing up a storm', 'cool', 'bad', etc. After his gig at night he would go to anybody's house or place where there was an after hours jam session going on. I went to listen and dig his show many times when Lenny was working the Sunset Strip. Needless to say he was a very funny guy! A lot of his humor came from hanging out with jazz musicians. He would do 'inside jokes' that only guys in the band would understand. Most of the time, when I would hang out and play at these sessions, there was always 'hard' drugs being used, and that's one thing I never got into and refused to do. I saw a lot of weird stuff going on in those days as a result of guys shooting up and taking anything else they could get their hands on just to get high.

"I still put Lenny Bruce in the same category as Beefheart in that they were too far ahead of their time. Lenny broke down a lot of barriers with some of the material and language that he used in his act. It was just a little too soon for a lot of people. He spent the later part of his career in and out of court defending himself from the law and it really was a shame. Some nights he would improvise and really get a stream of consciousness going on a theme, just like a musician would, playing an improvised solo and you could tell he was 'right on'! He loved to analyze his material. It seemed to spur him on to create new material from stuff he had been using but never really developed. A true artist in the sense that he never stood idle – he always forged ahead regardless of whether it offended some people or not – especially religious people."

Ironically, in this last sentence Gardner could almost be describing Zappa himself.

Freak Out! went on to spend 23 weeks on the US chart peaking at No 130. Whilst very much in keeping with the times, it was far from being a collection of hippie anthems. Obviously with its anti-authoritarian tone, zany music and unique arrangements, here was something that the new breed of hippies could readily identify with. However, Zappa's intentions were far from the endless musical jamming mentality of groups like the Grateful Dead. Zappa's highly disciplined approach might have been in keeping with a budding classical avant-garde conductor but it was hardly what most people/musicians expected from the leader of a rock 'n' roll band. It was this misconception that was more often than not the reason why so many musicians fell by the wayside over the next few years. The first casualty was Elliot Ingber who left the band shortly after the recording of the first LP.

Roy Estrada recalls how, "One time we were playing in San Francisco, and Elliot wasn't even hooked up (connected to his amp). And he was going to town and

Frank was just looking at him (mimics Frank's disapproving look). I remember thinking, 'That's it right there – this guy is finished.' (laughs) But I swear I heard the guitar though – even though he wasn't even hooked up. Elliot was out there already, Frank just didn't know it at the time. Well... he did. As you can see Elliot blossomed into something after *Freak Out!*"

In fact, Ingber went on to form a group called The Fraternity Of Man and then played in Beefheart's Magic Band as Winged Eel Fingerling. He still plays music and now has his own home studio.

Ray Collins takes up the story. "The period I was in the band, I think that Elliot Ingber was the only person who was ever fired. He 'abused drugs', I suppose is the modern way of saying it, he maybe smoked a little bit too much, I think, and he got to the point where he didn't do the mechanics of tuning his guitar and playing on stage."

As well as being unhappy with his second guitarist, Zappa and MGM locked horns in the first of his disputes with record companies. The group was all too aware that promotion via the usual medium of radio exposure was out of the question. Zappa was convinced there were other possibilities and almost immediately started to complain about the way MGM was promoting the LP.

Herb Cohen described how, "We had a lot of very large battles with MGM. They would put out advertising copy that was totally disastrous – you know, sort of 'hep' – what they considered underground advertising. And they would say things that were so inane that it would turn off anybody. Anybody under fifty, let alone under twenty."

Not surprisingly MGM had little idea how to promote a group as wild and weird as the Mothers, but fortunately the underground press and new college magazines had a much better understanding and soon word was spreading very fast about the Mothers of Invention. However, despite Zappa's disparaging view of MGM, they must have stuck their necks out considerably in agreeing to the content and artwork to the group's first LP. In effect they had helped realise Zappa's vision of transforming the Mothers from a bunch of r&b hopefuls into a group of wild freaks whose music was an unpredictable collage of avant-garde sounds, r&b blasts, satire, improvisation and tightly structured arrangements. As a result the Mothers received considerable press attention and appeared a number of times on TV. During one notorious television performance by the band in Detroit, the group had to lip-sync to one of their songs or be thrown off the show. Annoyed by this insipid demand, Zappa instructed the rest of the Mothers to perform a "repeatable physical action, not necessarily in sync with, or even related to, the lyrics".

Ray Collins recalls: "Well, we had couches, and a picture, an actual framed, beautiful, hang-on-the-wall type picture, and chairs, and we just destroyed 'em. Just totally ripped them apart, and ripped the picture apart, just like Frank had instructed us to, with no relationship to any of the musical lyrics or changes. I think it was 'Who Are The Brain Police' that we did it to, and I recall either the disc jockey that hosted the show, or someone telling me afterwards that they were deluged with calls from irate parents, saying 'Get those guys off the air, out of town, off the planet!' We had a lot of fun."

As 1966 wended its merry way towards the musical explosions, psychedelic happenings and summer of love that 1967 held in store, so the Mothers started to launch themselves into a completely different musical orbit.

two

Following *Freak Out!* Zappa was looking to expand the Mothers of Invention to handle the increasingly complex music he was beginning to write. Most particularly he wanted a band that was versatile enough to respond to sections of free-form improvisation as well as highly complicated sections containing different time signatures. He was also keen to firmly establish his position as the group's leader and as a result began to bring in musicians with whom he had worked previously. One such person was Don Preston (aka Dom Dewild) who eventually got the job as keyboard player. The two met when Preston had attended an audition with a band Zappa had put together in the early sixties.

Don Preston recalls: "One day around 1962 or '63, I don't remember exactly when, I received a call from Frank Zappa. He was holding an audition at a club in Santa Ana and he needed a keyboard player, it was typical of the organ/tenor-sax/guitar trios that were popular at the time. So I went over to Frank's house and talked and then later we auditioned for this club. Well, we didn't get the job. We actually played 'Oh No' at the audition, which I thought was kind of bizarre because it wasn't that kind of club. During the rehearsals though, I happened to browse through Zappa's record collection and saw that he liked a lot of the same composers as I did, and that we had similar musical tastes. Several months after that I was having these open free sessions with Bunk Gardner, where we would improvise to films that I would get out of the library. I invited Zappa to come and play, so we jammed for a while. Zappa liked a lot of it and was actually in the process of starting to make films himself, so we would use some of his films to improvise on."

Zappa obviously remembered these improvisation sessions and out of the blue called upon Don Preston asking if he was interested in joining the Mothers. "By about late '65, I hadn't seen Zappa for a year and a half or so," Don Preston remembers, "and he suddenly turned up at my house looking just the way he did on those early Mothers albums, which was kind of shocking to me because I hadn't seen a lot of long hair at that time. I didn't know who it was at first. He started telling me that they were touring a little bit, and I asked if I could audition for them – which I did. But he just said, 'Sorry, Don – but you don't know anything about rock 'n' roll so you can't be in the band right now...', which was true. Right after that I started to get work in rock bands though, even went to Hawaii with one band called the Forerunners. A year or so later I was asked again to audition for Zappa's band, went down and got the job."

Donald Ward Preston (born 21 September, 1932 – Flint, MI) grew up in Detroit in a musical family. His father was a musician who had started out by playing saxophone and then switched to trumpet and was offered the lead trumpet part in the Tommy Dorsey Band. He then settled in Detroit and became the staff arranger for NBC. The young Don had sporadic lessons on the piano from the age of about five, although not from his father. When he joined the army he was shipped over to Trieste in Italy where he joined the army band which also included Herbie Mann, amongst others. He also shared a room with Buzz Gardner (Bunk Gardner's older brother), as Buzz remembers. "Don and I were roommates there. Don played some piano, so we would get together and play songs. About eight months later we got work in an officers' club with a rhythm section. Don also played bass drum and glockenspiel in the marching band. He had a creative quality that drew me to him – we even started to paint. Don was known then as 'Moon' Preston, maybe because he looked as if he was daydreaming quite often."

"In the days in the army, Buzz Gardner was like a teacher for me," Don Preston says. "He turned me on to all kinds of new composers – I'd never heard Bartok before. I learned about string quartets, Schönberg, atonal music, Alvin Berg, Anton Webern and on and on. He also turned me on to all the Russian authors plus Thomas Mann – and all these things I had missed because I quit school in the 10th grade, so I really never got exposed to that stuff. So that was kind of like a schooling for me. I learned so much from Buzz!"

Also a lot of Don Preston's army experiences revolved around music. "I suppose it was about 1951 when I started playing bass; I was over in Italy and I had these Benzedrine inhalers. I'll never forget it, they were extremely strong and I sort of did one of those and walked the eight miles into town. I went into this club where a group was playing. There was a bass stood up in the corner with nobody playing it, so I jumped up on the stand and started to play, which I'd never done before in my life. I played for, like, six hours and then walked the eight miles back to my barracks. I never did get a blister. I suppose my first band was the 98th Army band within which we formed small groups so we could jam and play jobs around Trieste. Herbie Mann was very helpful when I first started playing. I didn't even know what a bridge was, and after I learned what a bridge was I promptly forgot them a number of times."

When Preston got back to Detroit he hooked up with Elvin Jones for about a year in an after-hours club. He recalls how, "I got out of the army in 1953 and I believe I started playing bass with Elvin Jones in 1954. I started going to this after-hours spot where Elvin was working at, and the bassist was Milt Jackson's brother Ollie Jackson. He'd already been playing for four hours, so he didn't want to play anymore – he was tired. So he would play the first set or so and then I'd play the rest of the night, or up until six in the morning. Elvin was playing drums with Yuseff Lateef, Kenny Burrell, Pepper Adams – some of the greatest players ever! By that time I'd gotten so I could keep up with them (on bass) – otherwise they wouldn't have let me play. So I was able to do that for a couple years and that was probably the best experience in my whole life – musically. Milt Jackson came in and played the piano with two fingers and stuff like that – it was just remarkable."

Later on, through Elvin Jones, Preston had a chance encounter with saxophone legend John Coltrane. As Preston himself recalls: "Because I knew Elvin, I used to go over and talk with him when they [Coltrane group] were playing in town. One night when they were through playing and packing up, I cornered Coltrane. I said to him, 'I have something very important to tell you. Do you agree that everybody (in jazz and contemporary music) looks up to you as a main influence with your saxophone playing?' He said, 'I never thought of it that way.' I continued, 'I have a theory that music has evolved through time according to the natural harmonic series' – that is when you play one note and then there are all these other notes you hear – through the harmonic series. Like Mozart started using the 7th (seventh note added to a chord structure) and then they kept going to the next harmonic series (9th, 11th, 13th) all through time. I then said to Coltrane, 'The evolution of music – to change music and to play something new is the most important aspect of music. That's when music influences every other form of life – business, arts, everything. Now you've been playing and you play wonderfully and you are exemplary in the way you choose everything – except one thing – you've been playing the same way ever since you started playing with Miles. I think it's your duty to evolve and change musically.' And that's all I said. And he looked at me and went, 'hmmm – I'll have to think about that.' It was right after that Coltrane became this other person and changed his whole style of playing and everything and started playing this far-out music! So I felt I was in some ways responsible for that."

In 1958 Don Preston did a tour with the legendary Nat King Cole. "I was in a band called the Hal McIntyre band – kind of a white Count Basie band – played a lot of charts that were very similar to Count Basie. At one point, Nat had a tour going all across Canada and so of course he hired Nelson Riddle because that was the guy who wrote all of his arrangements. Well, Nelson hired our band. So we all just went and did this show and it was Nat King Cole, Connie Francis and the guy who had the dog who would never do anything – I don't know if you remember him, it's been a long time. Connie Francis was about 17 years old and someone lost a trombone part and she just about had a hysterical fit. That was around 1958."

Between the years 1958 and 1965, Preston worked with a variety of notable artists. "I played bass with Shorty Rogers. I had a duo gig in L.A. with Charlie Hayden at the Unicorn Club run by Herb Cohen, this was late 1958. Theodore Bikel owned this coffee-house and another one a couple miles away. I was playing piano there, which by the way was where I met my first wife. This was several years before Herb and Frank hooked up. So it was kind of a weird thing because I'd known Herb back then and I knew Frank as well, but separately. It all came together later on, which was how I got into the Mothers. Anyway, we played at the Unicorn for about a year and all kind of people would come by – Jim Hall, Scott Lafaro... I also formed a band back then called AHA (Athletic Harmony Assemblage) and in that band was Emil Richards and Paul Beaver."

Preston eventually moved to the Los Angeles area and started playing keyboards. Soon he developed an interest in electronic music, as he recalls. "I started to get into electronic music about 1960. I listened to Nono, Berio, Stockhausen and other composers like them." It was through his connection with Beaver (of Beaver & Krause fame), who was at that time the West Coast distributor for Moog Synthesisers, that Preston got involved with the synthesiser. "Paul had a wonderful studio full of all kinds of toys," Preston remembers, "Hammond Organs, Baldwin electric Harpsicords with their plexiglass cases, many synthesisers and other odd electronic gear. One device was the size of a briefcase. Paul claimed the Germans invented it during the 2nd World War and once filled a whole room but was now condensed to this small size. One was to sit in front of it with several electrodes connected to your body and when turned on it would crackle with tiny lightning bolts running over the surface of the circuit board. It was supposed to be able to cure you of about anything. Paul also claimed to have had sex with dolphins!"

Preston built his first synthesiser around 1966, mostly out of oscillators, filters, and tape delay. Early in the same year he joined the Mothers. As well as eventually getting Bunk Gardner into the Mothers, Preston witnessed the procession of guitarists that would run through the early line-up. "Right before *Freak Out!* was released I joined the Mothers. At first it was just the basic band – Ray, Roy, Jimmy, myself and Frank. Zappa always had another guitar player because at that time he couldn't play guitar very well. So he always had a really good guitar player in the early group like Henry Vestine and then Elliot Ingber – both those guys are monster players. Even when I joined the band there was some guy, I don't know who it was to this day, but he had like lightning fingers. But he was very, very straight looking and he really didn't fit in with the band. He didn't really know any of us and we never got to know him – so he disappeared real fast. I think Jim Fielder got into the band – when he first joined the Mothers he played guitar. Then I got Bunk into the band."

It was through Don Preston, that Zappa brought in woodwind player Bunk Gardner, who had also been part of the improvisation sessions that had taken place in Preston's garage. Not a native Californian, John Leon Gardner (born 2 May, 1933 to Thema and Charles Guanerra – why his dad changed their name to Gardner, Bunk still doesn't know) was the second of three children and grew up in Cleveland, Ohio. Like Preston, he started his musical education by learning piano at the age of five or six years old. "The lessons were right down the same block, West 95th Street," Gardner remembers, "and my piano teacher's name was Elmira Snodgrass [savours the name for a few moments] – she was cute. She used to give me little stickers when I'd played a good lesson. I took lessons from Elmira for at least two or three years, and then went on and took lessons from a couple more teachers – I guess in all, I had five or six years of piano lessons right up until I started junior high school. Incidentally, I gave my daughters Zoe and Zena violin and piano lessons. I also gave Zoe clarinet and flute lessons as well. I still do private teaching of piano and woodwinds at St. George's Academy in Laguna Hills, Orange County.

"As far as my earliest musical influences," Gardner muses, "well I guess having an older brother certainly helped. So, from a very early age I was listening to Charlie Parker, Dizzie Gillespie, Miles Davis and all the jazz greats. At the same time I loved classical music. It all had an influence on me. Rock 'n' roll didn't have too much appeal at all. When I was in elementary school, aged seven or eight, they came around the class and asked what instrument you wanted to play. My brother was already playing trumpet, so I said I'd play clarinet, maybe because I sucked my thumb until I was 12 years old and needed something to replace my oral fetish about sucking. Then later on in Junior High School I got my first tenor sax (a silver and gold Martin) – what a beauty! Then right into High School I started a combo with my brother. We'd play Stan Kenton arrangements and mix some be-bop jazz at dances. While still in High School I started to play bassoon and got a scholarship from the Cleveland Institute of Music, and eventually started to play professionally with the Cleveland Philharmonic Orchestra.

"Right after school, the Korean War was on," Gardner continues, "and I enlisted in the army by taking an audition on bassoon at Fort Knox, Kentucky. There I got my first culture shock of the difference between the North and South. Segregation between blacks and whites was in force in Louisville, Kentucky and in the army as well in Fort Knox. There was the white army band and the black army band and it was a complete surprise to me. The white band training unit was right next door to the black army band, which by the way had the Adderly Brothers, Junior Mance and a host of great black musicians. There were jam sessions almost nightly and I had some great experiences from that period in my life. After band training, I was sent to Europe and at that time all musicians were sent to Dachau, Germany before they were sent out and assigned to a specific band. I ended up in Stuttgart, Germany where we had a nice jazz combo that played at the Officers Club, which was fun. Also, every Sunday I was in a dixieland band that played a live radio broadcast, which was interesting. In my last year in Europe I would visit my brother on a three-day pass in Paris, France. Buzz, after getting out of the army, went back to Paris and was going to conservatory school and gigging around town and speaking decent French. After the army, in 1955, I went to Baldwin Wallace Conservatory of Music to get my BA. I did a lot of gigging and teaching until late 1955. Then Buzz and I decided to move to California and be with the big boys in the jazz world."

Having decided to move to Los Angeles to start their musical careers there, Bunk's first taste of recording came in the late 1950s – on an LP called *Themes From The Hip* on the Roulette label. The LP was made up of jazzy versions of TV themes of the day; like the theme from *Gunsmoke*, *Wagon Train*, *The Lone Ranger* and *Colt 45*. Bunk was featured on quite a few numbers, playing flute and tenor saxophone.

Having been in the army together, Buzz and Don met up again in 1960 or so and the three of them started to do some musical things together. Bunk Gardner remembers, "Don Preston had a projector set up in his garage and we would improvise on our instruments to the various collages he flashed up there. Frank made an appearance at one of those sessions. He brought his own music, of course – it was a no-holds-barred, do whatever you want kind of set-up, and from those sessions quite a few things evolved. I remember Don showing Frank how you could get quite a lot of different tones out of a bicycle wheel by putting differing tensions on the spokes and playing it with drum sticks. I can vividly remember going down to one of those TV stations to audition for a talent contest. My brother and myself, Don, Frank and a couple of other guys auditioned down there doing all these weird things for the people. They couldn't believe our band. I can remember seeing them calling everyone in to watch and hear us. Certainly we were dressed a little bizarrely. Frank was blowing through bicycle handlebars, getting all these weird harmonics and banging on bicycle spokes – that was one of our first encounters with the public. We did quite a few other things together, but then Frank moved to Cucamonga and started his own little band with Ray Collins, Jimmy Carl Black and Roy Estrada. It wasn't long after that that he started the Mothers and recorded *Freak Out!*"

Don Preston remembers the same event. "Somehow Frank's dad had a connection at ABC and we got to audition for this show. We got in there and we were doing this really weird shit. All the musicians that were on the television lot all came in and like stuck their heads around the door, and they couldn't believe their eyes. We were playing this really outside music – of course nothing ever came from that audition."

Consistent with the demanding musical taskmaster that Zappa was becoming, he also put Bunk Gardner through his paces before asking him to join the band. "I can remember going to Frank's house and spending just about the whole day auditioning for him," Gardner recalls. "He kept handing out music for me to play, 'play this – how fast can you play this?' I played my saxophone and soprano, I played my clarinet, I played my flute, my alto flute, my bass clarinet and I played piano, it was just one thing after another. At one point he said, 'Well, we've got some dates coming up and might be touring, do you want to join the band?' This would be late 1965, early 1966. We started right away by recording *Absolutely Free*."

With this strict auditioning process, the band was beginning to mutate into a 'rock big band' or 'an avant-garde orchestra of weirdos' depending on your interpretation. A mixture of both would be as accurate as any definition. Certainly as a rock big band, the Mothers avoided the starchy riffing of the Stan Kenton-influenced jazz-rock big bands like Blood Sweat & Tears and Chicago. Likewise, the avant-garde explorations were never as anarchic as the likes of Ornette Coleman. But by encouraging his new players to improvise wildly in the style of free jazz players, Zappa steered the band away from appearing too classically avant-garde, and by including satirical versions of rock standards like "Hound Dog" he ensured that the band was never too far outside the bounds of rock 'n' roll. In truth it was a clever balancing act that was probably as intuitive as it was calculated.

What seemed to concern Frank Zappa the most was the increasing differential in his band between the new band members who could read music and were capable of interpreting his increasingly complex arrangements, and those who could not read music and therefore had to learn the material by tedious repetition. As Bunk Gardner explains, "It was an experience that I really didn't expect in the beginning when Don Preston and myself joined the band, because we spent so much time rehearsing the music and memorising everything that was written out that I wondered, 'When does the fun begin? And where is all the money that we're supposed to make?' Later on we certainly did have fun along with a lot of hard work and bizarre experiences and partying from 1966 to 1970.

"Frank Zappa was not a particularly easy guy to work with for many reasons," Gardner continues. "He was definitely a workaholic who could rehearse hour after hour after hour and then make a critique and criticise all that hard work, and also display a complete intolerance for anyone making a mistake while playing his music. I can still remember him walking around in a rage after many concerts because someone fucked up and made a mistake, which Frank said was a lack of concentration and not being tuned into him. Still, everyone in that band got along with each other quite well and we all have memories that we'll cherish for the rest of our lives."

Rehearsals became more like mini-marathons. A minimum of eight hours was always expected from his musicians, and most of the time it was at least 12 hours. "I always had my notebook and manuscript paper to take down notes and rhythms," notes Bunk Gardner, "but on a day-to-day basis the music always changed. Because the rest of the band, other than myself and Don, could not read music, repetition was very necessary to memorise and retain all the notes and to remember the repertoire. Frank was always changing notes from one person's part to another, and changing the arrangements as he saw fit. So if there were any personnel changes then usually notes and arrangements changed. Nothing stayed constant. Parts were expected to be practised and learned before the rehearsals, so we could really make progress when we were together! Give Frank a cup of coffee and a pack of cigarettes and he would forget about time and food – and go on, and on, and on. It was exciting and very consuming – my whole life, 24 hours a day, was into the band. There was no reading music on stage – everything had to be memorised and as I've already said Frank did not tolerate mistakes!"

The difficulty of learning the material was compounded by that fact that the group's repertoire was enlarging with new songs like "Anyway The Wind Blows", "Absolutely Free", "Motherly Love", "Hungry Freaks Daddy", "I Ain't Got No Heart", "Status Back Baby", "Electric Aunt Jemima", "King Kong" and "Help I'm A Rock". For jazz musicians like Bunk Gardner it was a huge learning experience as he'd never really played rock music before.

"I could see how Frank put a song together," Gardner explains. "He would sometimes get on the drum set and demonstrate the kind of beat that he wanted in a particular section of music. He would then play a couple of passages of 5/8 (rhythm) to 7/8 and show how he wanted it played. I had never played odd time signatures before and it was not easy to do at the speed he wanted it played sometimes! It was all a learning process for everyone because most of his songs were weird with hard rhythms and required total concentration. Frank had a habit of jumping up in the air in the middle of a song and coming down and then starting another song. He expected you to know what song he would go into. Mental telepathy was part of his focus as far as total concentration for playing his music. Everywhere we went, rehearsals were part of our daily routine – sound checks and rehearsals."

"From that daily routine came nights that I considered magic," Gardner continues. "Where everything came together unbelievably great! But then there were nights where everyone took turns making a mistake, including Frank! Up to that point in my life I had never played with a band that combined humor, weirdness and avant-garde music together. With all that going on, you also had to master all the hand and finger signs that Frank would throw at us. If he held up 5 or 7 fingers, it meant for the rhythm section to play a 5/8 or 7/8 rhythm (in correlation to the number of fingers held up.) If he held up his index and little finger it meant vocalize with a 'blahhhh!' Frank was really into hand and finger conducting the band."

In the beginning, rehearsals were held at the Lindy Theatre on Wilshire Boulevard, near the corner of La Brea Ave. It was a beautiful place and had a huge backstage area with enough space for the band's equipment and instruments. Bunk Gardner remembers that, "The Carnation Company restaurant was just minutes away on Wilshire Boulevard and usually we would go there to eat on our only break from rehearsing. Just about everyone in the band was finding it hard to make ends meet financially. We were not getting paid to rehearse, so money was tight. We were all ready to hit the road so we could make money for food and gas at least, and to get away from this schedule of rehearsing 8-12 hours a day, every day of the week! Jim Fielder was playing rhythm guitar, but he really was a bass player originally. He was not too happy to be in Zappa's shadow playing guitar. So as soon as we got to New York, Jim got a job playing with the Buffalo Springfield and then eventually got the job playing with Blood, Sweat & Tears."

Don Preston explains how, as a leader, Zappa set himself apart from the rest of the group. "I think there was a psychological thing that he did, that he chose to be that way so that he would be the leader. And he was tough on people on occasion. On the other hand, he had a great sense of humor, and was always breaking up at various things that we did. We found ourselves doing things just to make him laugh. Also, Zappa was a very powerful person, and he demanded perfection. Sometimes we weren't capable of giving it to him, but sometimes we did."

"As far as learning a song went," Preston continues, "there was no method untouched. Sometimes he would pass out music; sometimes he would just show us the song note by note. Sometimes we would figure out ways of improvising with various hand signals and other things. Sometimes we'd play a concert and we'd play for two-and-a-half hours, and we'd only play three songs! Because from all the intense rehearsing the band was so in tune with one another that we could do that. We would never have a set list. We always had to start the right song in the right key and the whole thing, and we got so we could do that. It was conditioning. But you have to remember that we rehearsed for six months, eight hours a day non-stop, including Christmas. Right through New Year's Day, every day of the week. That was the kind of loyalty that he would demand. 'If you don't want to do it, then don't be in the band.'"

"Even after rehearsing, I'd have to go home and practise some of this stuff," Gardner recalls. "There are things you can play, let's say, on guitar, and if you write it out and try to play it on another instrument, your fingers fall off. Frank would write things where there was no place to breathe. And there were things technically that I had to work out that were just mind-boggling."

With the limited recording equipment that was available in those days, it was testament to both Zappa's compositional and arranging skills, as well as the Mothers' instrumental skills, that the records turned out as well as they did. Zappa's long-time friend, and early Mothers roadie, Euclid James 'Motorhead' Sherwood recounts. "Actually recording sessions were just a lot of work. You'd go in and play your music, and Frank would stay back and engineer. I'd go in with Frank a lot of times to help out on the engineering. The early years, when the band had just started, recording studios weren't as good as the more recent ones. The only good thing about those was that you'd go in and they'd smell like a bar. There'd be booze all over the place, cigarette burns on the counter. They had funky old microphones. Everybody stood behind these little cages. These days, there's not a whole lot to doing sessions. Someone comes in, lays down their tracks and leaves. You'll have the drummer and bassist go in and lay down the basic tracks, then the guitarist goes in to lay down solos, then you'll have horns or vocals or whatever. Nobody even goes in at the same time anymore. The only really interesting things that I had with recording was in the very early days with the Omens. We'd go into the studio, and everyone would set up and play in one room, with the singer off in a booth, with a window where he could look out. While we were playing, I'd have to give the singer signals to tell him when to start singing, and when to stop. They only had a couple of mics that they set up and we all jammed at the same time."

By November 1966 the Mothers line-up had expanded considerably. The nucleus of Frank Zappa, Jimmy Carl Black, Ray Collins, Roy Estrada, Don Preston and Bunk Gardner had now been joined by a second drummer, Billy Mundi, and former roadie Jim Motorhead Sherwood. Of all the Mothers in the new line-up, Sherwood (born 8 May, 1942 in Arkansas City, KS) had actually known Zappa the longest, having been an old schoolfriend. Jim Motorhead Sherwood remembers how, "Frank used to sit out on the front lawn at the high school when I was a freshman and he had this old beat-up guitar. It was an old acoustic, with the frets really high. It had been in a fire and was all burnt up. I think his uncle gave it to him. Frank used to sit out and play guitar most of the time, because he was in his sophomore year (second year) and he didn't have any classes."

Sherwood soon found out that Frank's brother Bobby was in one of his classes. "Bobby found out that I collected blues records and he introduced me to Frank," Sherwood continues, "and Frank and I sort of got together and swapped records. This was in 1956. Frank had a band at the time called the Blackouts. I went over and saw them at the Moose Lodge or something, but the group disbanded right after that. Frank and Bobby moved down to Ontario, and he would come up for 'battle of the bands' all the time. It was kind of a kick. It was mostly involved with swapping records. Frank was working at the record store, and we'd go down and try to get all the blues records we could before Frank got hold of them."

Motorhead first became reacquainted with Zappa and involved with the Mothers when they were starting as a band and were playing at the Whiskey-A-Go-Go and other clubs around the Los Angeles area. He would go down and jam with them at certain clubs. He appeared briefly on *Freak Out!* just making sound effects on some of the songs. Because of the unusual sounds he could achieve from the saxophone, Zappa subsequently asked him to join the Mothers as a band member performing odd atrocities on stage during their performances. He also became master of a unique vocal stylisation known as the snork. Motorhead says that, "The snorks were actually Dick Barber's [the Mothers road manager] idea. He came up with that stuff. It's just a nasal thing. You just sort of snort through your nose, sucking air in through your nose. Dick Barber did that for a while on the road. I don't remember exactly how that started, but Frank wanted us to make some sound effects."

Although christened with the rather distinguished name of Euclid James Sherwood, his nickname Motorhead predated his involvement with the Mothers, originating while he was hanging out with Frank Zappa and Ray Collins. As Motorhead explains, "That actually came from Ray Collins. Frank had Studio Z in Cucamonga in Ontario, and I'd go down and do a little jamming with them every once in a while. I even lived in the studio with Frank for about six months. Frank and I would get a lot of people over there to do things, and he knew Ray Collins who would come over and sing. Ray was always joking with me because I was working on cars and trucks and motorcycles. He would say, 'It sounds like you've got a little motor in you head,' so they just called me Motorhead and that seemed to stick. I've been called that ever since."

Motorhead joined with all the other Mothers as they convened in November 1966 at TTG studios in Los Angeles to record the group's second LP *Absolutely Free*. The LP was recorded in an amazingly brief 25 hours over 4 sessions – unsurprisingly, the group's recording budget had been cut from the amount they had received from MGM for the *Freak Out!* album. Because of this fact, the production suffered to some extent with all the vocal parts being recorded in one session. As Frank Zappa recalled: "One day with 15 minutes per tune to do all the vocals on that album. That's right. It's called 'sing or get off the pot'." Even so, in typical grand style, the idea was that the music was intended to be part of two rock musicals entitled *Absolutely Free* and *The MOI American Pageant,* much of which was to provide the basis of the music that the band played at subsequent concerts. "I remember that we recorded *Absolutely Free* at TTG Studios on a four-track," says Don Preston. "I'm pretty sure that's what it was. I certainly remember that it took an unbelievable amount of takes – every eight bars we would do about 28 takes, because there would always be something wrong. The whole band was playing live and since about half the band couldn't read music and were playing from memory, there would be a lot of mistakes made. We would just keep going over and over stuff. Since you only have four tracks, you have to kind of play it live."

Just as they had invited an array of guest musicians to play on *Freak Out!* so *Absolutely Free* featured Jim Fielder on guitar, while Bunk Gardner's friend, John Balkin, played acoustic bass on a few songs. Balkin had played with the St. Louis Symphony and also Tim Buckley. Don Ellis played trumpet on "Brown Shoes Don't Make It", one of two songs, the other being "Call Any Vegetable", which were written in Hawaii just before *Freak Out!* came out.

Bunk Gardner remembers how the album was put together. "I was really excited about my first recording session with Frank and the band. Tom Wilson was the producer. The studio was a fairly big studio, but it was always crowded with people hanging out! I had all my horns there – tenor and soprano saxes, flute, clarinet, bass clarinet and bassoon."

Ray Collins recalls that, "Frank had this beautiful tune called 'And Very True,' and when we went in to record it, being a little crazy at the time, I just ad-libbed on the spot. The original lyrics I think were something like 'Moonbeam through the night,' something very loving, although Frank didn't like love songs. And I changed it to, 'Moonbeam through the prune, in June, I can see your tits.' I just made it up on the spot. So later, after we recorded it – you can hear Frank cracking up on record – it was fun. In fact, that's my favorite Mothers album, the *Absolutely Free* album. So later, after we recorded it, I told Frank, 'Well, you know, I just made up those lyrics as we went along, so if not money, I should at least get album credit for it.' I didn't say, 'Don't pay me'. So he says, 'Well, just tell me what you want to put on the album.' And so a couple days later, I said, 'Well, just put Prune: Ray Collins.' And he added the 'Side 3' part. That was out of his own mind." [There is a credit in the *Absolutely Free* album that says 'side 3 PRUNE: Ray Collins'.]

"'Call Any Vegetable' was a favourite of mine," says Bunk Gardner, "because I always got to play a solo and usually a long one. I had a King Soprano that only went up to a concert high D – most sopranos now go up to a high concert E flat. Anyway on take one, Frank played a long solo and then gave me an even longer one – it really felt great. The band was cooking and I was really pumped up and just kept playing and playing. Frank finally came back in and we took it out to the end of the song. Frank went into the control booth to listen to the playback. I thought it sounded great and I loved my solo! Then Frank said, 'Let's do another take.' So we went back out for take two. I didn't think we captured the excitement so well the second time, but I think Frank thought he played a better solo on take two. So that's the one that ended up on the album."

Gardner's multi-instrumental talents were fully on display on the LP, playing bassoon on "Duke Of Prunes" and getting his soprano out for "America Drinks and Goes Home". Gardner describes the latter as, "a kind of a corny jazz version. I remember a lot of people making noise and the cash register going off every couple of seconds. There was a lot of simulated drunk crowd noise. It took a few takes before we got it right. Ray's ad lib for the end section was great – it just fit perfectly. 'Brown Shoes Don't Make It' and 'Status Back Baby' were both tenor sax tunes for me. I had a little solo on 'Status Back Baby' – but 'Brown Shoes' was the real hard production number that had to be done in sections, and then put together. It is still a hard song to play live on stage."

On occasions the group still stuck close to their rock 'n' roll roots. Don Preston recalls how, "Most people, when they hear the version of 'Plastic People' on the *Absolutely Free* album think it doesn't bear any resemblance at all to 'Louie Louie', but that's how it started out – as 'Louie Louie' with 'Plastic People' lyrics. Then when we recorded it, Frank completely redesigned the song and made it completely different."

Absolutely Free remains a favorite album for fans, and particularly the band themselves. Bunk Gardner considers that, "this album represented some of Frank's most creative and original writing. I do remember in the early days that most of the time Frank was always writing wherever we went. As soon as he would write something or finish writing something he would bring it over and ask, 'Can you play this?' A lot of the time after I would play the piece he'd ask, 'How fast can you play it?' Anyway, I thought *Absolutely Free* was a classic – a mini-masterpiece."

If recording the album was difficult, there was also the problem of how to recreate its complex material live. "It's one thing to record an album," Gardner explains, "but when you go on the road and have to play all the songs on the album, the orchestration really requires some thought as to how to utilize the band and get this big sound with just seven guys! Especially when the repertoire was always changing. When I look back at some of the song titles I can't really place the song in my memory. Frank changed the names of the songs many, many times. When we first started rehearsing at the Lindy Theatre I remember a lot of the melodies that later Frank changed the titles of. Like 'Transition' later became '20 Small Cigars', and 'Never On Sunday' became 'Take Your Clothes Off When You Dance.' In the beginning the repertoire was maybe 20-30 songs, but because we rehearsed so much and so long, that list continually grew week by week."

The reason why the album's finishing touches were done in New York was because the band had taken the step of trying their luck on the East Coast. They started off in December by playing at a place called The Balloon Farm in New York, which along with a place called The Dom had become the places to be seen.

Celebrities like Andy Warhol would regularly hold court, often going out to see bands like his protégés The Velvet Underground. Much of the central focus of these New York happenings were based around the gay scene, or as Jimmy Carl Black puts it: "That was the first time I'd ever been exposed to gay people. These guys pinched me on the ass and I didn't like it."

To their surprise New York audiences immediately took to the Mothers with perhaps even more fervour than the West Coast hippies. Perhaps New Yorkers with their tougher, more abrasive sense of humor were more receptive to the group's brand of satire having been softened up by the likes of comedian Lenny Bruce.

Later, Zappa in his usual fashion summed up the typical Mothers' fan as "a boy, 18 years old. He had acne. He was Jewish, came from Long Island or its equivalent, was extremely lonely. He was alienated from his parents. He was worried about his glands, the war, being drafted, you-name-it. Insecure. He needed a friendly big brother image to emulate."

In any event, by Xmas 1966 instead of returning to L.A., the band's engagement at The Balloon Farm was extended and they went on to play a memorable concert there on New Year's Eve. Don Preston remembers: "That night, New Year's Eve, The Fugs came to the concert. I knew them several years before when they all stayed at my house for several days. They would distract a champagne vendor and steal several bottles and send them up to the band while we were playing. That night Allen Ginsberg came on the bandstand and brought in the New Year. I also remember Andy Warhol being in the audience that night, and when someone introduced him to me he gave me the once over. I didn't know whether to feel flattered or insulted."

Although successful, it was remarkable that a certain member of the band made the concert at all, as Jimmy Carl Black recalls. "The afternoon of New Year's Eve we were coming back from rehearsal. Roy had been up for about three days and a blast of wind hit him and knocked him on his ass. Man he fell flat on the sidewalk. Then he came back to the hotel and fell asleep, and we couldn't wake him up to go to the gig. Then Bunk said, 'I've got a couple of uppers Roy,' and his eyes came wide open. That's the night he was making it with that chick and he bounced right out of the bed onto the floor. He was laughing so hard he couldn't get up. She was kind-of propped up on the side of the bed, her tit hangin' out saying, 'What are you doing down there?'"

"While living in New York I got a large jar of uppers which were all different colors – red, green, brown, and yellow," Gardner remembers. "Roy would love to try and decide which ones to take and recount them over and over again. Being on the heavy side, Roy was always concerned about his weight. In the early days his weight was around 175lbs, but slowly it started to climb up and over the 200 mark. I think that was one of the reasons why he liked speed so much because it helped to keep his weight down. Roy also denied everything – 'I didn't do it' was one of his favourite phrases."

"I remember the bottle of tri-coloured uppers," says Roy Estrada. "Even before we got there I'd empty out the jar and I would separate the colours – it was brown, red, yellow... I loved the colours. (laughs) I must have fallen asleep during one point in the show that night. It had to be sleeping, because I remember starting one song and then before I knew it I was ending a different song. I had to have fallen asleep. (laughs) That was weird. I asked Frank if I missed anything and he said, 'No, you were all right,' – apparently I didn't miss a note. (laughs) But I could always get Frank pissed off at me."

"Roy Estrada was one of my favourite guys in the band," Bunk Gardner says, "and always provided the humor for Frank and everyone else. Jim Black and Roy were always doing their thing which could be like stuff that nobody else could understand – like making faces at each other or just speaking a little Spanish in Pig Latin. Roy had a liking for speed and coca-cola and never seemed to sleep. Sometimes he would get down about himself, and his self-esteem at times was not very high. Mostly this involved his inability to perform up to Frank's expectations. He would say, 'I'm just a dumb Mexican who can't read music.'"

"He was always taking things apart or putting something back together again or re-tuning his bass," Gardner continues. "One night in Toronto, Canada, Roy took the air conditioning system in his hotel room completely apart. He then cleaned it and put it back together again. Another time Roy got caught peeking into one of the transoms in one of the rooms by the lady that owned the boarding house he was staying at while we were in Montreal. The owner moved Roy right next to her room so she could keep an eye on him."

Estrada, for one, was at times oblivious to Zappa's insistence that the group remain drug free. Being the sixties there was a lot of drugs around, both for recreational use and increasingly as compositional aids. Drugs were inextricably linked with the whole pop music culture that exploded around the mid-sixties in America. What drugs a band were into tended to define the type of music they produced. The Velvet Underground's music was clearly constructed from a familiarity with heroin and amphetamines, whilst The Grateful Dead's music was just as clearly linked with LSD and marijuana.

As the Mothers were often linked with the psychedelic scene it was assumed that because of the type of weird music they played the Mothers were generally taking all sorts of drugs. If they were, Zappa probably wasn't aware of it and most certainly wasn't joining them – preferring caffeine and nicotine to anything stronger. Clearly, with a mind as intelligent and creative as his was, he was in no need of hallucinogenic assistance. Ever the consummate professional Zappa had no time for the sloppiness that indulgence in drink and drugs brought out in musicians.

Don Preston explains: "Although the band wasn't drug free, we weren't over indulgent. I made a rule for myself to never take acid more than twice a year. And when I did I made sure the environment was safe and non-threatening. This was a valuable learning experience as later on I sat up with a number of people who were freaking out, and I reassured and guided them through their experience." This is confirmed by Bunk who recalls running into a person years later that told him, "Don Preston saved my life when I went through a bad acid trip!"

Ray Collins recalls another incident that epitomised Zappa's view of drugs. "When we were getting ready to go on tour, we were all in a waiting area ready to board a plane, and Frank had just just delivered a monologue to the guys in the band on why they should not smoke or take any drugs with us, and not to smoke on tour, and all this same old stuff, not to do it. I didn't smoke a lot – just occasionally when I was with the band, but I didn't smoke regularly, or take any kind of drugs regularly. So after he gave this 'talk' to everybody, we were in the airport, waiting to board a plane to go on tour, and he was sitting down, drinking a cup of coffee, and Billy Mundi was standing near him, reaching into his shirt pocket to pull out his cigarettes. Next to his cigarettes he had a marijuana cigarette, so when he pulled his cigarettes out, the marijuana cigarette flew out and into Frank's cup!"

Although drug usage by the Mothers members was minimal at best, indulgence in sexual promiscuity was another matter altogether. The sixties as well as being notorious for its mind altering chemicals, was also a period of sexual liberation and experimentation. And it was the whole language and subculture of being in a band – groupies, getting the crabs, the clap, etc. – that became the subtext to many of Zappa's songs. So rather than singing about getting high, the Mothers more often than not sung about getting laid – the more lurid and lewd the suggestiveness the better.

"Roy was also always trying to get a little nookie any way he could," Gardner recalls. "While living in New York, I had a girlfriend named Peachie, who had a sister by the name of Mindy. I can still hear her saying to Roy, 'Stop that!' He always followed her around drooling over her body and asking for 'just a little kiss'."

Tapes of various band members "getting it on" would sometimes punctuate the group's material. The most notable of these was a tape of Bunk and a vociferous sounding girl called Peggy ("Oh, Yes Bunk!"), which became known as the Bunk sex tape. This found its way into live performances and subsequently onto *You Can't Do That On Stage Anymore Vol. 4* (as well as Roy Estrada's private tape collection).

Bunk Gardner explains how, "While in Columbus, Ohio and playing a club called the High Low Spot, I met a couple of young girls, Sandy and Peggy, and we became good friends. After I left Ohio, I found out Peggy was living in Florida. I don't remember how many times I went down there to see her. She was pretty vocal, and it was just a lark that I recorded it. Through the grapevine Frank heard about this, and he heard it and it cracked him up, and then he started using it on stage. Actually, she was good-natured about it. I didn't tell her I was going to do this. I still get a card from her every Christmas. Roy really loved to hear that tape! Some of Roy's pet phrases were – 'Got enough for you honey?' and 'Can you get a stiffy in a jiffy?' He always wanted to know every detail of a sexual encounter – 'How's she go Bunk?' he would ask. After that night of sex that I recorded, from then on Roy would bug me to listen to that tape and finally Frank heard it. Roy used a few of those phrases from that tape to make me and the rest of the group laugh. Sometimes on stage he would go into his routine, 'Right there Bunk!', 'Oh God right there, oh God Bunk! Yes! Yes!'"

Don Preston recalls one of his encounters. "While we were staying at the Albert Hotel, I was in my hotel room; a room trying to look respectable but failing with its worn carpet and old cigarette-burned furniture. I had just taken a shower and was drying myself when there was a knock on my door. 'Fuck it,' I said and went over and opened the door wide only to behold a totally beautiful girl standing there wearing a light turtleneck sweater and very short mini skirt. She looked me up and down and said, 'Well, aren't you going to invite me in?' She came in and I wrapped the towel around myself. She then introduced herself to me and we proceeded to make passionate love for several hours. She told me she was an interior decorator, but had been a Vogue fashion model during her teens. We lived together for six months. She was a beautiful soul that I regret separating from."

One of the increasing problems within the original Mothers was that some members were not adhering to Zappa's idea of the discipline he wanted in his band. It continued to irk him that a faction within his ensemble couldn't read music. He felt this restricted the band's ability to communicate the more complicated sections. It was somehow a strange paradox that perhaps the wildest and weirdest looking bunch in rock 'n' roll were expected to act and perform like very conservative, professional almost classical musicians.

Ray Collins states that, "Most great conductors and band leaders, Duke Ellington and all those people, have a reputation for being pretty hard to get along with. I believe they're very demanding. Maybe everyone is, or anyone is, if they get that kind of authority to be able to hire and fire people. Maybe they do all get crazy like that. Maybe I would, maybe you would!"

In January the band took a brief trip to Canada where they found things far different from the reception they had received in liberal New York. Not only was the weather freezing, but the reception the band got with their long hair and beards was frosty to say the least, as Don Preston recalls. "When we arrived in Montreal in 1967, we stayed at a little hotel near the club we were playing at. After a day, we found to our surprise that not one restaurant would serve us in the entire city, except the one in the hotel where we were staying. The reason, of course, was our long hair and beards."

In February 1967 Zappa began recording his first solo work which was to become the LP *Lumpy Gravy*. In fact, this largely instrumental and orchestral work wouldn't get a release for another 14 months. Part of the reason for this was that Zappa had signed a solo deal with Capitol as a composer. Even at this early stage it was clear that his solo career and that of the group were very independent. Indeed the music recorded for *Lumpy Gravy* veered strongly away from the rock 'n' roll music prevalent at the time and was greatly influenced by *musique concrete*. Despite its bizarre yet humorous title, the music displayed a much more serious stance than anything the Mothers had so far recorded. It was a dense form of orchestration that aimed to establish Zappa as an avant-garde classical composer, as well as the leader of a freaky bunch of rock 'n' roll renegades. Although credited as a solo effort, Zappa still got various members of his band to appear on it, notably Bunk Gardner, Motorhead, Jimmy Carl Black and Roy Estrada. Bunk Gardner recalls that, "It certainly wasn't a collection of out-takes from *Freak Out!* as some people have suggested. I think Frank wanted something classical, almost ballet-like or something because it was difficult music to play. All the great studio jazz players were on that date, along with a lot of the members of the Los Angeles Philharmonic Orchestra and believe me, they were on the edge of their chairs trying to play the stuff that Frank had written. It was in the Capitol Records studio right on Vine Street and at Apostolic in New York."

Richard Kunc, the recording engineer who would help Zappa complete *Lumpy Gravy* at Apostolic studio in New York and would eventually become Zappa's full time engineer, remembers. "During the New York days Frank did lots of seemingly strange things in the studio, trying for a new effect or an unusual blend of instruments. As time went by, less and less of what went on seemed strange to me. One notorious experiment was called 'piano people' (some of which eventually ended up on *Lumpy Gravy* and later on the 1994 release *Civilization Phase III*). In the studio at Apostolic was a big grand piano, a nice instrument with remarkable resonance. With the pedal held down it would just ring forever. Frank discovered by accident one day that when you spoke near it the appropriate sympathetic strings would resonate. So we clamped down the pedal and draped tarps and rugs over the open lid, sort of forming a little cave. Frank would put people in there and tell them to talk about various topics and we'd record it. Then we'd chop up these ringing words and use bits and pieces here and there. It became a kind of standing joke after a while. Delivery people would show up and he'd run out and grab them and stick them into the piano. It intimidated a lot of people – there were actually people who fled from the studio crying! But Frank didn't care, they were all just grist for his mill."

Kunc also recalls how he never knew who was going to show up at the sessions. "That was always a surprise, and for me that was one of the most wonderful aspects of that whole era. I was getting to meet all those amazing people, some of whom are still around today, still being amazing. And they ranged from Eric Clapton and Rod Stewart to Tim Buckley and a few dozen more names you'd know. It was really neat meeting people like that!"

Although *Absolutely Free* was now completed, it had not yet been released either. There was a dispute between the group and the record company over the sleeve to the album. Zappa was insistent that he wanted the lyrics reproduced. The record company, sensitive that some of them might be considered risqué, balked at the idea. Many of the sexual references in much of the Mothers material were no doubt a particular problem to them. Even more problematic was the fact that part of the artwork on the back sleeve contained the controversial slogan 'War Means Work For All'. Eventually the dispute was resolved and a libretto of all the lyrics was enclosed in the original pressing.

Absolutely Free was released in May 1967. Obviously, a considerable percentage of the American public were either oblivious to, or actively enjoyed, the sexual content of some of the lyrics, and the LP reached No 41 in the US charts.

three

By Easter 1967, the Mothers were back once again in New York. Rather than checking back into the Balloon Farm, they had, rather unusually for a touring rock band, taken up a residency at a small New York theatre. It was one of the defining decisions of the group's career and marked them as a unique part of the sixties counter culture. Not only was this to give the group the opportunity to flex its musical and satirical muscles, but it also clearly established Zappa and his group as a potent live alternative to most rock 'n' roll groups of the time.

The Garrick Theatre in Greenwich Village was a long, narrow theatre that held about 200 people maximum. With its low ceiling and lack of air conditioning, it had the tendency of getting extremely loud and hot in there. The Mothers would rehearse everyday from 1:00 p.m. to 4 or 5:00 p.m. – rain or shine, seven days a week. They then played two shows a night – at 8:00 p.m. and again at 10:00 p.m. – including Fridays and Saturdays. The Mothers of Invention's run at the Garrick Theatre lasted for at least six months, and they would loosely perform two mini-operas, so to speak, entitled "Pigs & Repugnant" and "Absolutely Free (An Entertainment)". This was a time when the idea of "rock theatre" was almost totally unheard of – The Who's *Tommy* (widely accepted as the first rock opera) had yet to be released. Perhaps only Andy Warhol and the Velvet Underground with their Exploding Plastic Inevitable had attempted anything similar.

Although musically miles apart, the two groups had certain elements in common. Firstly, both Zappa and Lou Reed were equally single-minded about the way they approached their material and the direction of their respective groups. They were also both cynical about the whole new hippie scene. By coincidence they also shared a record label. However, whilst *Freak Out!* was released almost immediately, the Velvet Underground's first LP took a lot longer to surface and was the cause of considerable annoyance to the Reed/Warhol camp. Perhaps out of jealousy, Lou Reed referred to Zappa as "the most untalented bore who ever lived". The previous year, the two bands had actually shared a stage together on the Velvet Underground's infamous first 1966 West Coast excursion. With their dark glasses and leather jacketed cool they were booed off stage on a bill at Bill Graham's Fillmore West which was co-headlined by the Mothers Of Invention and Jefferson Airplane. (Incidentally, during 1967, Jefferson Airplane had asked Zappa to produce their upcoming LP *After Bathing at Baxters*. Zappa, not surprisingly, was too busy to oblige. Possibly, Slick, Balin & co saw Zappa as an ally in their hippie cause. In any event, *After Bathing at Baxters* features a short track called "A Short Package Of Value Will Come To You Shortly" which was a musical tribute to the Mothers.)

In an April 1981 interview, original Velvet Underground member Sterling Morrison had this to say about the delay of the group's first album. "The album says, 'Produced by Andy Warhol.' Well, it was produced in the sense that a movie is produced. He put up some money. We made the album ourselves and then took it around because we knew that no one was going to sign us off the streets. And we didn't want any A&R department telling us what songs we should record. Ahmet Ertegun liked it, but said, 'No, no, no, none of this – no "Waiting For The Man", no "Venus In Furs".' Then we took it over to Elektra, who said some of the content was unacceptable, and the whole sound was unacceptable. 'This viola – can't Cale play anything else?' The album was ready by April 1966, but I don't think it even made a '66 release, or at least not until the end of the year. We were going crazy wondering what was going on while things got lost and misplaced and delayed. I know what the problem was. It was Frank Zappa and his manager, Herb Cohen. They sabotaged us in a number of ways because they wanted to be the first 'freak' release. And we were totally naive. We didn't have a manager who would go to the record company every day and just drag the whole thing through production."

Of course this was purely speculation by Morrison and there is no real way of confirming that Zappa and Cohen had anything to do with the delay of the first Velvet Underground album – most likely they didn't, and this was just a simple case of artist rivalry.

The Mothers of Invention's theatrical move eastwards was greeted with much more enthusiasm than Warhol and his cohorts attempts at conquering the Wild West. Of course, as a motley crew of jazz and rock musicians who were mainly used to one night stands, the whole idea of playing the same theatre, night after night, was an alien concept. Jimmy Carl Black recalls: "In order to keep from getting totally bored of playing this place, we started to get theatrical. There were several things that happened, but I think one of the best ones that Ray Collins and I pulled off was the one with the tall giraffe. These girls in the audience had given us a tall stuffed model of a giraffe. We ran a plastic tube from behind the piano on stage along the floor, taped it to the leg of the giraffe, ran it up through the stomach and out through the tail and pointed it, the tail end of the giraffe, at the audience.

"Frank, by the way, didn't have any idea we were doing this. We'd gotten several cases of pressurised whipped cream and in the middle of the show, when Frank was doing some frenzied thing or another, we started squirting this whipped cream out through the tube. It squirted over at least the first three rows of people and since it was coming out of the giraffe's ass they thought... well, they thought it was a pretty funny thing. And I did too. The rest of the audience just couldn't believe it. People were splitting their sides with laughter and Frank was on the ground. He had to stop playing he was laughing so hard. There was something that happened after. The air conditioner broke down and for three weeks, six nights a week, in the middle of the summer, in Greenwich Village, New York City, that theatre started to get rather rancid from all that whipped cream that was all over the place that they never bothered to clean up. The place smelled like puke for three weeks, and pretty heavy duty puke. But yet, they still kept coming. It was like the *Rocky Horror Picture Show*."

In a 1975 interview with *Creem* magazine Frank Zappa commented on the Garrick performances, "We were really the first band ever to perform rock theatre, which was a lot different than today's rock theatre. Most shows today are inferior to what we did then because they're so plasticized and predictable. What we did was courageous in that we never knew what was going to happen. We knew that everyone in the band was capable of doing one theatrical event, or concept. Each show was for each audience. We changed to fit the mood of the crowd."

The band's shows at the Garrick became increasingly surreal, often improvising musical routines which included stunts, bizarre puppet shows and wild humor. In a 1968 interview with Jerry Hopkins for *Rolling Stone* Magazine, Zappa again commented about the Mothers increasing use of atrocities during their live performances. "Music always is a commentary on society, and certainly the atrocities on stage are quite mild compared to those conducted in our behalf by our government. You can't write a chord ugly enough to say what you want to say sometimes, so you have to rely on a giraffe filled with whipped cream. Also, they (the audience) didn't know how to listen. Interest spans wane and they need something to help them refocus."

Jimmy Carl Black remembers another occasion when, "we had three marines up on stage. This was at the height of the Vietnam War. There were these three marines who didn't want to go to Vietnam, so we invited 'em up on stage and Frank had them ripping the heads off baby dolls yelling "Kill! Kill! Kill!" – *Life* magazine was there filming the whole thing, so needless to say they got out of the service."

Jim 'Motorhead' Sherwood was there mainly as the group's roadie and was put on the Garrick's payroll, however it didn't stop him joining in the craziness as he recalls. "That was some incredible stuff. We were at the Garrick a few months, experimenting with music and ideas. Frank figured that most people's attention span was about five minutes at most, maybe a minute when you're playing music. So Ray Collins and I used to turn this piano round and put on little puppet shows and we'd do really bizarre things.

"I was doing the lighting and sometimes in the booth I'd take vegetables and hang them on a wire. Then I'd slide these water melons and carrots and tomatoes down onto the stage. The band would break them up and throw them into the audience and share them with everyone. Or we'd get bags of ice cubes and throw ice out into the audience during the summer when it was really hot. You could probably spend months talking about all the bizarre crap that went on there at the Garrick. There were just too many numerous things. I can't remember all of them."

"The Mothers were doing a lot of instrumentals," Ray Collins remembers. "A lot of times there was nothing for me to do, so I became sort of like the 'Jonathan Winters', where you throw him a hat, or three hats, and he'd do an hour routine or something. I just used to ad-lib things and do comedy with whatever was available. So, at the Garrick Theatre, we started using fruit on stage, all the way from bananas to a watermelon, and stuffed animals. The Fugs were in town at the time too, and they used to call us the 'West Coast Fugs' from what I've seen. We sort of mimicked some of the things they were doing and just sort of – you know how that is: 'Oh, you can do that? Well, I can do that, too! Check this! I'll do this, plus what I do.' So Frank brought in a doll, and that kind of started the whole thing. We started doing 'nasties' to the doll, and I'd have the doll crawling up my leg, like

I was a rock star and the doll was after my person. Or we would throw things at the audience and they would throw things back at us. I remember one night, The Monkees were in the audience, and I was making love to a piano stool, doing all these sort of sexual acts to a piano bench – that was a lot of fun."

Don Preston reminisces a bit about the Garrick Theatre as well. "My strongest memories about the Garrick are about girls and things that would happen as a result of playing there – not during the performances but afterwards. Just all kinds of amazing things would happen, like one time these three girls came before the show started and they asked me if I wanted to go for a ride. All of them were dressed in black, and had black hair, and black make-up, and drove this black Camero. So we got into the car and drove to some place in the Village and went up into this ultra-modern apartment – really space-aged looking. We all smoked a joint and did other things. That kind of thing would happen everyday there. That whole area and that whole era, I met so many really interesting people. I remember Richie Havens was playing downstairs most of the time we were performing there. I got to know him real well. Unfortunately, I don't believe any of those Garrick shows were recorded – it was just before I started recording some of the shows on my little tape deck. Of course, Frank filmed a few shows. I'm sure they're probably in his vault."

By Easter the crowds had dwindled somewhat, and often the band found themselves only playing to a handful of people. As Frank Zappa himself commented. "Some nights there were three, maybe five people in there and we'd still play. But we would do it just for them. In fact, there was one night when there were just a few people in the audience. Now the Garrick Theatre was located right above the Café Au-Go-Go and there was a connecting passageway down to the Au-Go-Go. So all the guys in the band went downstairs and got some hot cider and coffee and stuff, put little napkins over their arms, and each guy in the band went up, sat down next to each person and served them a drink, talking with them for an hour-and-a-half. That was the entire show. The Garrick was small enough that you didn't have to exaggerate your movements because of the size of the place. You could actually behave in a normal manner – be normally weird."

Bunk Gardner recalls that, "To be in the West Village in the summertime right next to the Village Gate and next to the Café Au-Go-Go and across the street from the Tin Angel was incredibly exciting. People were everywhere, all the time! It really was a happening place. I lived in a second floor apartment above an Italian Social Club, which was interesting (they checked everyone out before you went upstairs). I could go home for the intermission and get a 'quickie' and go back for the second show re-vitalized! After the gig I'd be ready for night life in either the East or West Village which were packed with clubs that had just about any kind of entertainment you could ask for!

"The Garrick really was a happening place," Gardner continues. "Frank usually tried to get somebody from the audience up on stage and create a little weirdness, and make it interesting for the band and the audience. We established a reputation at the theatre for most of the stay there to 'expect the unexpected!' Sometimes we would have an opening act before we did our thing. One week we had Tiny Tim – that was a trip. He was 'out there' to say the least. We had Richie Havens for a week, a few comedians that I don't remember and also 'Uncle Meat' – Sandy Hurvitz (Essra Mohawk, who was temporarily a member of the Mothers during the Garrick shows. Frank Zappa produced one album for her called *Sandy's Album Is Here At Last!*)."

A typical set at the Garrick might include songs like "Mr. Green Genes", "Uncle Meat", "King Kong", "Stravinski", "Charles Ives", "20 Small Cigars", "Octandre", "Orange County Lumber Truck" and a medley featuring, "Baby Love", "My Boy-friend's Back", and "Gee", as well as other songs like "Louie Louie", "Mother People", "Brown Shoes Don't Make It", "Status Back Baby", "Absolutely Free", and "Hungry Freaks Daddy".

Bunk Gardner also remembers how, "there was always somebody hanging around or near the band at that time – the Fugs, Blood, Sweat & Tears, Jimi Hendrix, Linda Ronstadt, Simon & Garfunkel. I met Salvidor Dali, Bob Downey the filmaker, and Glen Gould the piano player. It was a never-ending array of artists who wanted to see if we were as weird as everyone said we were, and if our music was as avant-garde and out there as they said it was! We played classical, r&b, jazz, rock and made fun of everyone. We always combined satire and humor with the precision playing of Frank's tunes. People didn't know what to think of us at times, or take us seriously. We were like the Spike Jones of rock 'n' roll!"

The very first week at the Garrick, Don Preston bought a ten-speed bike and was riding it to work. Before the first show, he chained the front wheel of the bike to a fire hydrant right in front of the theatre. When he came out after the first show the chain and front tire was still there but the rest of the bike was gone. That was pretty representative of New York – nothing is safe!

"There was always something to do in New York," Gardner continues. "Both the East and West Villages had several jazz clubs and just a lot of clubs period. Movies, dance, art – the Village alone was a hotbed of entertainment. I lived right around the corner from the Garrick. My girlfriend 'Peachy' had parents that lived in Woodstock, so some of us spent leisure time there and then eventually moved up there. Roy, Ray and myself rented a house there and commuted back and forth to the city. Upstate NY was one of the most idyllic places that I have ever lived. I still remember how one night after our last show at the Garrick, Don and I went across the street to the Tin Angel and decided to hang out with one of the wait-resses. We did a lot of things that night like smoking hash in the women's restroom and then taking acid at 6:00 a.m. and deciding to go to the Guggenheim Museum of Modern Art. What a night and what a day at the museum that was. There were so many great things to see – all these great collections of art and trip-ping at the same time!"

Although a critical success, the group's run at the Garrick was hardly a financial triumph. There was even talk that they were so broke that they left the Van Rensler Hotel in New York where some of them had been staying without paying the bill. Rather than a percentage of the door receipts, the band were being paid a monthly salary that hardly covered their expenses.

Bunk Gardner says: "I heard stories that, in some places in the early days, our hotel bills were never paid! I believe it. We voted to pay ourselves $175 a week, and at the end of the engagement we would split up the rest of the money we had earned and divide it amongst the band. We all thought that we did so well that summer, that we would all have a couple thousand dollars a piece to be able to finally enjoy our hard work – to be able to splurge and spend some money on ourselves! As usual after the engagement ended we were informed that 'there is no money'. In fact we had lost money. We were dumbfounded and couldn't believe that it was actually true."

However, financial problems aside, in terms of the exposure the group was now receiving the theatrical run had reaped considerable dividends. The band members were having a great time and their new found notoriety meant that they were not only getting attention from the press but also from the opposite sex. However, Zappa himself was wary about the New York experience and wondered whether the audiences were just there to see a freak show, thereby ignoring some of the more serious messages behind the satire, or perhaps more pertinently ignoring the quality of the music the band was playing. After all, underneath it all Zappa wanted the group to be thought of as serious musicians. It was typical of his increasing belief that no-one quite understood or appreciated what he was trying to do. The Garrick run finally closed in the summer of 1967. Despite Zappa's dislike of New York, the band stayed on and started to work on their next LP, as well as continuing to work on his solo project *Lumpy Gravy* which he had yet to complete.

We're Only In It For The Money was recorded at the Mayfair Studios and Apostolic Studios between August and October of 1967. By now Richard Kunc had become an innovative recording engineer and had begun working full time with Frank Zappa. He would go on to help Zappa with his *Lumpy Gravy* project as well as record/engineer several of the Mothers and related artists' albums.

Richard Kunc recalls: "Over on 53rd or 55th Street (somewhere around there) in New York City, there was a studio called Mayfair – maybe still is. In the bowels of this studio the Mothers of Invention had been holding forth for quite a while. Frank Zappa was using their eight-track to create *We're Only In It For The Money* and *Lumpy Gravy*. He was always working on at least two albums at the same time. He'd heard about Apostolic and our twelve-track machine. He'd also heard that you could take a one-inch tape with eight tracks recorded on it by an 8-track machine, put it on our 12-track machine, and add four more tracks."

Using the 12-track meant shaving off some of the existing tracks, but they still ended up with twelve very mixable tracks, all of which still had very acceptable signal to noise ratios. This was a big selling point for Apostolic who sold a lot of studio time because of this trick.

"Being a cutting edge kind of guy, Frank decided to book some time with us," Kunc continues. "He said, 'I wanna come over and make some noise.' He brought some of the tapes he'd been working on at Mayfair. I guess he thought, 'I'll just see what it's all about – it probably won't be anything, and I'll go back to Mayfair and continue where I left off.' For reasons I can't recall, Tony (Bongiovi – older brother to Jon Bon Jovi and engineer at Apostolic) chose not to work with Frank, which fatefully put me in the proverbial right place at the right time – it must have been early 1967 – there was an immediate affinity, a meeting of eyeballs and passions for electronic toys. He made his noise – we had a great time and he loved it!"

As a result Zappa booked more and more time at Apostolic and eventually he transferred all his tapes there. "Pretty soon he was booking the studio by the week, and then by the month," Kunc recalls. "He liked to work at night, and we had a wonderful time. The engineer at Mayfair, who may still be there for all I know, was Gary Kellgren, a hell of a nice guy and damn good engineer. He did a lot of work with Hendrix and other monsters. You'd think he'd be bent out of shape, watching Frank transfer his flag, so to speak. On the contrary, he was most helpful and very nice to me. He was there, doing it, and I was just beginning – still wet behind the ears. He couldn't have been nicer or more gracious about my essentially stealing one of his biggest clients. Bless you, Gary."

Bunk Gardner recalls that, "Dick Kunc was a good engineer who considered himself somewhat of a comedian. From 1968 on, he recorded most of the concerts that we played right up until we disbanded in 1970. But he rarely hung out with members of the band and I really didn't get to know him that well personally. Apostolic Studio was up on the 2nd or 3rd floor of a building near the Village section of town and very small in comparison to most studios. I remember we had time restrictions on the use of the studio and could only go so late at night because of people living in the building at the time. I think the police came a couple of times to tell us to keep the noise level down a little." (Just such an incident can be heard on *The Lost Episodes* released in 1996.) Don Preston continues, "I liked Dick, he was a good-natured guy who was kind of glib. He was with the band for a number of years, and he toured with us and recorded the shows. I thought he was a really nice person and really knew what he was doing."

Much of the music recorded for *We're Only In It For The Money* benefited from the new found tightness the band had acquired from their residency at The Garrick. In fact, the band could now almost operate on ESP. Time and key signatures could be changed with the briefest of hand signals from Zappa. "I always loved those 5/4 & 7/4 rhythms we'd use," remembers Roy Estrada. "They were never used by other people at the time – everyone else played in 4/4 or 3/4. It's math-

55

ematics, it adds, eventually it comes back. There was a thing we would play and at one point it would stretch out (the rhythm) but then eventually would come back. That was nice. Frank's whole thing was that. He was into the time signatures a lot. That's what made it interesting to me."

The group also acquired a new member. Ian Robertson Underwood (born 22 May, 1939) was a New Yorker who had witnessed the group's show at the Garrick. As a classically trained multi-intrumentalist he very much appreciated what Zappa and the Mothers were trying to do. As a result he went down to the Apostolic studios to ask if he could work with the group. Zappa was so impressed with Underwood's credentials - he had Bachelor's Degree in music from Yale and a Master's Degree from Berkeley, but most notably he could play a whole array of instruments (such as sax, organ, clarinet and flute) and read music - that he was immediately hired.

Bunk Gardner recalls that, "Ian was an excellent musician who never really fit in with the band. He tried real hard to be 'one of the guys' but never succeeded. He spent most of his time hanging out with Frank. There was really no area in Ian's personality that was bizarre or weird. He tried but he was never a source of laughs or genuine humor for the rest of the band, although he tried hard and wanted to be liked."

Preston agrees: "I always liked Ian very much. I felt he was very, very talented. He had a lot of technical ability on the piano, and he could play sax and really get 'out'. I think he felt more comfortable around Frank than anybody else – his father was president of US Steel and I think he might have felt Zappa was more on equal terms than the rest of us who were all under-earners and lowlifes. (laughs) But Ian spent more time in the studio with Frank than the rest of us."

It was also at this point Dick Barber was hired as road manager, as Bunk Gardner recalls. "Dick Barber joined us in New York at the Garrick Theatre. He came on our first European tour and became the road manager for the rest of the time the band was together. We used to call him the 'Gnarler' and was the guy who did those snorks on the early albums. [Motorhead eventually took up the position as resident snorker.] Dick's basic duties were to keep the band happy and make sure the press didn't get any interviews from us – Frank was the sole spokesperson for the band."

As well as trying to finish *We're Only In It For The Money*, Zappa and the group went on their first European tour in September. Zappa had prepared the way with a promotional trip to London the previous month where he announced to the press that, "I may bring six or eight or fifteen Mothers with me – it depends on how many cats want to come to England."

As the group flew off to London that September for a highly publicised concert at the Royal Albert Hall, Zappa was wiry thin from overwork and the pressures of his recently getting married and becoming a father for the first time. Jimmy Carl Black, whose wife was already expecting their fifth child, knew all too well the pressures, financial and otherwise, that being in a rock 'n' roll band was beginning to exert. Nonetheless, the group's creative energy went on unabated as did the tightening of Zappa's hold on the group. For the purposes of touring abroad, Zappa was not only making his views about the carrying of drugs increasingly clear to the rest of the band, but he also laid it in on the line that he was to be the only spokesman and that no-one else would be doing interviews. In Zappa's mind, he was the only one who could best discuss his work with the press. The band now included both Pamela Zarubica as Suzy Creamcheese and Motorhead as roadie/band member.

Jim Sherwood: "I was with the Mothers in 1967 when we did the first trip to London, and that was when they officially put me into the band. I was taking care of the equipment, and they couldn't decide if they wanted me as equipment manager or as a musician in the band, so they decided to make me a musician who took care of all the equipment."

Bunk Gardner explains that, "Motorhead, or should I say Motormouth – give Jim a pack of cigarettes and a cup of coffee and he could talk non-stop all night about anything and everything – was a gopher for Frank. Anything Frank wanted Jim would get and spend endless hours talking about the old days with Frank in Lancaster, CA – the highschool days with some of their buddies and some of the early bands that Frank started. I think Jim was always a little frustrated that he couldn't play that much with the band. Jim couldn't read music and couldn't play very well and most of the time was just a roadie. Every once in a while Frank would have him come up on stage and let him 'Freak-out' on the microphone or on his baritone sax."

There was now a clear division between bandleader and his band, so much so that the band now stayed in a different hotel than Zappa himself. In London, the band generally enjoyed themselves whilst Zappa lost no time in an endless round of promotion. In England the group was already being treated as a collection of celebrities and as a result was introduced to a whole host of stars, as well as Zappa himself appearing on the front cover of *Melody Maker*.

The Mothers settled into a week of rehearsals with ten members of the London Philharmonic Orchestra who were to accompany the group on their date at the Royal Albert Hall. The concert was an unqualified success mixing up the usual satire with wild improvised sections and complex arrangements. Don Preston surprised everyone by playing, at Zappa's suggestion, a version of "Louie Louie" on the Albert Hall's enormously ornate pipe organ, as Preston remembers. "When we arrived at the Albert Hall, I noticed the pipe organ up behind the band. I went over and looked at it and a person who worked there came over and said, 'Do you want to play it?' Stifling my every urge to scream, 'Yes!', I mumbled, 'That would be nice.' He turned it on and left. I sat down and pressed down a key on the second largest organ in the world! A deep penetrating pure tone emanated from the ceiling. I looked at the five tiers of keyboards and all the tonal controls for each keyboard – I was in heaven! I spent the next four hours experimenting and figuring out how it worked. Of course during that evening's concert I played 'Louie Louie' on it." [This version eventually ended up on the *Uncle Meat* album.]

Ray Collins and Roy Estrada also performed an impromptu version of The Supremes' "Baby Love" which became a regular part of the show on the rest of the tour. Many leading musicians were in the audience that night, including Jimi Hendrix and Jeff Beck. It proved that Zappa and the Mothers had truly arrived, both in the eyes of the public and their musical contemporaries.

Bunk Gardner remembers that, "the first gigs and tours were interesting because musically I got a chance to solo all the time on any song that Frank decided to open up for solos. Most of the time, harmonically, it was just soloing on one chord, which was a real challenge to find different ways to work over the same notes and tonality. Between trying to retain and memorise everything we rehearsed and trying not to make any mistakes on stage, it was very demanding! I played soprano on 'Motherly Love' which is a song I liked very much. But we concentrated more on 'odd time' songs and going from one song to another with an interlude in between or just going in the middle of one song to another by Frank jumping up in the air and coming back down and starting another song or playing a riff that established a thread of a melody, and tweaked it a little, and we could go off in another direction – melodically and rhythmically! The first UK tour was fun and my first time in the Royal Albert Hall playing music. We did get a per diem of $10 or $15 a day, but we never got paid for the whole tour."

The group then headed off to the other capitals of Europe's burgeoning hippie scene, most notably Amsterdam and Copenhagen. The rest of the tour was an immediate success and European audiences took to the band's blend of jazz and avant-garde music like ducks to water. The band played many memorable concerts including a couple at Copenhagen's Tivoli Gardens where the legendary Don Cherry sat in with them. Many of these concerts, like the one in Stockholm, have been released subsequently in their entirety. From very early on Zappa had begun to religiously record all the group's live performances. Initially intended for his own use, many sections of these recordings began to appear on records and CDs over the years, most notably on the *You Can't Do That On Stage Anymore* series in the 1980s as well as the Rhino release *Tis The Season To Be Jelly Stockholm '67* and the 1993 release of *Ahead Of Their Time* CD.

Mostly the rest of the band were happy to let Zappa deal with the press, as they had some partying to do. As Don Preston recalls, "There was this time when we were in Amsterdam and Jimmy Carl Black got totally tanked on beer and decided to go down to the red light district and get laid. He came back a little later and told us that he would see a beautiful girl sitting in her window with the red lights on and go up and knock on her door, but she wouldn't answer. When he looked back at the window, she had closed her drapes. After this happened ten or more times, Jimmy gave up and went home totally pissed off. He must have been a sight, this tall drunken Indian dressed in these wild clothes."

Back in New York, the recording hiatus continued unabated. *We're Only In It for The Money* was completed but yet to be released and work had already started on the project that was to become *Uncle Meat*. Zappa was also still trying to complete his solo project *Lumpy Gravy*. Zappa explained how his first solo record deal came to be. "Originally what happened was that right after the completion of *Absolutely Free* in '66, the basic tracks were cut for *Lumpy Gravy* in Los Angeles. This guy Nick Venet – a producer at Capitol – heard I could write orchestra music and asked me if I'd like to do an orchestra album for Capitol because my MGM contract didn't preclude me from conducting. I wasn't signed as a conductor and since I wasn't performing on the album, there didn't seem to be any problem. He gave me a budget for a 40-piece orchestra, x-number of studio hours, and said go do it. And I did."

Unfortunately, MGM's legal department did have a problem with *Lumpy Gravy*. When Zappa brought the album's tapes to New York for mixing and editing, MGM complained. This was after Capitol had spent over $30,000 on the project. Eventually, after 13 months of litigation, MGM paid Capitol back $30,000 for the master tapes to *Lumpy Gravy*. In fact, MGM, who had disputed Zappa's solo contract with Capitol, after buying the rights to the original tapes discovered that they had been cut and spliced about by Capitol's engineers. Zappa set about the unenviable task of trying to piece the project back together again.

Frank Zappa again: "In fact, if you're looking for rare collectors' items, there are 8-track tapes with the Capitol label of *Lumpy Gravy* that have a different *Lumpy Gravy* than the album. Those have only the orchestral music and they do exist." When not recording or editing, Zappa and the Mothers carried on touring. With their increasingly bizarre looks the band could even turn heads by just walking down the street. In many places where they toured, very long hair was still relatively rare in 1967 and inevitably the band met with some hostility.

Jim Motorhead Sherwood recalls: "There was one deal once when we were in the L.A. airport getting ready to fly out. There was Jim and Ray sitting around at one table and Frank and us were at another one. This marine came up with a handful of peanuts and just threw them all over the table, and he says, 'Here you monkeys, eat!' Jim Black, who'd been in the Air Force, just freaked. He jumped up and was going to kill this guy, and we had to hold him down. Everyone was trying to keep Jim from doing this guy over. Eventually this guy discovers there are another five or so of us at the next table, so I guess he felt a little overwhelmed and he decided to back off."

Another time in Philadelphia, Bunk, Roy and Jimmy were standing on the curb and they started to walk across the light. A cab driver came whizzing across all four lanes of traffic and tried to run them over. "We always had to walk to work as we could never get a cab," Motorhead continues. "Strange things like that went on all the time. We'd get on airlines and the stewardesses wouldn't talk to us for about half the trip until they found out we were a band, and then they'd start bringing us drinks and peanuts and extra little snacks. Touring in the early days was really tough and really bizarre. It was kind of hard to deal with."

However, within the artistic community the band were much better received and commissions for scoring work were beginning to come in. On one particular occasion the band went to Montreal at the invitation of the National Film Board of Canada where they were asked to do the score for a documentary film called *Ride For Your Life*. "It was about a bike racer and his family," Preston remembers. "We arrived at the complex; a very large brick building containing several sound stages, recording studio and remix facilities. I was very excited because two of my favourite filmakers worked there – Norman Mclauren and John Whitney (from the films we used to improvise to). Mclauren pioneered animation using real people and objects. Many of his ideas were stolen and used in various films. Whitney pioneered the use of computers in animation. His son now owns a large firm in Hollywood, where computers are used for films like *The Last Starfighter*. Anyway, we set up in the recording studio and they showed the film on a large screen. We watched it several times and then proceeded to improvise to it with Zappa giving us the customary hand signals. We did two or three takes and then packed up our gear and left."

Later in 1990, when Bunk, Don and Jimmy Carl were touring as the Grandmothers they found out that this biker documentary had won first prize in a European film festival for short music films. They finally got a copy of the film and for the first time watched it on video, 23 years later!

In December it was all change in the Mothers camp once again, Billy Mundi had been replaced by Artie Tripp as the group's second drummer/percussionist. Mundi's tendency to speed up during a number may be one of the reasons his services were dispensed with. He went on to join the obscure band Rhinoceros. (Mundi recorded two albums with them, *Rhinoceros* and *Satin Chickens*.) Mundi would make a brief appearance with Zappa again in 1970 for the premier of *200 Motels* with Zubin Meta and the L.A. Philharmonic, as well as having a cameo in the *Uncle Meat* movie.

"Billy wasn't with the band too long," Bunk Gardner recalls. "He left after the *We're Only In It For The Money* album. Some of the things I remember about Billy – he was always playing with his hair. It would take him two hours to get ready for a job and most of that time was spent on his hair. He always wore a hat – he was losing his hair and a little sensitive about it. In his drumming, Billy was always pushing and driving the beat, and it seemed that we always ended up a song with a faster tempo then when we first started. Billy Mundi and Jimmy Carl Black did not work well together when we used two drummers. For quite a while we used one drummer – Billy – and Jimmy was playing bass trumpet (yes, he had to practise daily!). Jimmy's confidence level got very low during that time, when he wasn't playing drums and was getting a lot of criticism from Frank about his trumpet playing. From the beginning Billy was very unhappy about the little money we were making, in spite of being famous, and always expressed that unhappiness to Frank. So periodically we would get a speech from Frank or Herbie – 'You've got to hang in there just a little longer. We're all in this together – be patient – it's gonna happen and then we'll be rich and famous. It's only a matter of time!' Billy got tired of this, and told Frank he couldn't take it any longer."

Mundi's replacement, Arthur Dyer Tripp III (born 10 September, 1944 in Athens, OH) had the added advantage that he could read music (he had played with the Cincinnati Symphony Orchestra) and could also play the xylophone and marimba. For Frank, Artie's additon enabled the band to explore more complex rhythmic ideas within the music.

"Art was another Virgo," Bunk Gardner recalls, "which I seem to have an affinity with or for. I liked Art right away when he joined the band. Art read whatever Frank wrote and improvised solos like a true Mother of Invention. Art fit in right away. He loved John Cage and true experimental music. He played drums and marimba equally well and really was an asset to the band. Artie was a regular at Barney's Beanery when in L.A. – he loved to drink a few beers and shoot pool which he was very good at. Art used to wear female panties over his head, dye his moustache green and wear wing-tip shoes – fairly unusual for a rock 'n' roll drummer! I remember having Art over to the house one night and we had a few beers – just talking music. I remember telling Artie that Glen Gould, the famous pianist, had just died the day before and Art was absolutely stunned. He kept saying, 'I just can't believe it,' – it ruined the whole night for him. He loved Glen Gould and classical music so much. He was really very sensitive about a few things and at the same time a very likeable guy and easy to relate to. Most of the time while we were travelling, Art was always checking out percussion accessories. Anything that might make a weird or unusual sound Art would buy it for the drum set. He would then try to figure out how to mount it so he could play it, or use it in a particular song in just one measure or beat."

With the addition of new drummer/percussionist Art Tripp, Jimmy Carl Black was once again relocated to the drums – a position he was much better suited to. "I guess that Zappa felt that Jimmy could never grasp anything harder than the rock 'n' roll stuff," Don Preston says, "so Frank always had another drummer in the group who could play a little more technical. I always liked Jimmy's time very much – he had (and still has) a lot of power and good feeling in his playing. Eventually we ended up with Art Tripp which was pretty good because Art could play anything. He'd been playing with John Cage and an orchestra – he was very accomplished."

Bunk Gardner concurs. "Jimmy was never a technician playing drums – no flash but always Mr Steady. Jimmy always concentrated on keeping the time.

That's why having two drummers (Artie and Jimmy) seemed to work so well. Art Tripp played around the time and Jimmy kept it steady."

Ray Collins also left the band for a few months which explains why he is not featured on *We're Only In it For The Money* which finally got its release in January 1968 – the delay was partly due to the controversial nature of the album's sleeve. In fact, throughout the years with the Mothers, Ray Collins would quit and rejoin the group several times. Don Preston also quit the Mothers after the recording of *We're Only In It For The Money* only to return a few weeks later.

Bunk Gardner recalls how, "Ray Collins quit the band because there was always a difference of opinion about the direction musically and the new material that Frank was writing was just too far out for Ray's tastes. Ray was kind of a loner. He really never saw eye-to-eye about a lot of things with Frank. Ray was more a traditionalist in the sense of just wanting to sing all the past hits and your normal rock 'n' roll orientated songs. When Frank started writing some of his weirder material it didn't sit too well with Ray. They had many arguments about the musical direction of the band and the selection of material to be sung. After an argument Ray would quit, and then later come back again. I remember a few times when we were all together just hanging out and Ray would say, 'Somebody here is giving off bad vibes.' Then we would all look at each other and do a double take like, 'What the fuck is he talking about?' or 'Where is he coming from?' and 'Who's giving off bad vibes?' Later we would make fun of it when Ray wasn't there, and make like one of us was giving off bad vibes. Then we would crack up over it. At times Ray did not seem to possess a lot of humor, and was fairly serious. Then there would be times on stage when he was the funniest guy you ever saw! So it was difficult to understand where he was coming from."

Don Preston remembers Ray Collins as being "a truly amazing comedian. All during the time he was in the band he would be doing things on stage that would break me up every night! I've worked with some big name comedians before and they wouldn't crack me up like Ray because they did the same routine everyday. With Ray it was like completely different – sort of like a stream of consciousness type of comedy – always very fresh and innovative. It just flowed out and was totally off-the-wall. He had a very weird sense of humor which in turn was very appealing to Zappa. As far as Ray and Frank's relationship, well of course it's been said many times before, Ray wanted to do the r&b-type stuff and Frank wanted to go into just about every direction possible. Also Ray had no prior knowledge or concept of avant-garde or jazz music, or anything associated with it. It's odd because you would think since Ray's humor was so bizarre and innovative it would have matched up with his musical tastes – but that just wasn't the case at all."

The original outside cover for *We're Only In It For The Money* was a notorious spoof on the artwork of *Sergeant Pepper's Lonely Hearts Club Band* with the Mothers in women's clothing standing in front of a rogues gallery just like The Beatles had done. This was later confined to the inside after record company jitters about the legal ramifications (black bars were even placed across the eyes of those people featured in the collage who were still alive). The cover by Cal Schenkel was therefore reversed and the outside featured the equally arresting close-up image of these long-haired, bearded, freaky looking guys dressed as women.

"One of the interesting things I remember doing the album cover," Don Preston recalls, "was that we all had to wear dresses; my dress was I think $200 which at the time was quite a large amount of money for a dress. They were all like that, and the set itself was quite incredible, all these mannequins and vegetables that you can see on the sleeve – it was really amazing."

Bunk Gardner remembers that, "the photo sessions for the *We're Only In It For The Money* album were done in New York, mid-tour, by Jerry Katzenberg – a famous photographer at the time. I liked Cal Schenkel's artwork on the album, but the photos were the main theme."

Many of the songs on the album were actually adaptations from instrumental sections that the band played live, Zappa only adding the lyrics and vocals in the studio after the instrumental was recorded. Interestingly enough, Don Preston's name is featured on the sleeve with the word 'retired'. In a fit of pique Preston had upped and left the band to go back to L.A.. As he recently commented to *Mojo* magazine, who incidentally had just voted *We're Only In It For The Money* as 55th greatest album of all time, "I decided, fuck all this shit in New York, I'm going back to L.A. to my wife and kids. So I went back to L.A., found out where my wife was living, and this big guy answered. And I said, 'Fuck this shit too'. So I called Frank and said, 'Let me back in the band', and flew back to New York. I was gone for about a week, but during that week, they did the liner notes."

After working on *We're Only In It For The Money,* the innovative Cal Schenkel began his stay as resident artist for Zappa and the Mothers, as he remembers. "For about three years in the late sixties I was essentially Frank's art department. When we were in New York (during the recording of *We're Only In It For The Money*) my art studio was basically at Frank's house. Frank was either in the studio, onstage or asleep. He wasn't the kind of guy you would get together, go out and have a couple of drinks. He was always the person who was in control whenever you're around; everything revolved around what he was doing. But that was my relationship with him. He had vision and he knew how to create it. On the other hand, I think he did allow for a lot of other input. He was able to draw out people's talents, but he knew how to put it all together."

Schenkel's artwork would soon become an intrinsic part of the visual concepts Zappa had developed alongside the music. Whether it be cartoonish drawings and paintings, bizarre collages or twisted pen and ink sketches, Calvin's artwork is in a class by itself.

The music that accompanied the artwork to *We're Only In It For The Money* was loosely a concept album. Essentially an intense political satire on the burgeoning West Coast hippie culture, it featured such tracks as "Flower Punk", "Are You

Hung Up" and "Concentration Moon". The latter featured a middle section which officially christened Jimmy Carl Black as the "Indian of the group". It also rather eerily predicted the Kent State University killings, a full two years before they actually happened.

Again, various ideas were adapted from popular tunes of the day, as Don Preston recalls. "Actually a number of those early songs were the same chords as other tunes. 'Flower Punk' for instance – that is totally based on 'Hey Joe'. But see how different it is – it's almost the same music, but Zappa put the rhythm in 7/16 and 5/16 and of course different lyrics."

With the LP's delicately poised blend of phoney hip lingo, political commentary and zany interludes, many consider it to be Zappa and the Mothers finest work and it reached numbers 30 and 32 in the US and UK respectively. The LP featured the Mothers line-up of: Frank Zappa, Jimmy Carl Black, Roy Estrada, Billy Mundi, Don Preston, Bunk Gardner, Jim Sherwood, and a young Ian Underwood.

Don Preston recalls one incident that summarises not only the acceptance that the LP had garnered, but also Zappa's contempt towards the tampering of his material in any form. "We had gone to Sweden and after performing in Stockholm we were asked to attend an awards ceremony the next day. We went to this person's elegant house where the award for 'best album of the year' was going to be presented. All these dignitaries were milling around the modern Swedish furniture. The award was displayed on a cabinet along with the album (*We're Only In It For The Money*) and you could hear the album being played in the background. All of a sudden Zappa said, 'Stop the music and play that last section over again!' We listened to the section in the song 'Let's Make The Water Turn Black' again and Zappa said, 'There!' Apparently some record executive decided to delete the line that referred to a mama with her apron and her pad. His thinking was that 'pad' meant Kotex pad instead of the pad we all use in the kitchen to handle hot items, which was what Zappa had meant. Frank then announced that we couldn't accept the award because the album had been altered. Everyone in the room was shocked. We left the party as all who had attended watched with disbelief."

four

No sooner had *We're Only In It For The Money* been released when the group embarked on recording another LP, as well as mixing the recordings for *Uncle Meat*. MGM's contract specified that the group owed the record company two more LPs, but *Uncle Meat* was proving to be a huge recording and editing undertaking, so instead Zappa took the group back into Apostolic Studios in New York in January 1968 to record something quick as a way of fulfilling their contractual obligations. The result was an album which surprised many people.

Although Mothers' concerts were known to feature versions of "Blue Suede Shoes" and "Hound Dog" in amongst the satire and improvisation, *Cruising With Ruben And The Jets* was pure authentic '50s style rock 'n' roll (with a bit of humor thrown in for good measure).

Richard Kunc, once again brought in as engineer, remembers how, "Frank never seemed to work on just one album at a time – two was the absolute minimum. He'd start on one and a little ways into that he'd get an idea for another one. Then he'd start that one and then maybe a third and a fourth. He'd work on them bit by bit, going back and forth as ideas flowed through his head. So whenever I came to work – this was true in New York and L.A. – I never knew what I'd be doing. One of the best examples of this is the album *Cruising With Ruben and The Jets*. During a break at a session for some other album, we were sitting around talking about old high school days and doo-wop tunes. Ray Collins and some other people just started singing them. Then someone sat down at the piano, someone else played drums, and so forth. All of a sudden Frank said, 'Hey, let's make an album of this stuff!' Right then and there *Cruising With Ruben and The Jets* was born. He came in the next day with charts for the whole album."

Frank Zappa devised a plan whereby the LP was to be a Mothers Of Invention album loosely working under the pseudonym of Ruben and The Jets, and this was enhanced by the bubble caption coming from the Cal Schenkel drawn cartoon of Zappa on the cover which asked the question as to whether this was just a ploy by the Mothers Of Invention to get their music played on the radio.

Ray Collins was brought back into the fold for the *Ruben* LP. This was just as well, as his high falsetto was ideally suited to the material. "I brought the 'style' of being raised in Pomona, California," Ray Collins remembers, "being raised on the Four Aces, the Four Freshmen, Frankie Lane, Frank Sinatra and Jesse Baldwin. The early influences of r&b came into the Southern California area when I was probably in the tenth grade in high school. And I remember Peter Potter's show, and I think I recall the first r&b tune on there was 'Oop-Shoop'. Frank actually had more influences from the 'real blues', you know, like Muddy Waters, those kind of people. But I wasn't into that in my early life. I was into more of the pop culture, pop radio things, and it's always been more of a favourite of mine than the early blues stuff – even though I love John Lee Hooker and all those people."

In a rare 1968 interview with Jerry Hopkins for *Rolling Stone* magazine, Frank Zappa talked a little about his then Mothers. "Ray Collins, the lead vocalist. I've known him maybe 10 years and he's been singing r&b for 15 or 16 years, which makes him about 30 now. He has a very bizarre sense of humor, as shown when he performs his magic tricks, which don't work. Prior to joining the Mothers he was a part-time bartender and carpenter. Roy Estrada is the bass player, 26. He's been playing r&b since he was 16, lived in Orange County most of his life, and was driving a lumber truck before joining the group. Jimmy Carl Black is the drummer, is around 30, and up until recently was an extremely ambitious beer drinker

– 10 quarts a day. He's about 90 per cent Cherokee (his Indian name is James Inkinish) and was working in a gas station in Kansas. Ian Underwood is 29, has a masters in music from Yale and Berkeley and is an accomplished woodwind player and concert pianist, specializing in Mozart. I met him in the studio one day and he wanted to join the group. I said, 'What do you do that's fantastic?' He played the piano and alto sax and I hired him. Bunk Gardner I don't know much about. He's obviously conservatory trained, manicures his beard, combs his hair, and likes to take his clothes off when he's counting money. Euclid James 'Motorhead' Sherwood I've known 12 years. We were in high school in Lancaster together. He used to play baritone sax in the Omens (early Zappa band). He has the ability to perform a dance known as the bug, which resembles an epileptic fit. He's one of those guys you say, 'I know this guy who's really weird and I want to show him to you.' He was our equipment handler for a while and when we started the atrocities we started handing him our instruments to see what would happen. He played things more imaginative than the proficient musicians could lay down. It was just him against the machine in his mouth, a saxophone. He is also very proficient at dolls and visual aids. Don Preston plays electric piano, electric organ and electronic music effects. His main claim to fame is he loses money – hundreds of dollars a month. Art Tripp played for two years with the Cincinnati Symphony as a percussionist. He toured the world for the State Department. He has performed solo concerts of stuff by Stockhausen and John Cage. In spite of all that, he's just as creepy as the rest of the people in the band."

Cruising With Ruben And The Jets was released in August 1968, and it was certainly the most straightforward music that Zappa and the Mothers had so far produced. In fact it was so faithful in its recreation of '50s music that some radio stations took it be some unearthed '50s LP. The songs were straight pastiches of the doo-wop and rock 'n' roll that Zappa and most of the rest of the group loved so much (although on closer inspection tinges of Stravinsky can be detected in there too). Apparently recorded by Ruben Sano and his group The Jets – the full line-up was Frank Zappa, Ray Collins, Jimmy Carl Black, Roy Estrada, Don Preston, Bunk Gardner, Jim Sherwood, Ian Underwood and Art Tripp.

"*Cruising with Ruben and The Jets* was an easy album to record," Bunk Gardner recalls. "We were recording it at the same time as *Uncle Meat* because the songs were easy and very simple and didn't require a lot of time for arrangements and technical overdubbing. It was the beginning of the end for Ray Collins because all the new material Frank was writing was a little too far out and away from Ray's roots – which was *Ruben*-era material. Motorhead too was in his glory during the recording of this album. He loved *Ruben* and that was really his kind of music to get nostalgic over – on stage and doing the dance steps and playing that music – heaven. I really enjoyed playing a solo on Ray's tune 'Anything'. I remember Frank, Ray and Roy standing in the control booth while I recorded my solo. Frank was telling me after the first take to keep it simple. So I nailed it on the second take and everyone was happy! Then I went on to other things because we were recording stuff for *Uncle Meat* at the same time. It probably didn't take more than a total of three weeks to make *Ruben and The Jets*, plus another month for *Uncle Meat*."

An early high school photograph of Zappa replete with pencil moustache appeared on the back cover as Ruben and it might have been easy to assume that with typical Mothers humorr they were gently poking fun at the musical style with its simple songs about unrequited love and "Jelly Roll Gum Drops". However this was much more than a cursory pastiche or throwaway project. Zappa's low doo-wop vocals mixed with Collins' high falsetto lead vocal, remarkably closely approximated the sound of the originals. It was a set of Zappa songs (although Collins also actually wrote a couple) stripped of the jazz improvisations, complex arrangements and bizarre satirical edge, concentrating more on the melodies. If *Lumpy Gravy* emphasised Zappa's interest in the orchestral and avant-garde, *Cruising With Ruben And The Jets* took an altogether different element of the Mothers pot-pourri of musical styles and brought it under the microscope. It was clear that being a Mothers fan necessitated some dedication – literally within months there was the prospect of trying to unravel concrete music symphonies and pastiches of '50s doo-wop.

In June of 1968, Zappa and the Mothers were featured in the June 28 issue of *Life* magazine. With bizarre pictorials of Zappa and the Mothers surrounded by screaming babies, the magazine also featured the highly acclaimed article written by Zappa entitled 'The Oracle Has It All Psyched'. Don Preston fondly remembers: "Of course, I was very proud to have my photo with the other Mothers in *Life* magazine. That was *the* magazine at that time. I thought it was great – it was another step in the band getting somewhere!"

With both *Cruising With Ruben and The Jets* and *Lumpy Gravy* having been released and with *Uncle Meat* mostly finished, the band moved back to L.A. where they played a triumphant return gig at the Shrine Exposition Hall on 6 and 7 December, 1968 in Santa Monica. Billed as a *Gala Pre-Xmas Bash* the show also featured the Alice Cooper group, the GTOs, Wildman Fischer, and Easy Chair (an unknown group that was never heard of again after this gig).

Don Preston remembers this wild yet historic concert. "I remember that there was this girl there on stage who liked to be whipped, and there was this guy there also who took his belt off and began chasing her. She was running all over the stage and he was really flailing at her! It was unbelievable – I couldn't even stand to watch it. It was during the Mothers set and Wildman Fischer also performed with us at that gig as well."

For Bunk Gardner the journey back from New York was an eventful one. "Just before moving back to Los Angeles I bought a 1955 Chrysler New Yorker with the hemi engine," he recalls. "Don bought a TR3 and Jimmy a Volkswagen Beetle – all used cars we wanted to drive back to L.A.. I had my car checked out completely and spent a lot of money fixing it up with new tires, a new fuel pump, oil change, etc. The only thing I didn't do was drop the oil pan and have it completely cleaned. Our last week in New York we played a concert at the Fillmore East that was great! It was like saying goodbye to New York for the last time. Anyway, I drove up to Woodstock that night after the concert with Gigi, a girl I'd met while living in Woodstock. I decided to try some magic mushrooms the next day just to see what it was like. I'm sitting at the edge of this small stream with my feet in the water and just tripping out when I heard this voice. I turned around and didn't see anybody and wondered what was going on? The voice said, 'I'm not going to make it.' I finally realized that my car, which was about ten feet away, was talking to me. At first I cracked up and thought it was very funny, but then I started to ask it questions like, 'Why are you saying you're not going to make it? Tell me why aren't you going to make it.' We had a long conversation, but my car never told me why it wasn't going to make it all the way to L.A..

"Two days later Roy and I started taking turns driving to Los Angeles. When we got to Springfield, MO the engine seized up and blew a head gasket and we had to get towed to a garage. The mechanic said the oil pan had too much sludge in it and oil was not getting up and lubricating the engine. So he offered me $300 for it and I took the money. Then, Roy and I had to charter a small plane to fly us to Kansas City where we were playing a concert before going back to L.A.. I almost wanted to go back to Springfield to buy back my car when I got back to Los Angeles. But time did not permit making that move, but I will never forget that car and that conversation or the time spent in Woodstock!"

The Mothers of Invention's whirlwind work rate of recording and playing live, while Zappa edited live tapes for possible release, carried on relentlessly through 1968. The amount of material that was now released, along with all the live material which was now being accumulated, was a sign of things to come – namely Zappa's continuous outpouring of creative genius and the release of a wealth of material with no stopping in sight! Even Zappa's old pal Captain Beefheart would comment on Zappa's intense work schedule. "I enjoyed him whenever I saw him but I could only enjoy him for a few minutes because he'd say, 'I've got to get back to work.' And I thought, 'God, it's a shame that you have to work so hard,' but if he has to work that hard, he has to work that hard. Some people do."

Zappa still refused to adhere to his fans' expectations – the audience would never be too sure exactly what sort of set the Mothers would deliver. On record too they would continually try the patience of their fans and record company executives alike.

Zappa was quoted as saying, "Most of the stuff that I did between '65 and '69 was directed toward an audience that was accustomed to accepting everything that was handed to them. I mean completely. It was amazing: politically, musically, socially – everything. Somebody would just hand it to them and they wouldn't question it. It was my campaign in those days to do things that would shake people out of that complacency, or that ignorance and make them question things."

It wasn't surprising that people were finding it difficult to cast the Mothers of Invention into any specific musical category. Although such impressive diversification may have kept musical integrity intact, it was not reflected in terms of commercial success. Whilst *We're Only In It For The Money* was an exquisitely achieved balancing act, both *Lumpy Gravy* and *Cruising With Ruben and The Jets* represented two very different extremes of the musical spectrum. As such both were only moderately successful in commercial terms of the time, the latter only reaching number 110 in the US charts. Nonetheless, both LPs highlighted some fine playing. In particular, *Ruben And The Jets* features some of Ray Collins finest vocal performances (he was to leave the group for good shortly after although he did resurface briefly as vocalist for Zappa's new incarnation of the Mothers in 1970 for the live premiere of *200 Motels* with Zubin Meta and the L.A. Philharmonic. He also appears on Zappa's 1974 LP *Apostrophe*).

As a footnote to the whole *Ruben* project, in a typical piece of mid-80s tape tampering, Zappa re-released *Ruben and The Jets* on CD having replaced the original bass and drum rhythm section with new recordings. It was typical of the way that he liked to play about with his original work, often reworking old songs or incorporating old sections of live material into new recordings.

Bunk Gardner: "But you know what, when he took the rhythm section out of *Ruben And The Jets* and put those other guys on... When I sat down and listened to the CD I got sick in the pit of my stomach, man. It wasn't so much sterilised, but the music was from one era and you could tell the rhythm section was from the 1980s, it didn't make sense at all to me. And the thing that blew my mind was – didn't Frank hear that? I mean it might have been technically an improvement on the rhythm, but it didn't make sense. I mean when I started talking to the fans that is the one thing that they express."

Roy Estrada echoes a similar sentiment. "I think it was because he was going out of his way to correct something. I know it. I would think anybody would notice it – didn't he?"

"We asked Zappa why he did that," Don Preston continues. "He said that the bass and drum tracks were irreplaceably damaged and that he had spent a considerable amount of money trying to get them back to normal but was unable."

Exactly a year after their first tour of Europe, the Mothers went on a return visit, mostly for a series of gigs in Germany. It was another unforgettable experience, sometimes not for exactly pleasant reasons. "I suppose though, the European tour of 1968 was probably the most memorable of all the tours that the Mothers ever did," Jimmy Carl Black says. One event that stuck in the memory of the group and fans alike was when the Mothers arrived for a gig at Berlin's Sportspalast, a place where Hitler used to make regular speeches during the war. Far from being a normal gig, the whole thing turned into a frightening event, as Jimmy Carl Black explains.

"The SDS, Students For A Democratic Society, had contacted Frank and asked him to get the audience excited that night and then tell them to all go burn down the Allied supply dump. Frank informed them that we were a musical band and we weren't into doing that kind of thing, plus of course we wanted to go back to the United States after the tour and if we'd done something like that we would never have gotten to return home. So they told us that in that case, they would destroy our show. We were about fifteen minutes into the show when we started to get showered with eggs. Then came these green pears that were like baseballs hitting us all and we didn't know where they were coming from.

"There was 10,000 people in the hall, and it was jam packed. After the pears came a can of green paint; it went all over my drums, all over me. Roy Estrada had this pair of white pants on which immediately turned green. It was then that they started ripping the iron railings from around the balconies, ready to throw those down onto the band. At this point Herb Cohen kicked the railings out of the way just as they threw them and instead of dropping onto us, they took out the first few rows of people. I mean these railings came crashing down on a lot of people. We got off the stage pretty fast and went back to the dressing room, but we couldn't get in because all the seventy or eighty security guards were hiding in there. Pretty soon a message came down that if we didn't get out on stage to finish the concert, they were going to come and get us. So we went back on. We played the last part of the show with about twenty SDS members up on stage with us – we couldn't even see each other to play. We eventually finished the show – and got the hell out of Berlin."

The band may have been rather unprepared for the intensely political atmosphere prevalent in Europe that summer (it was only a few months after the May riots in Paris). The German students had no doubt interpreted the Mothers' musical anarchy as a battering ram at the door of censorship and as a result conceived the group as a spearhead for anti-establishment rock. They assumed that Zappa would be happy to endorse their demonstrations. In reality, Zappa was interested in challenging censorship but not others' political agendas. Any political agenda the Mothers' music had was not intended to be used by any political party of whatever persuasion. In typical fashion the band's experience in Germany didn't go to waste artistically speaking, and the song "Holiday In Berlin Full Blown" was written as a direct result of this incident. The instrumental version of this song appears on the album *Burnt Weeny Sandwich*, although there are lyrics that describe the events that took place during that frightful show in Germany.

This rather unnerving experience aside, the group generally had a good time despite the obvious financial strains of keeping what was a fairly large rock and roll band on the road. On a more light-hearted note, Bunk Gardner recalls, "I do remember being on tour in 1968 in Germany, we were on a TV show and Motorhead and myself demonstrated the Buster Crabbe – a new sexual position that I had discovered one night in an Amsterdam hotel with a young American girl. We had fun with that one for a long time. Later on, in 1976, that girl became my wife (Bonnie)." In fact, Gardner has now been married twenty-five years, and has two girls, Zoe and Zena, who are twenty-three and fifteen respectively.

"I also remember after a concert in Vienna," Gardner continues, "Motorhead and I picked up two gorgeous girls at the Voom Voom club. After dancing half the night away with them, we brought them back to the hotel and I can't remember how it happened, but the girls ended up getting locked in the bathroom and becoming hysterical because they couldn't get out. So it ended up with Jim and I having to take the door off its hinges and practically destroying it to get the girls out. We had to pay for that little number."

The tour was also used as a way of compiling a film. During the day, the band would visit castles and historic places and shoot footage for the movie that would become *Uncle Meat*, whilst at night they would rehearse if they were not performing.

Although the *Uncle Meat* film would not get released for another twenty years, in 1970 Zappa loosely described the plot of the film. "The story line revolves around Don Preston, who is always changing into a monster; Phyllis Altenhouse who used to be Tom Wilson's secretary, who is now my editor's assistant on the film – who falls in love with the monster because she sees him on the screen with the machine everyday; Aynsley Dunbar, who likes to get beaten with toilet brushes, and wears a vibrator on a strap as part of his band uniform and Motorhead and Calvin (Schenkel) who have formed a group which consists of a guitar that doesn't play and cymbals... (which) are plugged with a pair of pliers, Motorhead had wings and a hat and Calvin had a tin reflector off a photographer's bulb that he wears for a thing. They like to play at the Hollywood Ranch Market; Tom Wilson who's running for President in 1972, and Suzy Creamcheese who wants to be the First Lady..."

Bunk Gardner vaguely remembers the filming of the *Uncle Meat* movie, "I don't know what it was all about. I remember Frank shooting a lot of film in the woods of Vienna and other locations. Also he used some of the live footage from the concert we did in 1968 at the Royal Festival Hall."

Gardner continues, "I would have to say that touring with Frank in the sixties bordered on the incredible when it came to the groupie situation. There was not only a sexual revolution, but social and political upheaval going on at the same time, which made things very interesting in more ways than I ever imagined! Just about every concert we played there was the potential to get laid or at least have a fairly intimate relationship for one night. After every concert there was always somebody who wanted to take you to a party or just talk or hang out and see what developed. Drugs were rampant and sex was available for the asking. Groupies were a part of the scene and acceptable to all rock musicians as a bonus for playing rock music and being a 'star'. I never dreamed in the beginning when I first joined the Mothers that I would have so many chances at having sex and fun and meeting so many new people and having such a challenge musically! There has never been a time like it, before or after!

"I certainly don't want to incriminate myself in any way, but you have to realise that we did have a reputation in the rock world, and everywhere we played there were people who wanted to know if we were really as bizarre and weird as all the stories they had heard. I can't go into detail for the readers, but strange experiences were commonplace for us because we did have individuals and groupies that would follow us around to every job that we played."

The band's tours were now more like a freaky rock 'n' roll circus where the stage show was a mixture of theatrics, satire, improvisation and extremely tight and difficult arrangements. In between numbers Zappa could bait the audience with put downs and acerbic wit, and Don Preston would amuse them with his ghoulish transformations (a sort of mad professor routine).

Sometimes the group was accompanied by other bands and musicians. "I remember the band going on the road to Buffalo, NY for a weekend, and Simon and Garfunkel came along for some fun!" Gardner recalls. "We did a lot of bizarre stuff in the hotel and in our rooms that Simon and Garfunkel filmed, like Motorhead and I demonstrating the 'Buster Crabbe' for them. Later on at the concerts, we would introduce them as our mystery guests, and while they sang, we did our usual weirdness right along with their singing. It sticks out in my mind because I remember it was my birthday, and after going to a party following the concert, I was driven back to the hotel by a gorgeous Virgo school teacher who decided to come in and help me celebrate by sharing a fine bottle of wine! Of course I couldn't help indulging in a few of my sexual fantasies as well!

"Also, I do remember a job we played out in Long Island with the Vanilla Fudge – it probably was Fudge territory anyway. We played first and halfway through our concert a guy in the audience screamed, 'You guys stink – bring on the Fudge!' That cracked everyone up and was the subject of infinite days and nights of humor for years to come."

By now the various members had established a sort of camaraderie, often as a way of relieving the tension created by trying to play such demanding music, as Bunk Gardner remembers. "For laughs in the band, you could always count on Motorhead, Jimmy Carl Black and Roy Estrada. They provided most of the humor for the rest of us, and in the early days it was badly needed because of difficulties dealing with Frank's strict discipline and the fact that we weren't making much money, but we were working a lot. We used to have a band meeting after almost every job to find out how much money we'd made – if any. All the expenses and bills had to be paid before the band did, and whatever was left went to us – if any. We were always being told not to worry when it came to explaining why we weren't making any money. It was always the old cliché about 'we are all in this thing together and if we just hang in there through the bad times, we would all eventually have the proverbial fame and fortune.' That was the constant message at the band meetings. Unfortunately the end came so soon, and later on the fame was acknowledged but the fortune completely eluded us!"

With Ray Collins having departed the group's ranks, Zappa began to look around for a possible replacement. Rather surprisingly, his choice was Lowell George, the future leader of the legendary seventies band Little Feat. George's gruff bluesy vocal style was nothing like that of Collins, and he was also a guy whose fondness for drink and drugs were somewhat legendary.

Neverthless in November of 1968, George took up the role as a Mother, as Jimmy Carl Black remembers. "Lowell had a band in California called the Factory, guys that had opened for us on several occasions. Lowell was very young at the time. He stayed with us for about four months, just up until the time we went to Europe [April/May 1969]. Frank gave him his walking papers so to speak. He told him he thought Lowell ought to start his own band. I told him at the time that if he did, he should call it Little Feet because he had little bitty feet. And as it turned out, that's pretty much what happened."

Lowell George described his stint with the Mothers in a March 1975 interview with *Zig Zag* magazine. "I got into the Mothers to replace Ray (Collins) – an impossible job, because no-one can replace Ray. He's a singer par excellence and has a sense of humor that I couldn't hope to get near. He did amazing things, very, very funny things. Well, I wound up playing more guitar than singing... We wound up doing a lot more instrumental stuff. I appeared on a couple of albums although I didn't get credited for the albums I appeared on, I got credited on other albums, because at that period everything was sort of in a state of flux that those moments were never chronicled. No-one ever scribed who did what and when. I sang on 'WPJL', a song on *Burnt Weeny Sandwich*, and I played on *Hot Rats*, and I sang something else. I wasn't on *Uncle Meat* although my photograph was. Very strange things occured at that period. I'm also on the 12-album set that Frank planned to release. I think I have half a side. I do a border guard routine. I'm a German border guard interviewing people as they cross the border. And I think I play one long relatively lame guitar solo, almost half a side. One of these days Frank will put that thing out – an Xmas album – that was when it was supposed to be. But nobody will take it. Nobody wants a 12-album set. It'll probably cost 30 bucks or something, and not many people will want to spend 30 bucks on a 12-album set of the history of the Mothers of Invention. What he might do is make it a limited edition." [Unfortunately the box set was never released.]

And so it was that George came and went. However, as the band were now recording every show they played, Lowell's performance of "Didja Get Any Onya" was captured for posterity on the subsequent compilation *Weasels Ripped My Flesh*. In recent years, some of Lowell's performances with the Mothers have surfaced, notably on the *You Can't Do That On Stage Vol.4* CD.

"I felt sorry for any guitar player that had to be in the band and play in the shadow of Frank Zappa," Bunk Gardner comments about Lowell George. "There was never any limelight because Frank had it continuously. So Lowell had to be content with being a back-up musician and didn't get much of a chance to contribute musically. Roy and Lowell hung out together a lot (both loved speed) and both were a little over-weight. They were always going out for breakfast at 6 or 7 a.m. in the morning to Rueben's deli and then just stay up the rest of the day. It was easy for Roy and Lowell to stay up for two or three days at a time. Lowell did a lot of writing at night after the concert was over. He had a lot of good ideas musically, but never got to use any of them because Frank was always doing his own thing and really wasn't interested if somebody wanted to try and contribute something to the music. If you had some verbal humor to offer then Frank was interested. He loved to be entertained with bizarre humor. Lowell was a funny guy and could get Frank to laugh fairly often. It helped Lowell feel more a part of the band, because most of the time Lowell was just in the background on stage and didn't get much of a chance to show what he could do – especially with his voice."

Richard Kunc observes that George was developing into a formidable musician in his own right. "While Lowell George was in the Mothers he was also part of an emerging group initially called Rocky Karma. Rocky Karma included most of what later became Little Feat. At the tail end of one session at Whitney, Lowell got Frank to let Rocky Karma come in and lay down a demo of a tune they'd been working on, just to see how it sounded. They particularly wanted to do it at Whitney (studio) because of that incredible organ. It was a really neat tune called 'Crack In Your Door.' We had a lot of fun recording that. Lowell was in the Mothers for just a short while, but I got to spend some time with him on tour. What a talent! I had tremendous admiration, affection, and respect for Lowell. I miss Lowell, may he forever rest in peace."

At the same time Lowell George was a member of the Mothers, Charles Buzz Gardner, Bunk's brother, joined the band and toured with them throughout 1969. Buzz beefed up the horn section, giving the jazzier sections more of a big band feel. Being Bunk's brother and the fact that he had been in the army with Don Preston meant that he already knew the guys in the band pretty well. Just like his younger brother, he had been brought up on a staple diet of jazz music.

"In 1938 when I was seven years old, I forget where I was," Buzz Gardner recalls, "but I heard someone playing cornet, and the sound of it enthralled me. The tone was clean, and it had some heroic aspects. As a result I decided I wanted to play trumpet. My folks bought me a trumpet and I had to pay it off from my paper route. About that time I started listening to the Big Bands – Harry James, Tommy Dorsey, Elliot Lawrence, Claude Thornhill, George Paxton, Count Basie etc. Later on I started listening to individual players – Charlie Parker, Dizzie Gillespie, Miles Davis, Al Cohn, Zoot Simms, Charlie Christian, and Benny Goodmans Sextet."

When Buzz was thirteen or fourteen he put together his first big band. At that time you could get stock arrangements of what the Big Bands were playing. With this band he played dances, sometimes hospitals, or whatever gigs they could get. Then when he was sixteen, he got his first professional job and went on the road with Jack Wilson and played the midwest.

Buzz then moved to New York and went to Mannes School of Music. After a year there he moved back to Cleveland. Shortly after that national service beckoned and he did his stint in the army.

Bunk Gardner describes his elder brother's musical path. "I know more about my brother than anybody. Buzz started trumpet in elementary school and progressed rapidly. By the time high school came Buzz had a 14-piece big band and a small combo that played all over Cleveland. Also while in junior high school he sang in the choir and also sang the lead in *Pirates of Penzance* by Gilbert & Sullivan – a featured production in junior high. Right out of high school Buzz was drafted into the army during the Korean War. He was sent to Trieste, Italy (1951-1953) where he met Don Preston and played in the Army Big Band, which consisted mainly of jazz musicians and many notable big names like Herbie Mann.

"After the army stint, Buzz went back to Paris, France and studied for two years at the Paris Conservatory of Music. He also played in clubs there, meeting many French jazz musicians as well as traveling around with a famous jazz band of French musicians. He continued to broaden his scope of music in general and ended up speaking fluent French. Buzz returned to the United States in 1955 and went to the Manhattan School of Music. He graduated in 1959 with a BA in music. In 1959 Buzz and I packed up and moved to California. We settled in L.A. and started our careers in music. Buzz played in Latin and jazz bands for about five or six years before he joined Frank and the Mothers."

Buzz remembers how it came about, "I used to take Bunk to rehearse at Frank Zappa's house. As I knew Don and Bunk, I had a few conversations with Frank. At that time they were going on tour in Europe. Frank told me I would be added to the band after they came back."

"Buzz was very excited about joining the band", Bunk remembers, "but he also knew he had his work cut out for him because most of the music that Frank was writing for horns was very difficult to play. Buzz struggled when he first joined the band mainly because I think Frank intimidated him a little. Frank would come in and say, 'Can you play this?' Then after you played it Frank would say, 'How fast can you play it?' Things written that seem very easy to play on guitar can be incredibly difficult on trumpet or sax. So needless to say there was always something to woodshed or practice and memorize to play for the next concert. Buzz fit in right away, but he just was not as weird or bizarre as the rest of the guys. But he loved being around the guys and it was a new experience that he enjoyed. I think the main plus of being in the band was the attention from groupies and large crowds to play for. It was real easy to score and still play challenging music with one of the best bands around. Buzz was in his glory!"

Buzz's trumpet playing is featured on *Uncle Meat, Burnt Weeny Sandwich* and *Weasels Ripped My Flesh* and latterly on *You Can't Do That On Stage Vol. 4.* Zappa was obviously keen to include him in the band because like his brother he could sightread music – now a prerequisite for all new members of the band. Buzz Gardner also confirms that, "Frank would usually get annoyed with the band because Don, Bunk, Artie, Ian and me were the only ones that could read music. Considering some of the long numbers the band would play, I think the guys did well."

Perhaps Zappa hoped Buzz would also be a bit of a sobering influence on some of the younger members of the group. In any event, Buzz remembers a memorable occasion when the rest of the band had a brush with the effects of LSD. Buzz Gardner: "I think we were in Philly when a detective climbed through the window looking for drugs. He found nothing. Another time, without Frank, the band went to a party. They didn't know it but the punch was spiked with LSD. When I went back to our room, they had all come back and were sitting on the bed holding hands and scared to death. Nobody in the band ever carried drugs."

five

The double album *Uncle Meat* was finally released in April 1969, nearly eighteen months after it had been started. The LP consisted of studio sessions recorded between October 1967 and February 1968 at Apostolic Studios in New York and Sunset Sound in Los Angeles. These were mixed with various live recordings made in Los Angeles, Copenhagen, London and Miami, along with social commentary and even an angry Jimmy Carl Black, during a band meeting, asking his trademark question of Zappa, 'When do we get paid?!'

After the dense *musique concrete* of *Lumpy Gravy* and the breezy doo-wop of *Ruben*, at last fans had an LP which was far closer to the unique experience of a Mothers' live performance.

In fact, so successful was the mixture of live and studio recordings that this was to become the template for Zappa's future practise of editing together live and studio sections, sometimes literally lifting solos or segments from live performances and grafting them onto studio recorded backing tracks. This was so skillfully executed it often became quite difficult to tell which parts were which.

Don Preston recalls: "One time, he [Zappa] was listening to the group record parts for *Uncle Meat* and writing a harmony part for the song also, and if somebody made a mistake, he'd stop them and make them go over that. I always thought that it was quite amazing that while he was writing another piece of music that he could still be listening to the one being recorded. Frank had the stamina of a bull. We'd do 50 takes of eight bars, and then 50 takes of another eight bars. I always liked to say that he was a compulsive editor. I saw him three months after an album was released, put that same album together in different ways, and re-editing the album when it's not even going to come out. He used to love to sit there and edit anything."

In a 1968 interview with *Rolling Stone* magazine, Zappa discussed the continuity that ran throughout his work. "It's all one album. All the material in the albums is organically related and if I had all the master tapes and I could take a razor blade and cut them apart and put it together again in a different order it still would make one piece of music you can listen to. Then I could take that razor blade and cut it apart and reassemble it a different way and it still would make sense. I could do this twenty ways. The material is definitely related."

"During those wonderful Apostolic days," Richard Kunc recalls, "we made and released *We're Only In It For The Money, Lumpy Gravy, Uncle Meat*, and *Cruising With Ruben & the Jets*. Two of my personal favorite album projects, however, were *No Commercial Potential* and *Ever Shall It Be*, both completely amazing six-sided beasts. Outside of me and Frank and the Mothers and other musicians involved, I doubt if anyone has ever heard either one of them. They probably don't exist anymore. Frank was forever pulling apart unfinished albums and rearranging and redistributing the component parts."

This piecing together of songs like a jigsaw was facilitated by the increasingly sophisticated recording technology that was now becoming available. Some tracks on *Uncle Meat* were so extensively over-dubbed, containing as many as forty tracks, that at times the music sounded like a full orchestra rather than just the product of ten rock musicians. As Jimmy Carl Black puts it, "*Uncle Meat* was a leap forward in technology because Frank had more toys to play with. That was on 12-track as opposed to most of the 8-track studios." The reason why *Uncle Meat* wasn't released on MGM was because Zappa had already agreed to fulfill the group's contractual obligations with the release of a LP called *Mothermania*. This was a compilation of material from the first three Mothers of Invention albums, although some of the versions are slightly different from the originals, such as "Mother People" and "Idiot Bastard Son". (Apparently obligations weren't reciprocated and Zappa had to sue to get royalties.)

In any event, Zappa and the Mothers were now free to change labels. The constant disagreements, not to mention delays in releasing material, meant they were wary about repeating their experience with MGM. As a result Zappa and Cohen set up Bizarre Records which they then licensed to Reprise Records which was a division of Warners.

Herb Cohen commented: "The contract with MGM expired in '68, and so we decided that what we would do, instead of signing directly with a company, was build an independent structure, where we would have total control of everything, and all that a major company would do for us would be distribute the product. We talked to a few labels and finally decided that Warner/Reprise would be the most flexible situation for us. Warners at that time had just acquired Reprise – before that it had been Sinatra's label – and I had known Mo Austin for a number of years. I had done business with Warners before and they were very nice people. They understood to a great degree what we wanted to do and they were willing to give us the facilities – and the money, ah ha! – with which to do it. And they were willing to accept the idea that Frank was capable of designing his own projects."

Cohen never got round to mentioning how much money was involved, but summed up by saying, "What we signed was a contract for them to distribute Bizarre Records; it wasn't like them signing the artist to their label. But they gave us enough money for us to start a project for our label. The distribution deal was for four years. And it meant, of course, that Frank got to own his own masters – no-one can put out crummy compilation albums of his material against his wishes any more like MGM did." (In the early 1970's without Zappa's consent MGM released two inferior quality "best of" MOI albums – *The Worst Of...* and *The #%&*# of The Mothers*.)

However, *Uncle Meat* ran into problems almost immediately when Pye (Warners distribution company) refused to handle it because the record featured the word 'fuck'. Zappa and Cohen immediately responded in turn by setting up Straight which would also release records by other like-minded artists who were anything but straight, musically speaking that is. Straight had a distribution deal through CBS. When *Uncle Meat* was finally distributed by way of this new arrangement with Warners, the cover alluded to the idea that this was music from a Mothers movie called "Uncle Meat" which they hadn't the money to finish. It indicated that Zappa was about to add a celluloid release (much of which had been recorded in Europe) to his vast array of output. In keeping with the LP's soundtrack possibilities, much of the music was instrumental, notably the "King Kong" suite which took up all of side four. However, the album also contained such classics songs as "Dog Breath", "Cruising For Burgers" and "Electric Aunt

Jemima", marking a return to the sort of wackiness and sexual innuendo that people had come to expect from the Mothers. As a result it scored much better commercially and reached number 43 in the US charts. The full Mothers line-up listed on the LP reflected various members and ex-members in keeping with the period of time it had taken to record. The full line-up was: Frank Zappa, Ray Collins, Jimmy Carl Black, Roy Estrada, Don Preston, Billy Mundi, Bunk Gardner, Jim Sherwood, Arthur Tripp, Buzz Gardner and Ian Underwood.

Bunk Gardner recalls that: "On the main title theme 'Uncle Meat', Frank wanted me to play clarinet through the Maestro box. So it was hard to tell what instrument I was really playing on that song. Even today people are amazed to find out that I was playing clarinet on my solo in 'King Kong.' Most of my memories of Apostolic Studios are of recording *Ruben & the Jets* and most of *Uncle Meat*. Hour after hour – many days I remember putting in anywhere from 10-16 hours recording. Give Frank a cup of black coffee and two packs of cigarettes and he was good for hours on end. I did write a clarinet duet on a version of 'Dog Breath' and recorded it at Apostolic, but Frank never used it. When I look at a lot of the song titles and try and remember particular things about any one song, I'm kind of struck by the fact that a lot of times we – the band members – would sit around and come up with weird titles for songs and lyrics. It also strikes me that Frank recorded a lot of our conversations on the bus, and during band meetings and other informal settings. He actually used a lot of our material and things that we said and put them on albums. Like the taped conversation from the band meeting where Jimmy said, 'If we'd all been living in California', or Lowell George acting like the customs agent at the border saying, 'Where's your papers?' and 'We can't shoot you'. Frank had a talent for taking all the ideas floating around and making it into his own unique creation. This was very much the case on the *Uncle Meat* album. To this day, *Uncle Meat* and *Absolutely Free* are my favourite albums."

To coincide with its release, the Mothers were back in New York in April, and headed off for a full tour of the UK in May, including Zappa giving a lecture at the LSE (London School of Economics) which was far from well received. The LSE students (like those in Germany the year before) had been expecting Zappa to be full of support for radical politics. Instead they got such observations as, "I'm not big on demonstrations" and "Revolution is just this year's flower power." The gist of Zappa's argument seemed to revolve around his belief that it was actually more subversive and successful to try and alter society by infiltrating from within, imploring his audience to make movies or become lawyers. The LSE students with their reputation for outspoken rebellion (including one very well publicised sit-in) were less than impressed and there was much hissing and booing.

Throughout 1968-69 Bizarre Records became a fully-fledged record label that contained a roster of artists that truly lived up to the label's name – BIZARRE. A statement issued proclaiming the company's motives set the scene: "We make records that are a little different. We present musical and sociological material which the important record companies would probably not allow you to hear. Just what the world needs... another record company." Such budding new talent the ambitious label boasted were the Alice Cooper group, Wildman Fischer, and the GTOs. Even the redoubtable Captain Beefheart recorded probably his most aspiring and notorious album for the Bizarre label – *Trout Mask Replica*.

"Frank's album work was done in various studios on both coasts," Richard Kunc recalls. "I think it was early '69 when we all moved to Los Angeles – lock, stock, and record company. In L.A. we made *Hot Rats*, *Burnt Weeny Sandwich*, and *Weasels Ripped My Flesh*. We also did a few strange non-Mothers projects, like *An Evening With Wildman Fischer* and *Permanent Damage* by the GTOs."

For a long time it had been Zappa's dream to build his own studio. "That was the grand and glorious plan," Kunc remembers. "I drew up dozens of designs and equipment lists in the early Los Angeles days. That wonder-studio, alas, never happened. In the late, late years, long after my time, he built a pretty space-age facility into his house. It was probably close to what our dream was way back when. Anyway, after moving to L.A. we used places like the Record Plant, TTG, Sunset Studios, and some others."

Every time they heard about a new studio, Zappa and Kunc would check it out. "It was a hell of an education," Kunc says. "The one that stands out, the place where we did lots of really interesting things, is a place in Glendale called Whitney Studios – maybe it's still there. I had stumbled upon it accidentally – I think I saw it in the Yellow Pages. I called them up and went over to take a look. It had been primarily a religious music and gospel kind of place. The main room, which was really big, had a well planned, well constructed studio. They had a huge full-blown Wurlitzer organ with dozens of pipes, tambourines, violins, drums, and other crap behind the walls of the studio. There were grills at the upper levels of the walls all around the studio where the sounds of these various things came out. That organ was used on many, many albums by groups you know.

"They had a very fine 3M 16-track machine, and a really fine console. Not fancy, but extremely well thought out and versatile. And the more we and our ilk used the place, the more neat new equipment they added, often at our suggestion. That was very smart marketing on their part and it kept us coming back and sending our friends. We cranked out lots of stuff there. We did the first Alice Cooper album, *Pretties For You*. We did Captain Beefheart's ground-breaking *Trout Mask Replica* there. A lot of the later non-Mothers Zappa stuff that involved the *Hot Rats* material with people like Jean Luc Ponty was also done at Whitney."

Many of the bands on the Bizarre label were certainly nowhere near as musically proficient as the Mothers. Zappa's main criteria appeared to be based around notoriety rather than musical acumen.

Bunk Gardner remembers the early the Alice Cooper group. "Since Herb and Frank had signed the group to the Bizarre label, they played on the same bill with us at some gigs in 1969. They were pitiful musically – even embarrassing, but it was 'Theatre Of The Absurd' and the kids loved it. Forget the music – it was the weird show that the kids loved. But I still cringed at how bad musically they were. A nice bunch of guys, but they were just starting out and really just novices in a lot of ways. I didn't understand why Frank and Herbie signed them to begin with. But later on I could see as their stage act got better their popularity started to rise. Although I thought the stage thing was a little corny, most of the young kids didn't. They were all teeny-boppers themselves and most of the guys in Frank's band were older, more mature and certainly much better musicians. So we really didn't hang out with any of the Alice Cooper group members."

Michael Bruce of the Alice Cooper group confirms that Zappa's interest was somewhat fleeting. "I remember Frank came to only one recording session for the *Pretties For You* album. He was so bored with the project that he turned it over to Ian Underwood, who did the rest of the producing, even though he didn't receive credit on the album. I think because we were signed to Shep Gordon it meant that Frank and Herb couldn't control the group, and they quickly lost interest. But we were the only act on the Bizarre label that really went on to become very success-ful."

In a recent interview with Russell Hall of *Goldmine* magazine (May 19, 2000 issue), Alice Cooper Group drummer Neal Smith reminisces about the *Pretties For You* album. "I like *Pretties For You* for its originality. When you create music that sounds like other music that's going on at the time, it becomes dated. On the other hand, when you do something that's different, it has a better chance of hold-ing up over time. Unfortunately, when we went into the studio, we were very green, and we didn't know anything about the recording process. Frank Zappa said he wanted the album to sound like a car driving past a garage while a band was playing. That was his goal, and I think he more or less achieved it. He had us set up our amps around the drum set, so there was total leakage. We would run down the song – setting the dials on our amps and stuff, just trying to get a proper sound going so that we could record – and Zappa would say, "We got a take." We would be like, "What? We didn't even play the song yet."

Bunk Gardner describes his encounters with the very much less successful Wildman Fischer. "Wildman was always out on the street. I would run into him everywhere – from the Whisky to the all night Jewish deli Cantors. When we played in L.A. there were the GTOs, Vito and his dancers and Wildman Fischer. Frank would have him come up on stage and just let him be his normal weird self – making up songs as he went along and trying to be funny. He always reminded me of somebody with a 12 year old mind in a 25 year old body. He always seemed a little paranoid about something. I didn't know if he was making things up or he had a very fertile imagination or maybe he was just on acid or some mind expand-ing drug. Anyway, he seemed to make Frank laugh and in the end Wildman did an album of his songs on Frank's label (*An Evening With Wildman Fischer*).

Years later, I played at a club on Hollywood Boulevard called Legends of Hollywood and we were called the Hollywood Allstars. Wildman would come in once a week and say "Hi", and show me some of his old clippings of articles on himself. He'd also talk about the old days and how he thought the Mafia was out to wreck his career (more paranoia). He thought he would eventually take his act to Vegas and really hit it big. He's still crazy as ever, but probably still as naive as ever."

Don Preston remembers Wildman as well. "Poor guy – he does have serious mental problems, like a lot of homeless people today. They're not completely crazy where they go out and hurt people, but they are too crazy to go out and make a living. We used to have places for people like that, but unfortunately the government took away the funding. The thing is, Wildman used to stand on the street corner and strum on an album cover like a guitar (presumably his own) and sing these songs like 'Merry Go Round' and whatever. He had a bunch of songs and people would give him some change to sing, and that's how he survived for those many years. I think he's probably still doing that."

Frank Zappa himself commented. "He needed some structuring, someone with an appreciation of what his craft was, to sit through the problems of making the album and then have the patience to put it together in the continuity the listener could pay attention to. Listen, the people who bought the *Saturday Night Fever* album probably won't like *An Evening With Wildman Fischer*. But that album was made for the people who like that kind of stuff and all the rest of the albums I make are for people who like that kind of stuff. If they like it, fine. If they don't, there's other stuff."

The GTOs (short for Girls Together Outrageously) were another bunch of Zappa proteges who recorded only one album for Bizarre called *Permanent Damage*. Bunk Gardner remembers, "They always looked so vampirish; black lipstick, black mascara, black everything – a little bit too unattractive for my taste. They were always at most of the concerts in Los Angeles that we played. Only one of them was very appealing – her name was Jerry and she wore a white nurse's uniform sometimes. She was cute and had real thin lips and loved to get high and hang out. I think most of them wanted to be different, and we represented an alternative to most rock bands at that time. For the most part nobody wanted to be mainstream. There were a lot of people who came to our concerts and just stared at us – the GTOs, Vito and his dancers – we were different in so many ways! From the music we played to the entourage that surrounded us!"

Pamela Des Barres recalls, "I first met Frank at the Shrine Auditorium in Los Angeles for a big '60s freak-out scene with the Mothers and all these other bands. I was just mesmerized. Frank wore these bellbottoms with flowers all over them. He was always poking fun at whatever was happening, and he continued to do that right to the end. He was wandering around after the show and I made a point of slamming into him on the dance floor. A bunch of us used to dance at all the local rock shows. We called ourselves the Laurel Canyon Ballet Company. One of the girls who danced with us was Moon's [Zappa's daughter] governess, so she started inviting us up to Frank's house, which was very exciting. Frank was like the ruler of Laurel Canyon. He lived in Tom Mix's old house. People would just congregate up there and, in his words, 'freak out'. And not only were you allowed to, but Frank would just pull that stuff out of people. He made them become their true, freaky selves. He didn't need drugs either. In fact, he'd get mad if anyone was using. I lived at his guest house in the back when I was governess for the kids. It wasn't what you'd call normal but it wasn't what people thought either. It was a very free-form household – loose, but very loving and warm. He was very much a family man."

Another Bizarre signing was an altogether different kettle of fish. Zappa's old friend Don Van Vliet (Captain Beefheart) had a much more fertile and successful recording career – one that has continued (like Zappa himself) to exert a strong influence on new generations of musicians. In a 1968 interview with *Rolling Stone* Magazine, Zappa talked about his early relationship with Captain Beefheart. "Don and I used to get together after school and would listen to records for three or four hours. We'd start off at my house, and then we'd get something to eat and ride around in his old Oldsmobile. Then we'd go to his house and raid his old man's bread truck and we would sit and eat pineapple buns and listen to these records until five in the morning and maybe not go to school the next day. It was the only thing that seemed to matter at the time. We listened to those records so often we could sing the guitar leads. We'd quiz each other about how many records does this guy have out, what was his last record, who wrote it, what is the record number."

Bunk Gardner recalls that, "I spent a lot of time hanging out with Don and his band. I always felt he was just too far ahead of his time to be appreciated. He was always very creative with his words and always talking. His creativity was endless. His freak-out solos on soprano and bass clarinet were sometimes just awesome, but some people just didn't know what to think. At one point, Don gave up playing the bass clarinet, so I bought it from him for $250 and I still have the instrument to this day. Don and Frank got along fairly well most of the time. I felt that Don had more dimensions and warmth to his playing and musical ideas. Frank's playing was a little calculated, like a mathematician figuring a solution to a problem, and felt a little cold. Even looking at Frank's music you really had to break it down mathematically to figure it out and play it and memorize it."

Don Preston reminisces about the good Captain as well. "I did hang out with Don a few times. One of the things that struck me about him was the fact that when you were just having a conversation on the street corner, he talked pretty much like his lyrics! That's just the way he talked, and that really blew me away. He was that off-the-wall – he just could sit down and write stuff like that, and I thought that was quite amazing. The other thing that I was aware of at that time was that this guy could really paint. He really is a fine artist. I had seen several of his paintings at that time, of course now they're selling for big bucks. I thought what he and the Magic Band were doing at that time was interesting – it wasn't really my cup of tea, in a sense I go for more organized music. But I could sort of see what he was doing and I appreciated the value of what he was doing. When Beefheart recorded the *Trout Mask Replica* album, Zappa told me that he was totally amazed at the band because they went into the studio and recorded the entire album (studio material) in one take – pretty much without stopping! They just played the whole album. But the thing was, Zappa wasn't so satisfied with that so much – Frank said he needed to have the band do a second take just in case he needed to switch things around a bit. So he asked them to do it again, and once again they did the entire album in one take! Zappa was completely amazed because the second takes were virtually identical to the first!"

It is no secret that Frank Zappa and Captain Beefheart at times had a rocky relationship. Don Preston speculates as to why. "Well, they grew up together and went to high school together. They also went for several years without communicating with each other. Both Frank and Don had two very extreme personalities, and how they ever did anything together is a mystery to me. Both had very strong personalities and they both had real definite ideas about the way things should be done, So one of them had to give a bit, I imagine. But, they did manage to put a couple things out together and that's amazing to me."

A common feature at the time was for Frank Zappa to host jam sessions in his basement to which a whole variety of musicians would be invited. Bunk Gardner again, "I do remember a couple of jams that we had in Frank's basement with Beefheart that were pretty wild and as always Frank recorded them. At some point in the future I'm sure these tapes will show up on CD. Don played harmonica and sang and everyone got to solo and work out a little. One of the things I liked about Don was how unconventional he was and how unorthodox his approach to music was – just unique to a degree that made it abstract and interesting at the same time."

The first Captain Beefheart LP to be released on Bizarre was the epic double-LP *Trout Mask Replica,* which was partially recorded at Whitney Studios in Glendale over one or two nights in 1968. "We were doing some recording for Frank in one studio," Bunk Gardner recalls, "and Beefheart was in the other studio just cranking out one track after another, like a production line. He knew what he wanted once he got into a studio and didn't waste any time doing it. Don didn't write most of his music out, so there was a lot of repetition in rehearsing the music until it was memorised and ingrained so you didn't forget it. His band was really the only contemporary rock band I heard in all my years playing with Frank in the '60s."

"I don't remember the exact day I met Don Van Vliet," Richard Kunc remembers. "'Captain Beerfart' we affectionately called him. Probably around the time we began planning *Trout Mask Replica* in Los Angeles. It was probably at Frank's house during the meetings we had before going into the studio. There was a lot of planning and stuff – rehearsing and listening to what they were going to do on the album and so forth. Don and I became good friends. We both lived in Woodland Hills. As a matter of fact, we lived just over the hill from one another, and I used to go over to Don's house a lot – partly on business, partly just for the hell of it. I used to take the little Uher tape machine with me and record all kinds of songs and stuff at their rehearsals to analyze them, to see how we should approach them in the studio. Most of the time I went over there it was just social. The band would just be waking up in the middle of the afternoon – and they would be playing inside or outside the house while they were having lunch.

"The sessions we did at Whitney for *Trout Mask Replica* were great! We had a wonderful time. Later, when the Zappa thing folded up and I was getting ready to leave L.A., Don says, 'When I do my next album I want you to record it!' I said, 'Great, I'd love to!' He says, 'OK, I'll send for you.' I kind of forgot that, and time went by – six months to a year. All of a sudden I get this call from Don, 'Come on out – I'm making a new album and I still want you to do it.' So I got on a plane and flew out there.

"A side note here – Herbie Cohen told me, 'OK, when you're doing these sessions we need you to be 'our man' in there. Beefheart has a way of wasting studio. So without upsetting him, we want you to kinda keep things moving so it doesn't get needlessly expensive.' Great. So now I had two roles.

"We got into the recording studio at the Record Plant. We were working on stuff, getting some tracks down, and things were going along fine. It was day three or four. We were working on a track and Don was asking me for some kind of really special 'locomotive' sound on his voice. We were experimenting with multiple microphones and strange placements and stuff. It got to a point where I had to make a mild but obvious executive decision like, 'Let's move on, we're spending too much time on this' or 'Let's keep it rolling.' It wasn't a big deal. Well, Beefheart exploded! Went ballistic on me! Suddenly it was, 'I'm the boss here and you have nothing to say about this! Who do you think you are? You're done, you're fired, get out of here, beat it!' Wow, this is a guy I'd been real close friends with up until that instant. I never did understand that – that was that! I went to see Herbie, got paid in full, and went home! And Don and I haven't spoken since. To this day I have no idea what that was all about. It hurt. I mourn the loss of Don's friendship and never got an explanation. But maybe a lot of people go through this with him – I don't know."

Through the summer of '69 the Mothers were back in the States touring. The standard now being each and every show recorded for possible use by Zappa for later album projects.

Richard Kunc recalls, "There was one amazing road recording experience, I think it was 1969. The Mothers were going on an East-coast tour, and those of us who were not going, which included me, drove everybody else to L.A. airport. A couple days went by and I got a call from Frank saying, 'I've changed my mind, I want you to come and record the rest of this tour.' I said, 'Frank, you may not have noticed but we don't have any equipment!' He said, 'I know – just buy what you need and put it together.' To him it was buy a screwdriver and a pair of pliers and that's it – you're off, what else do you need? So he said, 'Fly to Miami. Herbie will take care of all the financing – just tell him what you need. Fly to Miami and buy all the stuff – assemble it into a recording package, and we'll meet you there and you'll go on the rest of the tour with us.' – which was by bus.

"So off I went to Miami, which was my old stomping ground so that wasn't too bad. In Miami I bought a Uher five-inch-reel battery-operated two-track stereo 7¹/2 ips recorder, a little portable thing with a shoulder strap. It came complete with a one-piece stereo microphone which we used on the road a lot, mainly on the bus and in all those hotels and motels. You need to ask Bunk Gardner about an epic field recording he made with it in Miami with the help of a nurse named Peggy, a work entitled 'Right There, Bunk!' Anyway, it was an amazing little machine. Many miles of recordings done on that machine ended up in various albums – the quality was that good!

"For Monitoring I bought a Dynaco preamp and a Dynaco power amp, which were kits, so I had to build them. I also bought some KLH-6 speakers which were in vogue at the time, a couple of Shure mixers, and about ten microphones ranging from some medium-priced Sony condensers down to a bunch of Shure and various other brand dynamics. It was a selection designed to handle everything from vocals to bass drums.

"I flew to Miami and bought all this stuff, plus a few basic tools with which to build it. I took it all to my motel room and over the next two days I built all the Dynaco kit stuff. No way to test it, of course; it just had to be right.

"Now the one missing ingredient was a microphone cable 'snake' that would reach from whatever back room I would be in, out onto the stage where we'd place our microphones. So I bought a ton of shielded balanced cable, Belden 8451 I think it's called, and made a snake that accommodated ten microphones – the whole thing being a hundred feet long. So that's a total of ten one-hundred-foot lengths of cable with Cannon connectors on both ends – a lot of cutting and a lot of soldering. All this measuring out the ten one-hundred-foot lengths had to be done in my dinky little hotel room, and of course there were none of those nice nylon cable ties to bundle it all together. I ended up lacing the ten lines together with string, which worked great but looked like something done by a stoned marionette. With this instant portable studio we recorded whole concerts in Miami, Philadelphia, the Fillmore East, Boston, Yale in Connecticut – a whole bunch of cities. That tour went from city to city on a Greyhound bus driven by a guy named Jake. He was the company's 'stunt driver' and had made some TV spots doing 'donuts' with a Greyhound SemiCruiser! Jake was cool. He fit right in, and we were glad to have him along. But that's another story."

Frank Zappa had started recording his second solo LP *Hot Rats* in August 1969. Meanwhile the *Mothermania* compilation was released in September and all seemed to be going favorably for the Mothers of Invention. Zappa, as well, continued with various side projects like the *Uncle Meat* movie and his continuous composing of orchestral music.

Richard Kunc remembers: "In the later years, when we were in L.A. and Frank was living in the 'log cabin' – Tom Mix's old log house up in Laurel Canyon – he would occasionally want to hear live musicians play some charts he had written. These weren't charts for the Mothers, but for classical players. Frank would put out the word that he wanted musicians to come and voice some new charts. It was amazing – I remember seeing carloads of symphony players show up with their french horns and bassoons and everything. I mean there must have been twenty or twenty five of these people from the local symphonies with all the instruments you learned about in 'Music 101'. Gail would put out a bunch of folding chairs and music stands probably rented a few hours earlier. The musicians would sit down and tune up, and Frank would pass out the charts and climb up onto his little homemade podium with his baton. They weren't being paid, but Frank had such a reputation as a composer that these people volunteered to come and play just so they could read his charts! Whole days were spent doing this. I just sat there and watched the faces of these players. It was like they'd been turned loose in some sort of musical Disneyland or Oz! We never recorded any of it that I recall. It was amazing – a wonder to behold!"

Ironically, just as it seemed as if the Mothers of Invention were finally going to reach that pinnacle of success they had worked so hard over the past six years to achieve, suddenly in October 1969 a Warner Brothers press release was issued under the headline, "Whatever happened to the Mothers of Invention?" and read like this: "The Mothers of Invention, infamous and repulsive rocking teen combo, is not doing concerts anymore... It is possible that, at a later date, when audiences have properly assimilated the recorded work of the group, a re-formation might take place."

It was Zappa's way of saying that he had fired his band. Officially, the reason given was that audiences applauded for all the wrong reasons. More pertinently the costs of keeping a 10-piece band on the road was becoming expensive (Zappa was allegedly $10,000 in debt at the time and paying each Mother $250 a week in salary). He was depressed and broke, the last four years had been a whirlwind of constant touring and recording and he felt he had reached a dead end. The rest of the Mothers were understandably confused and angry at Zappa's decision.

"Concerning the break up of the original Mothers," Jimmy Carl Black states, "we had just got back from an East Coast tour, we'd been back about a week when I called Frank to ask him some question or another. We talked for a while and pretty soon he said, 'Oh, by the way I've decided to break up the band. You guys are now unemployed.' I thought that was really cold, but that's the way Frank did it. It wasn't a very pleasant experience at the time – we felt we were being very successful and didn't think that was called for, but hey... I think that Frank considered that the Mothers of Invention weren't good enough musicians to do the things that he wanted to do at that particular point. I don't think that was true, but then again I wasn't writing the songs. In fact, the Mothers of Invention were really the only band that Frank Zappa ever had. All the rest of the guys have just been sidesmen. We weren't sidesmen – we were partners. With the Mothers, it was at the time I think the best band in the world, the most avant-garde and innovative band with sort of commercial potential – even though we were always seen as the ones who had no commercial potential. And Zappa, back then, he was twenty-eight or twenty-nine; what can I say? He was a genius."

Jimmy Carl Black ends by saying, "I still think that if we had stayed together we could still be there just like the Rolling Stones, and made a lot of very, very good records along the way." Don Preston agrees: "If he'd stuck with the original band, we would be making about ten million a year now. Look at the Grateful Dead!"

If part of Zappa's decision to disband the group revolved around musical ability, what he had failed to grasp was that half the charm of the original Mothers came from the lack of ability of some members to play the complicated sections. Looking at it purely from a technical point of view, he obviously felt that this was giving the music an amateurish edge, but it was exactly that spontaneous anarchic feel which made the music so appealing. After all, many of the great bands have featured musicians that aren't exactly virtuosos on their chosen instrument. Ringo Starr springs to mind – the Beatles would never have sounded quite the same without him.

It's anyone's guess as to whether the original Mothers would have continued to develop and produce fine records if they'd stayed together. Perhaps Zappa was right and this configuration of musicians had gone as far as they could and if they'd carried on they would have simply outstayed their welcome. Certainly, some commentators remain convinced that the most conceptual, bizarre and reliably consistent of Zappa's records were those which he made with his original band.

However, Zappa himself obviously felt it was time for a change of direction. Bunk Gardner believes that, "Frank decided that he wanted to go in another direction. I think he was just tired of the band, certainly we were criticised many, many times about how badly we played his music. He was very unhappy with certain members of the band. He probably thought it would be less of a drain financially as well, because at that point we were making a salary of $250 a week and I think it was just too much of a drain on him. But it was his doing and there wasn't much we could do about it. Everybody went their own way – I certainly played with a lot of different bands around that time, but nothing could match the musical challenge with Frank! But I do remember that when the band broke-up, we all went up to Frank's house for a meeting to find out how things were going to be divided up (amplifiers, equipment, etc.) and how much money we would get. Herb Cohen passed out financial statements and informed us that instead of us getting any money, that the band had been losing money for the last eight months and that we were actually $20,000 in debt! We were all totally in shock, shaking our heads. Then Frank said he would forget about the twenty grand and 'let's just call it even.' And that's how our final meeting ended."

"You know I remember going up to Frank's house after the band broke up and we were going to organize another tour. We all went up to Frank's house and we had a meeting. We said, 'Is Herbie (Herb Cohen) coming along?' And he said, 'Yes' – so nothing ever happened with that tour."

Motorhead thinks that, "Frank was just tired of touring and playing. He wanted to go in a different direction. We talked about it. He asked everybody to just go out and join other groups and play different styles of music, and then we'd get back together later on and do our thing again with a lot of new ideas and new material. Nobody wanted to, because at that time, we were starting to make pretty good money. The name the Mothers was really big, and Frank said, 'Hey, if you don't want to do that, then that's it. We quit.' He just broke up the band and that was the end of that.

Don Preston was one of the members who got hired for subsequent incarnations of the Mothers. "To explain how that original band broke up is really hard. There are many, many reasons. I think Zappa was dissatisfied with some of the performances of the band, the limited nature of some of the people like Roy Estrada and Jimmy Carl Black who couldn't read music. They did play some very complicated stuff, but it just wasn't complicated enough. Zappa wanted the very best sight readers in the world to read his music, and unfortunately when he got these sight readers they had absolutely no personality, which is why the band sounded the way it did after that. That's certainly why it looked the way it did, anyhow. But who knows what the real reason was in the end? I really don't know. But it was a big shock to all of us. It was like when you've been married ten years and all of a sudden your wife leaves you. It was the same feeling, because we were all of us very close and we'd been doing this for quite a while and it was just a big shock. Myself and Ian Underwood appeared in the next two bands that Frank put together."

Don Preston, when pushed to sum up his experiences in the Mothers, seems to echo all their sentiments when he says, "Bittersweet memories of having great music to play, great women, being in the limelight, and having to deal with Zappa's strict discipline most of the time."

Ray Collins emphasises the contributions of the other members by saying, "Well, a 'personal ensemble', in many cases, probably in most cases, does it exactly the way the composer wanted, but the ensemble that made up the Mothers of Invention not only played it the way Frank wanted, we shaped it also. We incorporated our ideas of ways of doing it. I've seen a lot of Frank's bands, and I haven't talked about it too much, 'cause it would sound sort of like sour grapes – all the guys in Frank's band seem to do what *they* think the Mothers of Invention are supposed to do. They all try to act zany. They'll have some bit of clothing that's cuckoo, that they envision the Mothers would do 'cause it would 'be funny'."

Richard Kunc describes his view of the break up. "Well, that was really strange – I don't really know all the business facts, but I can tell you what my recollection is. It was about 1970 out in L.A. and we'd all reached the stage where the band, the Mothers – the actual real honest-to-goodness Mothers – almost never really played together anymore. Frank was busy with studio musicians and symphony people and movie deals and this, that and the other thing. The band just kind of withered away. And then one day he had Herbie Cohen call all the members of the band and just tell them they were through – they were fired – that's it... pick up your checks... we'll see you later... boom! Goodbye. I wondered if the same would happen to me, and it did. I got a phone call from Herbie, 'Your services are no longer required.' And that was that. It was very cold! There was no, 'Gee, thanks for all the good times... we really enjoyed the association.' Nothing! Just, 'We don't need you... we're done... goodbye.' That was that – the end of the Mothers of Invention!"

In a 1975 interview with *Creem* Magazine, Frank Zappa gave his side of the story by describing his reasons for the break-up of the original Mothers. "I was frustrated. When you play your music before an audience interested in only one thing, the ultimate pumping of the rhythm section, it can piss you off. It also pissed me off that the band could never drive the way I wanted it to. It sounds rather irrational, but I was constantly torn between two ideals. I didn't like the idea of firing people from the group. At this point, there was only one person I had fired from the first Mothers and that was because he was too stoned to play. No matter what the other guys did I wouldn't fire them. I kept on bringing in new people to make the musical end of things more proficient.

"But the band was always down on me because I was their employer. If I'm the guy who's paying the bills, how can I be a human being? I've had the problem with all of the bands. It's strange. Finally it got to the point where I just said, 'Fuck it.' I like to play blues. I like to get out there and boogie. But I like to do other stuff, too. I want musicians who can do both, have the same range of interest as I have.

"By the time our last tour ended I was $10,000 in debt. But the band got paid their salaries whether they played or not. I had to pay the expense of shipping the equipment and guaranteeing them $250 a week even if we didn't work. I couldn't do it. When I told them I couldn't do it they hated me because suddenly they were unemployed.

"It was painful at times. There was always such a vast difference between what would happen in the studio and what would happen on stage. Most of the people could not play live on the same level as the album. Ian Underwood, for instance, was a very academic musician who could play everything you could give him. He wasn't funky, though, and wasn't into the blues at all. Art Tripp was the same way... a good percussionist who could play his butt off but couldn't do a shuffle. Bunk Gardner was somewhere in between. He was a jazz musician who could play a variety of woodwind instruments but had limitations in other areas. Don Preston could really improvise in all kinds of weird situations but could not sight read music. He had a mental block about that. Seeing all those little notes on paper frightened him to death. All the rest of the band, myself included, was musically illiterate."

Zappa also talked about the break-up to music reporter Jerry Hopkins. "It all started in Charlotte, North Carolina. We'd been booked by George Wein on a jazz concert date as bait to get a teenage audience. We went into a 30,000-capacity auditorium (Park Center) with a 30-watt public address system, it was 95 degrees and 200 per cent humidity, with a thunderstorm threatening. It was really horrendous. After that I had a meeting with the group and told them what I thought about the drudgery of grinding it out on the road. And then I came back to L.A. and worked on *Hot Rats*. Then we did one more tour – eight days in Canada. After that I said, 'Fuck it.'

"I like to play but just got tired of beating my head against the wall; I got tired of playing for people who clap for the wrong reasons. I thought it was time to give people a chance to figure out what we've done already before we do any more.

"At first they (the Mothers) were extremely angry at me for breaking up the band, not because they wanted to play the music but because I had been supporting them. Suddenly I had taken away their income. I said to them, 'Look, am I supposed to kill myself going out and doing this over and over again? Well, it's not any fun for me anymore.' I was really depressed about it, I couldn't do it anymore."

After the break up, two LPs of unreleased live and studio material were released almost immediately. Despite Zappa's worries about the musical abilities of his original band he had seemingly no qualms about using live performances by the original Mothers as the basis for these two collections. (Not to mention the snippetts of live performances that appeared as late as the '80s and '90s on various releases.) The title *Burnt Weeny Sandwich* possibly referred to that fact that this was a mixture of live and studio recordings from 1968 and 1969 sandwiched between two 1950s cover versions (as well as a fond name for one of Zappa's favourite late night snacks – a slightly burnt hotdog sandwiched in between two pieces of white bread). The LP was released in December 1969 and features the classic "Holiday In Berlin (Full Blown)" referring to the incident on the European tour of 1968. In total the LP featured contributions from the Mothers line-ups of: Frank Zappa, Jimmy Carl Black, Roy Estrada, Don Preston, Bunk Gardner, Buzz Gardner, Jim Sherwood, Arthur Tripp, Sugar Cane Harris and Ian Underwood.

"*Burnt Weeny Sandwich* was recorded in various places," Jimmy Carl Black remembers, "including a lot of live recordings, as was *Weasels Ripped My Flesh*. For the last two years of the band, we recorded every show that we played and recently Frank has put out those *You Can't Do That On Stage Anymore* samplers, one of which (Vol. 4) I understand from a friend of mine has about 70 minutes of the original Mothers of Invention live stuff on it."

Weasels Ripped My Flesh was again essentially a mixture of live and studio recordings from 1967 to 1970 and was released in September 1970. Featuring the classics "My Guitar Wants to Kill Your Mama" and "Oh No", it highlighted the Mothers big band line-up of: Frank Zappa, Jimmy Carl Black, Roy Estrada, Ray Collins, Don Preston, Bunk Gardner, Buzz Gardner, Jim Sherwood, Arthur Tripp and Ian Underwood, augmented by Sugar Cane Harris and Lowell George.

From 1965 to 1969, the Mothers had produced some remarkable music. Zappa managed to create a complete aura around the band as the dirtiest, weirdest and most technically proficient (even if he didn't sometimes think so) rock 'n' roll band in the world. He constantly reworked and recycled themes (and continued to do so) from this period, whether it be Suzy Creamcheese, groupies, all manner of sexual innuendo, improvisations or complex rhythmic ideas and interpretations. He pioneered a general wackiness that both confused and intrigued, sticking two fingers up at the authorities, successive record companies, the hippies, and ultimately his own band.

Zappa summed it up saying, "I wasn't happy with the first Mothers as a group of musicians. But they were the only people I could get. I didn't think of them so much as musicians than as people. It was their idiosyncrasies that made the group, not their musicianship. I've very seldom been happy with any of the bands.

"The main thing to remember about the first batch of Mothers is a) they didn't want to do it, b) they didn't know what they were doing when they were doing it and c) if they knew what they were doing, they wouldn't have done it in the first place. Most of those people were extremely straight. Jimmy Carl Black used to hide his hair down his collar when he walked through an airport so no one would know he had long hair. I'm telling you, people had such fantasies about what the band was like but they were really deep down conservatives. They just had these little idiosyncrasies which I tried to amplify into a large, idiosyncratic unit which I presented to the public. They're all nice guys. The freakishness that most people attributed to the group was all highly exaggerated. It came across onstage because I made it come across onstage."

In any event, by the end of the sixties much of the craziness that had surrounded the hippies and the freaks had been assimilated into mainstream culture. Rock 'n' roll had become a million dollar business churning out superstars by the month. However, undoubtedly as the iconography of rock gained momentum, so Zappa's moustached sneer joined Morrison's tousled pout, Lennon's bespectacled look and Hendrix's spaced-out glare as lasting images of what some see as this century's most enduringly fascinating musical decade.

six

Despite the fact that Frank Zappa buried the first incarnation of the Mothers of Invention as a musical unit, the name refused to lie down and die. As a new decade dawned Zappa launched himself into a solo career which included finding time to play with Pink Floyd and his old school friend Captain Beefheart. He also played a second date at the Royal Albert Hall. In May conductor Zubin Meta and the Los Angeles Phil-harmonic offered to play a concert of Zappa music – the premier of music from the *200 Motels* suite – the only proviso being that he was to reform the Mothers of Invention to play as well. This oppor-tunity was too good to turn down.

Seemingly, here at last was recognition of his position as a serious classical avant-garde composer. As regards to reforming the Mothers of Invention, only Ian Underwood, Don Preston, Billy Mundi, Motorhead and Ray Collins got a call. Also in this temporary Mothers (who also did some gigs in New York, augmented by violinist Sugarcane Harris) was drummer Aynsley Dunbar, as well as Jeff Simmons and Ruth Underwood.

Don Preston remembers: "There were two separate concerts we did there with Zubin Meta – I remember one was with Ray Collins, Aynsley Dunbar, Billy Mundi – I also remember Ruth Underwood playing percussion. She sat in the percussion section, and I remember she was so good! That group played some gigs in New York as well. Zappa then formed a temporary group called Hot Rats which featured Aynsley, Max Bennett, Sugarcane Harris and I think Ian."

Some of the material this line-up played was "How Could I Be Such A Fool", "Son Of Mr. Green Genes", "A Pound For A Brown", "Call Any Vegetable", "My Boyfriends Back" and "Duke Of Prunes". Zappa would later describe this historic concert as such, "A lot of people said it sounded like movie music. Well in a way it was – for a movie they haven't seen yet, the movie that I was living while I was out there on the road with the Mothers. I'd go back to the motel after the job and write whatever I was thinking about, it was more like a musical diary, a two-year orchestral diary."

This historic concert was held on 15 May, 1970 at UCLA's Pauley Pavilion. Ironically, in attendance at the L.A. Philharmonic gig were ex-Turtles, Mark Volman and Howard Kaylan (Flo & Eddie). Both would become fully fledged Mothers in the following months.

In a 1986 interview, as told to journalist Alan Vorda, Mark Volman had this to say about his and Howard Kaylan's joining of the Mothers. "Howard and I got an offer to join Frank Zappa's band, the Mothers of Invention, and go to Europe. The Mothers included Frank, Ansley Dunbar, Ian Underwood, Donnie Preston, and Jeff Simmons. It seemed like a great vacation for us to get out of town, so we did. One of the things that was happening was that we couldn't use our real names. Once we went into litigation (a lawsuit between the Turtles members and their former record company Blue Whale) we slapped a suit on our record company based on an auditing. When the group (Turtles) split up we sued them for royalties, estimated punitive damages and so forth and they re-sued us because of our non-knowledge or lack of investigating. We signed as a group collectively and individually which is the way groups signed with a record company. When we broke the band up it was collectively and they didn't own the Turtles except individually. If Howard and I made a record they owned us individually for any recording profit. The only way we could get out of it was to sue them and win the lawsuit so we could use our real names on record. Basically, they owned the names Turtles and Mark Volman for our records. That's when the litigation began. It took four years to free up our names individually. We couldn't use our real names

Above: Mothers of Invention, circa *Uncle Meat.*
Below: Mothers 1969 promo photo. Bottom row: Lowell George, Roy Estrada, Frank Zappa, Ian Underwood (standing), Art Tripp.
Top row: Jimmy Carl Black, Don Preston, Bunk Gardner, Motorhead.
Photos: Michael Ochs Archive.

Above: Jimmy Carl Black, Frank Zappa and Roy Estrada during the recording of *Beat Club* in Hamburg for German TV in 1967. *Photo: Petra Niemier/Redferns*.

Top right: On tour, 1969. (l-r) Jimmy Carl Black, Frank Zappa, Motorhead, Buzz Gardner, Bunk Gardner, Ian Underwood. *Photo: David Redfern/Redferns*.

Bottom right: Garrick Theatre, 1967. (l-r) Ray Collins, Bunk Gardner, Frank Zappa, Ian Underwood (above FZ), Motorhead, Roy Estrada. *Photo: Chuck Boyd/Redferns*.

Top left: The Mothers on stage at the Ford Auditorium, Detroit Michigan, May 1969.
Photo: Copyright © Brian A. Bukantis.
Middle right: Frank Zappa with rubber chicken, from the same show.
Photo: Copyright © Warren Leach.
Middle left: Bunk Gardner on sax (right), Stuttgart, Germany, 1953.
Bottom left: Buzz Gardner, 1973.
Above: Promo photo from the cheesy, low-budget sci-fi *Ogo Moto*, starring Don Preston (shown above in full mad-scientist attire), directed by Brooke Connors.
Right: Roy Estrada, January 1982.
Below: Bunk Gardner and Ian Underwood, 1 June 1981 at the LA Roxy debut of The Grandmothers.

Above: Grandmothers at Rhino Records, 1981. (l-r) Bunk Gardner, Motorhead Sherwood, Buzz Gardner, Don Preston, Jimmy Carl Black, Elliot Ingber.
Photo: Robert Matheu.
Below: Grandmothers in Germany 1993. (l-r) Ener Bladezipper, Bunk Gardner (pointing), Don Preston (above Bunk), Jimmy Carl Black, Roland St. Germain.

The Grandmothers on tour in Europe, 1994.

Above: (l-r) Bunk, Don and Jimmy.
Right: Don Preston.
Below left: Jimmy Carl Black.
Below right: Bunk Gardner.

Photos: A. L. Schoone.

Top left: Motorhead Sherwood photographed in the early 1990s.
Top right and middle: Bunk Gardner and Don Preston on tour in Germany, 1993.
Photos: A.L.Schoone.
Bottom: Ant-Bee and The Grandmothers, Chapel Hill, North Carolina,
29 August 2000. *Photo: Barb Dye.*

on the album we did with Frank Zappa. The first LP we did with Frank was called *Chunga's Revenge*. We only did three or four tracks on that album. That was because he had a bunch of stuff in the recording can and when we came along Frank said, 'Wow, let's put them on.' We sang a few numbers on that album and we're listed as the Phlorescent Leech and Eddie. The two guys were actually road managers with the Turtles. One was very flamboyant and freaky looking while the other was real straight. We named the Phlorescent Leech for the wild one and the other guy Eddie. We jokingly kept saying we'd make an album for them on our own production company which was Blimp. When we joined Frank we needed two names so he could give us credit on *Chunga's Revenge*. On the credits we're listed as The Phlorescent Leech and Eddie because it was the only way we could get credit. On the next album, which was coming out about four months later after the European trip, Frank asked us to play for a while. We stayed in the Mothers for two more years and did three more albums: *Just Another Band from L.A.*, *Fillmore East*, and *200 Motels* which was also a feature film."

Howard Kaylan, in a 1990 interview with producer and MC of the Dutch radio show called *4FM*, also relates the story of how Mark and he joined Zappa's Mothers. "Frank heard through the Hollywood grapevine that the Turtles had broken up. We didn't know what we were going to do. When the band broke up, we called our lawyer, and we said, 'We just broke up the Turtles,' and our lawyer said, 'You guys are idiots! You're idiots, because now you can't use the name Turtles to record, you can't use the name Mark and Howard to record... you can't do anything.' And so, we were really depressed. We didn't know what to do, but we were offered the West Coast lead parts of the Broadway production of *Hair*. We almost took it. I can't imagine how scary my life would be if we'd have gone into *Hair*. (It should be noted that Howard was also offered the gig as lead vocalist for Steely Dan at this point as well, which he declined.) Instead, we went to see Frank Zappa and Zubin Meta and the L.A. Philharmonic do the previews to *200 Motels* at U.C.L.A.'s Pauley Pavilion. It was a very nice program, and after the show, we went backstage to shake hands with Frank and the members of the original Mothers that Frank had gotten together, and Frank said, 'He-e-e-ey! I hear the Turtles broke up.' We said, 'Wow! That was quick! Yes, we did. We broke up about two weeks ago,' and he said, 'I'm putting a new band of Mothers together. We're going to go to Europe. We're gonna do this special in Holland.' That was the first thing we were scheduled to do. And he said, 'We're gonna play a bunch of shows, and then we're going to make a movie. Are you interested?' And we said, 'Yes! Absolutely interested.' And he said, 'Do you play instruments?' And we said, 'Yes.' We both played saxophones at the time, and he said, 'Well, I'm having a barbeque on Sunday. Why don't you come over and bring your saxophones, and we'll have a little audition.' So Sunday rolled around. We went over to Frank's house. We couldn't figure out why he wanted us to bring our saxophones. We knew he had Ian Underwood in the band. He was the best saxophone player we'd ever heard in our lives, but he brought us, during the course of this barbeque, down into the basement, and we took out our saxophones. We honked around a little bit. We did this audition, and after we played a little bit, Frank just said, (with a sarcastic tone), 'Yeah, that's real good, you guys. Okay. Put away the saxophones. Let's just try singing for a little while,' and that worked out really well."

Kaylan continues: "I'm sure when we first joined the Mothers of Invention, there was a certain amount of resistance from the audience, because we were always percieved as being these light-weight sort of AM poppy sort of singers. You bring us in, and you teach us 'Holiday In Berlin', and all of a sudden, you change the texture of what we brought to the group, too. All of a sudden, you could tell, 'Hey! These guys can sing, and these guys are funny if you put them in the right context. If you know what to give them to do, they can do it.' And so, we learned. We learned an awful lot about how to use our voices as instruments, and how to become more of a part of a band. When we would finish a section, like 'Holiday In Berlin', and it was real good and it went down well in concert, you'd get a look of approval from Frank that was almost fatherly. Really! He would look over at you like, 'My boys! I'm so proud of you! You did it so well tonight,' that it was like a pat on the head. It was a very nice appreciation. Frank really had an appreciation for the members of our particular band."

The other ex-members of the first Mothers of Invention initially tried recording with Tom Wilson in L.A. in 1970. Rumour has it that they did record a song called "High and Mighty" which also featured Lowell George, but nothing came of these recordings. Having relied on Zappa's songwriting skills for the previous four years, they gave up any thought of keeping the band together and went their separate ways. Over subsequent years, a few got recalled into the ranks of Zappa's backing bands, most notably Roy Estrada, Ian Underwood and Don Preston.

Zappa's recorded output through the early '70s remained notoriously prolific and innovative as ever but in some people's eyes never really recaptured the spirit of his original band. Or as Roy Estrada puts it, "He couldn't recapture what he had with us, man. The style of it was still there but it wasn't the craziness he had with us." Inevitably, as he matured, Zappa found it increasingly difficult for his new ensembles to maintain the zaniness and spontaneity of the earlier Mothers LPs. On occasions he proved he was still capable of biting satire, most notably on the 1971 LP and movie *200 Motels* which was recorded at Pinewood Studios, London in February 1971. A double LP of the music from the film was released in October 1971 but is not exactly the same music or in the same order as it appears in the screen version. The music had been written over a period of four years, most of it, appropriately enough, in motels while touring. The film was intended to be Zappa's vision of life on the road (based around various tours the Mothers undertook in the 60s). In the movie, Jimmy Carl Black portrays redneck Lonesome Cowboy Burt while Don Preston acts the Mad Scientist. Motorhead has a romance with a vacuum cleaner played by Dick Barber, the Mothers original road manager and snorker. The album was dedicated to anybody who was ever in the Mothers.

Motorhead recalls the making of the movie. "My part in the movie was just really strange. Frank wanted me to play a newt rancher and I was supposed to be in love with a vacuum cleaner. That was my deal in the film. I don't know what that had to do with anything. Frank just wanted to put that in it. The rest of it was based on supposedly abstract ideas of how the band is on the road, how strange it is to tour, and all the bizarre people you encounter and all the weird things that go on.

"*200 Motels* to me was a take-off from a movie that Frank was going to do a long time ago with Captain Beefheart [presumably *CB vs the Grunt People*]. Don and I were supposed to be in the movie and it just kind of evolved from that. Frank added his own bizarre things about his ideas on travelling and music in general. There's not much you can say about the film. It was just Frank's idea about how things were."

Don Preston remembers that, "I didn't play in the band at the time, but I was in the movie. I don't know why, but Frank always thought of me as some sort of charismatic character. Maybe Frank thought that I had some sort of acting ability. I was always doing these weird things with transforming, vile foamy liquids and all that stuff."

Mark Volman told journalist Alan Vorda: "I think *200 Motels* was always in Frank's mind, but it heightened when we were able to provide him with a pop music band that he had never had before. He had always had this idea to do a satire of an anti-pop band and now he had the ability to mock pop through the faces of a pop band. It became a satire on satire. It was really perfect for what Zappa wanted. There's a story in *200 Motels* about a rock star and the groupie singing a big hit record. I always say to Zappa fanatics, who understand or have seen *200 Motels* and who know the concept, to listen to *200 Motels* and listen to side three. We sing a song called 'Daddy, Daddy, Daddy' about going to a club where he meets the groupie at the club. At this point you have to take out the white *Fillmore East* album and hear the song 'Do You Like My New Car?' If you insert the entire white album at this point in *200 Motels*, where the rock star and the groupie are going back to the hotel and singing the new big hit record with a bullet, then it ends the white album with us singing 'Happy Together' and the groupie finally getting her thing. Unfortunately, in the movie we never got to shoot that. That was all part of the script and it never appeared in the film. So for the Zappa fans, the continuation of the movie takes place on an album we recorded a year before the movie was made. And that was supposed to have been in the movie with me dressed as the girl. When we leave the club I'm dressed as a girl and I do this whole thing about the size of your penis. We even have this whole orchestra playing it."

Howard Kaylan, in a 1990 interview with Co de Kloet, relates his memories about the epic film. "It was a movie about a movie about a bass player quitting, and then the bass player quit! When he read the script, he couldn't stand it anymore. So it became a vicious circle. We couldn't even tell, when that movie was being made, what was real and what wasn't real. I mean, we were already into rehearsals at the time when Jeff Simmons quit the band. We had to make this movie. We only had five days to shoot the movie in, and we were in our third day of rehearsal when Jeff walked out, and we had no one to play his part. Frank brought in Wilfred Bramble, of course, from *A Hard Day's Night*, to take the part over, and he freaked out after a couple of days, and just couldn't say the lines. We were all sitting around in this dressing room and Frank said, 'The next person to walk through that door, I don't care who it is, is going to play the part of Jeff Simmons.' And we all just sat there waiting. 'Oh God! What's gonna happen?' We all waited for the door to open, and when the door opened, it was Ringo's chauffeur Martin Lickert. He already had a rudimentary knowledge of bass playing, and he had his cute little English accent and everything. Frank just went, 'Okay. That's it! This is perfect!' And it was! It worked out very, very well for everybody, but it was one of the luckiest things I've ever seen! And then, I'm sure you know Martin Lickert abused his privileges, as far as Ringo was concerned, and thought he was a real movie star! I mean, after *200 Motels* was made, he went back to Ringo's house, and Ringo went on tour or on holiday, and Martin Lickert threw a bunch of parties at Ringo's house, and drank all of Ringo's liquor, and trashed his furniture, and Ringo just finally said, 'I don't know who you think you are, but you're fired!' And so, I don't know what ever became of Martin, but he wound up not even being a driver anymore. It just all went to his head."

In retrospect *200 Motels* is a musical and visual masterpiece, perked up by appearances from Ringo Starr and Keith Moon. However, like a lot of Zappa's work, because of its complex nature, inside jokes and surreal plot, many people including the critics didn't understand the movie. Even to this day, Zappa's vision and genius are misunderstood by many. One can't help feeling that Zappa was somewhat delighting in poking fun at his band by putting them through a rather ridiculous set of scenarios. It was almost like an exorcism of the previous four years on the road. Dialogue like Jimmy Carl Black endlessly asking when he was going to get paid was presumably Zappa's way of reflecting past financial gripes by former band members. Admittedly getting the 'Indian of the group' to sing the cowboy song was a nice touch of irony. In general, the film displays how Zappa's humor could range from the sarcastic to the inspired.

It is notable that, with the exception of the straight musical sections of the band playing, Zappa himself only appears as a character in the film either in the guise of Ringo Starr dressed up as him or as a stuffed dummy. In fact, the sections where the band is actually seen playing work best. Shot with four video cameras, and edited with very fast cuts, it looks remarkably like a blueprint for some of the rock videos that are made today. The new Mothers assembled for the *200 Motels* film project included ex-Turtles Mark Volman and Howard Kaylan, George Duke, Martin Lickert, Aynsley Dunbar, and Ian Underwood.

However, *200 Motels* was undoubtedly a watershed. It was the last LP to be directly connected to the in-jokes and camaraderie of the original Mothers of Invention band. For future recordings, the general off-the-wall craziness that had surrounded early tours, and so often provided the raw material for many of his songs, would be supplied by Volman and Kaylan, later to be christened Flo & Eddie. However, the Mothers (he dropped the 'Of Invention') was a name that Zappa was to hang on to as a vehicle for some of his future recordings. Various line-ups of the Mothers would be reconvened at various times in the seventies, often comprising talented virtuosos.

In February, 1971 Zappa's new Mothers were scheduled to play a concert with the Royal Philharmonic Orchestra at the Royal Albert Hall to help promote the upcoming *200 Motels* movie. Unfortunately, the concert was cancelled due to the fact that the people in charge of the Albert Hall felt some of the lyrics to Zappa's songs were obscene. Zappa and Herb Cohen retaliated with legal action against the Albert Hall for the loss of money due to having to pay the Royal Philharmonic Orchestra and other concert expenditure. The case took four years to reach the courts and Zappa eventually lost, incurring an additonal $35,000 for legal costs. Don Preston vaguely remembers the incident. "I don't think I was aware of it at the time, but I don't think it was just because of Frank playing there. I believe they had several other rock bands play there that had misused the place. I also think the management didn't want any more rock 'n' roll there.

"I had maintained contact with Zappa after the break-up of the original Mothers because I did like what he was doing." We remained friends and I managed to play in two more of his bands after that. These new incarnations of the Mothers were completely different – different structure to the music and different people – everything was different. The only thing that was the same was sometimes we played some of the songs we were playing before (with original MOI) but basically it was pretty much different.

"The 1971 band was of course put together with Aynsley Dunbar and the Turtles members and they recorded *Chungas Revenge*," Preston continues. "At that concert at the Fillmore East (11 June, 1971) Zappa invited me to come and sit in. So I went down there and brought my mini-moog. I got up on the stage and then we played for a while. [Preston's mini-moog solo that evening was captured on tape and released on the *Live At The Fillmore East* album as a track entitled 'Lonesome Electric Turkey.'] So I was on that album but I wasn't in the band at that point. But after that concert, Mark and Howard asked me if I wanted to be in the band and I said, 'Sure,' cos I wasn't doing anything at the time. I had just finished doing a couple of tours with Meredith Monk and that was all over with. So I joined the band after *Live At The Fillmore East*, because some of the guys in the band didn't like the current piano player [Bob Harris].

"I thought Frank's new band was very good – of course Aynsley Dunbar was playing drums and the band sounded really good – Mark and Howard were hilarious. At first, I guess, I was a bit surprised the Turtles were singing with Zappa, but of course once I got to know them then it was perfectly understandable. Four or five weeks after the Gil Evans tour I finally joined Zappa's new Mothers. I came back to L.A., my wife, Tina, was back there so we got back together again. I hooked up with Zappa and he started telling me when rehearsals would be and what to expect – then I started rehearsing with the band. Of course, the pay was totally different than the early days. I now had achieved the position of band member and I got paid for rehearsals and the tours. Before in the early Mothers, we were all part owners of the band, if you will, we were all equal and never really made much money."

Don talks about the new members of the Mothers. "Mark and Howard are great singers and also very intelligent and warm people. I've had nothing but good relations with them ever since I met them, which was the night of the Fillmore concert. Howard and Mark obviously had been singing together since they were little kids – all the way through school. They were very professional in their approach to presenting music on stage, as well as comedy. In the old Mothers, we never knew what songs we were going to perform because there never was a set list or anything. When Mark and Howard joined the band, one of the major things that changed was that there was always a set list. We always knew exactly what we were going to play. It did take some of the sponteneity out of the performance, but because the musicians were better than most of the ones in the old Mothers, it didn't take as much rehearsals to learn songs.

"Aynsley Dunbar was a terrific drummer – I really loved his playing. He could play flat out rock 'n' roll and burn, on the other hand he was a very good sight reader. With all the time changes and complex rhythms, he could play them exact and do all that stuff. There wasn't anything I saw that he couldn't do. He was also a ladies man, there's no question about that. He loved to pick up the ladies, and these young girls were all very attracted to him. At one point, we were both staying at Frank's log cabin. I was there for a short period of time, and Aynsley never failed to bring girls home everynight. Also we roomed together when we were on the road and he always had some cute girl with him.

"We did a lot of touring for about a year, then at Montreaux there was a fire and all our equipment got burned and a week later (December 1971) Zappa got thrown into the orchestra pit at the London Rainbow and that was the end of that band."

The aforementioned fire has of course entered the annals of rock history as the subject of Deep Purple's classic heavy metal anthem "Smoke On The Water". The Mothers were playing a concert at the Montreux Casino in Switzerland, when a fire, allegedly started by someone in the audience shooting a flare gun up at the ceiling, burned the venue to the ground destroying $50,000 worth of equipment. The Rainbow incident refers to the now notorious concert in London when Zappa's leg and ankle were broken after being thrown from the stage into the orchestra pit by an outraged fan. There are two different stories this crazed fan gave to the police as to why he attacked Zappa. The first was that he believed that Zappa was flirting with his girlfriend from the stage – implausible as every musician knows it is impossible to see most audience members because of the bright stage lights. The second story goes that the attacker felt he wasn't getting his money's worth. The incident occurred after the band's encore while they were performing "I Want To Hold Your Hand". Zappa also suffered a fractured skull and spent the next few months in a wheelchair and surgical brace. (In March of 1974, Zappa's attacker received a one year jail sentence.)

"In that band I experienced the highest of highs and the lowest of lows," says Mark Volman. "The lows started with the Montreux festival. We played an afternoon concert and some kid shot off a flare gun and the casino burned to the ground. We had a band meeting and Frank wanted to come back to the U.S. He felt that the fire and losing all our equipment was an ominous sign. But we had ten dates ahead, all sold out, including four shows in London. The band felt we needed to make money, and it was Christmas time. So Frank went along with it. And then, the very first show at the Rainbow Theatre in London, Frank got thrown into the pit. I remember looking down at him from the top of the pit and his leg was bent underneath him like a Barbie doll; his eyes were open but there was no life in them. Two or three of us were cradling him in the pit and the blood was running from his head to his knees. We weren't sure if he would live through the night. Later at the hotel we got word he would live, and a few days later we got to see him in the hospital, just one or two at a time. We went in and there was Frank, on his back, arm in a sling, one leg in a cast on a sling in the air. His head was bandaged like a mummy. You couldn't see his hair or his moustache – just his lips where they had cut a hole in the bandages, and his eyes, which followed us to the foot of the bed. And then he said, 'Peaches En Regalia – one, two, three...' – you know, the way we opened the show. We died laughing. It was the sorriest of jokes. But it was his way of saying, 'It's okay'."

In the end two live recordings of the band featuring Flo and Eddie were released, *Fillmore East June 1971*, a landmark album with resurfacing themes from *200 Motels* and a grand rendition of the Turtles' "Happy Together". That same night the Mothers jammed with John Lennon and Yoko Ono and this was recorded and released on Lennon's *Sometime In New York City* album, as well as Zappa's later release *Playground Psychotics*. Zappa's experience with the legendary Beatle was an uneasy one. Both artists had agreed that they would release versions of this concert on their subsequent albums. Unfortunately for Frank, Lennon released the performance completely re-edited. "King Kong" written by Zappa, was retitled as "Jamrag" and the songwriting credited to Lennon and Ono. In the mid-90s Zappa re-edited this historic concert material back to its original form and re-released it with the correct credits intact. In retrospect, Yoko Ono is quoted as having fond memories of the event. "When John and I did a little thing with Frank Zappa in '71 at the Fillmore East, I discovered he was actually a composer who came into the rock/pop world. Both John and I hit it off with him very well."

Don Preston remembers the legendary Fillmore gig with the former Beatle and his wife. "It was very difficult for me at that time. My wife and I were going through some difficulties. We were in New York staying at somebody's house, and there were a lot of unusual things going on that caused a lot of pressure – so we were having fights during that time. I still wasn't in Frank's new band at the time. So anyway, I went to the gig with my equipment and sat in with the band. I had spoken to Frank that day and he said, 'Come on down Don and sit in at the gig tonight.' And so I did. My first recollection was I walked by one of the dressing rooms and Zappa was sitting there with John Lennon and Yoko Ono. They were just talking, but I didn't go in. So, later on, we went on stage and played the concert. After a while, John and Yoko came out on stage and the audience went nuts! And then we played the set. One of the things I remember, which is still very vivid, is that we played this song called 'Scumbag' and then Yoko got into this burlap bag and started jumping around on stage, singing the way she does. I thought, 'My god, this is so demeaning. Why is she doing this?' Then later on I played the mini-moog solo during the encore. Afterwards, I was still having a fight with my wife, so I didn't get really involved with Frank and Lennon. The next day I went on the road with Gil Evans for a few weeks. Then I came back and re-joined the Mothers."

The next Mothers' album, *Just Another Band From L.A.,* was a solid release featuring the legendary mini-opera "Billy The Mountain". Mark Volman recalls this conceptual Zappa masterpiece. "On the album it was only twenty-two minutes, but in our show there was another fifteen minutes. Frank wanted it to be a two-record set, but Warner Bros said, 'No way'. Sides one and two were supposed to be 'Billy The Mountain' with sides three and four the stuff that appeared on side two such as 'Call Any Vegetable' and 'Eddie, Are You Kidding?' They said no. So Frank cut it down to one album with all that material. 'Billy The Mountain' we learned over a three or four month period in pieces during rehearsals. Frank just made up a story about a mountain and a tree that lived on his shoulder whereupon they decide to take a vacation. Frank wrote a visual script of 'Billy The Mountain' and I have the script at home. I think Frank originally visualized it as an animation and to make a feature-like cartoon. It was fun to do as a live show. I believe it was the first or second live show of 'Billy The Mountain' that we recorded at Pauley Pavilion (UCLA, in CA.) in 1971. We recorded almost every concert we did with Frank live in person."

Howard Kaylan, in a 1990 interview, spoke about the humor they brought to the Mothers. "*Just Another Band From L.A.* makes all these local references to things in and around Los Angeles, that show would only happen in Los Angeles. When we took the show to New York, all the references were local to New York. So it was a customized show for every city, and that was our job. We had to go out and learn about the city or the town, and the celebrities, and get to know what streets the kids cruised, and got to know the hot spots that they went to, so that in the improvisational part of the show, we could say:

'Oh baby! Where ya goin'?

'Oh, I just came from the Paradiso.'

'Oh you did?'

'Oh, that's a hot place! Oh! Hey! Well, I gotta get up and fly outa here in the morning...'

All that stuff was modular. It was designed so that we could play with it a little bit, and when Frank laughed at something that we did, it was much more important than if the audience laughed or not. We existed in that band for humor, but not necessarily for the audience's humor, but for Frank's humor. When Frank laughed, we knew we were funny. The rest of the stuff we practiced for hours and hours, y'know, eight, ten hours a day. The improvisational stuff was the most fun because then we could really play around and keep an eye on Frank, and when Frank started cracking up, the shows really got good."

Not surprisingly the two incidents of the fire and Rainbow attack had a profound effect on Zappa, and this particular line-up of the Mothers was never rehired. As to why Zappa broke up this successful incarnation, Don Preston gives his opinion. "For some reason, and I'm not sure what it was, after that (Rainbow incident) Zappa never contacted anyone. He never really said, 'You're fired' or anything, he just never got in touch. He then got another band together with George Duke, the Fowler Brothers (Tom and Bruce) and Ruth and Ian Underwood and I went on tour with them throughout the United States, also did the album *Live At The Roxy* with that band. That was the last time I was in the band. I finally had a falling out with Zappa and couldn't do it any more."

In a 1990 interview with Co de Kloet, Mark Volman and Howard Kaylan both discuss the break-up of the Mothers and the formation of the first Flo & Eddie band. "Once Frank was in the hospital, we were asked to continue the tour without Frank Zappa – the Mothers were approached by the people involved with this tour saying, 'You guys sang all the material. The music would still be intact without Frank. You could at least go and do the shows,' and the band said, 'No!' says Volman.

Kaylan continues: "It would have been horrible! I can't even imagine what would have happened if we would have showed up at some of these shows as the Mothers of Invention without Frank, and that's what they were trying to get us to do. In the meantime, Frank was recovering. For months and months and months, we had no contact with him whatsoever, we had no contact with his office whatsoever. All these guys that were members of his band were sitting around their homes waiting for the phone to ring, wondering if they would ever work again, wondering if there would ever be another Mothers of Invention. We couldn't get an answer. No one would tell us if Frank was ever going to tour or work again, and eventually, the guys in the band, Aynsley and Jim and Don, they came to us and said, 'What are we gonna do?' And we said, 'Well, we've always wanted to make a solo album.' We had the stuff that was left over from when the Turtles broke up, and we said, 'Well, let's just go into the studio with you guys. We'll make the record.' We had a deal with Warner Brothers. We put the record out."

Flo and Eddie were subsequently offered a record deal with Warner Bros for their first solo album *The Phloresent Leach & Eddie*. In essence the Mothers minus Zappa and Ian Underwood became Flo and Eddie's backing band – Don Preston, Jim Pons, Aynsley Dunbar together with Gary Rowels on guitar. The group toured the States to promote the new album, bringing their special brand of humor and tight performance, not to mention some of the older Turtles material, to the stage. Don Preston fondly remembers, "I enjoyed playing in the Flo & Eddie band very much. It was a few steps back, so to speak – it was a lot more commercial. They weren't interested in doing anything unusal or Zappa-esque. Their first solo album was more a continuation of where the Turtles left off, sort of."

Admittedly Flo & Eddie (as well as the rest of the Mothers) had learned a lot from their former employer. Mark Volman explains: "We negotiated an album with Warner Bros to do Flo & Eddie (1972). We took the band that was the Mothers and we brought Gary Rowles into the band as the guitar player. We recorded the first Phlorescent Leech and Eddie album and that was how we prolonged our band since there was no Frank and therefore no Mothers. We went right out on tour in support of the album."

Flo & Eddie released a second album in 1973 – *Flo & Eddie* – which featured the same line-up as their first solo outing with the exception of Don Preston, who at this point went back and rejoined Zappa's Mothers for the third time. Don Preston admits, "I couldn't really handle the financial part of working in Flo & Eddie after the first album and tour. Unfortunately I never played with them again after that. The thing was when they were in a position to pay better money they never used me again because I kind of left them at a bad time. But I do remember playing on a German TV show called Beat Club with them in 1972. We played 'Feel Older Now' – that was fun."

In 1972 Don Preston recorded piano and mini Moog on Frank Zappa's third solo effort – *Waka Jawaka/Hot Rats.* – an album that showcased Zappa's new direction toward big band jazz compositions. Other musicians featured on this album were Aynsley Dunbar, George Duke, Tony Duran, Sal Marquez, Erroneous, Chris Peterson, Joel Peskin, Mike Altschul, Jeff Simmons, Sneaky Pete Kleinow, Janet

Ferguson and Bill Byers. Zappa, who was still in a leg cast and confined to a wheelchair, continued to record the next Mothers album – *The Grand Wazoo*. Considered by many to be Zappa's best exploration of his big band compositions, the LP once again featured Don Preston on mini Moog. Zappa then recruited a new group for the subsequent tour to promote the *Grand Wazoo* album, taking some of the musicians he used on the two recent album releases, as well as new members such as the legendary drummer Jim Gordon, but Don Preston was not among those called up. The *Grand Wazoo* band did several shows throughout the US and a most memorable show at the Hollywood Bowl which garnered rave reviews.

At this point in time, Don Preston formed a solo group called Raw Milk, as Preston relates. "It was an all synthesiser band except for drums. The music was pretty much rock oriented – there was a cut on the first Grandmothers LP (not released on the CD version) called 'I Can't Breathe No More'. One of the reviews at the time we got in the paper went, 'This band has all synthesisers – that will never go anywhere.' But of course, Tangerine Dream made a great living at it."

In 1973, Frank Zappa then released the critically acclaimed *Over-nite Sensation* album, which saw a return to a smaller ensemble as well as a large dose of Zappa's trademark humor. Although Don Preston was not featured on this album, ex-Mother Ian Underwood was, as well as jazz violist extraordinaire Jean-Luc Ponty. The touring ensemble, which gigged throughout the US and Europe in 1973, featured Ian Underwood, Ruth Underwood, Jean-Luc Ponty, George Duke, Tom Fowler and Ralph Humphry. 1974 saw the release of the only Zappa album ever to reach the US Top Ten – *Apostrophe* which featured the comical masterpiece "Don't Eat The Yellow Snow".

Apostrophe saw the return of both Don Preston on synthesizers and Ray Collins on background vocals. Legendary Cream member and rock icon Jack Bruce remembers recording the title track for the *Apostrophe* album. "At first, Frank wanted me to play cello on the album. They had this old cello, which I guess they rented, that wouldn't stay in tune. So I told Frank, 'This cello unfortunately is unplayable.' So Frank said, 'Why don't you play some electric bass, we'll jam a bit and see what happens.' Well, Jim Gordon (drummer) was there and we played some with Frank, and developed this riff that eventually became the 'Apostrophe' song."

Through late 1973 and early 1974 Zappa toured extensively with a new group of Mothers, later to be dubbed the *Roxy & Elsewhere* band. The new group featured Don Preston, George Duke, Chester Thompson, Ralph Humphry, Tom Fowler, Bruce Fowler, Walt Fowler, Napolean Murphy Brock, and Ruth Underwood. Ruth Underwood, now ex-wife of Ian Underwood, had been involved in a number of Zappa's projects, having first contributed to the *Uncle Meat* album.

Ruth Underwood remembers how she first met Zappa. "I went to college for seven years and did everything by the books until I met Frank. His *Absolutely Free* show at the Garrick Theater changed my life. I no longer wanted to be a timpanist at the New York Philharmonic, or a virtuoso marimba soloist. All I ever wanted from that point on was to play Frank's music. One night my brother and I went to the Village Gate to hear Miles Davis. We were standing around waiting for show time and Frank was just walking down Bleecker Street. This was before body-guards - he was just a guy on his way to work. My brother accosted him and said, 'You should hear my sister play! She's a great marimbist!' I was totally embar-rassed. Frank turned to me and said, 'Fine. Bring your marimba backstage and we'll check ya out.' The next thing I knew I was recording *Uncle Meat* at Apostolic Studios on East 10th Street. I was really active with him in the '70s. It was the greatest experience of my life and the most difficult experience of my life. It was educational and enriching, and also backbreaking, gruelling, sometimes lonely, terrifying – it was fucking unbelievable."

The new Mothers were an intensely tight ensemble able to pull off what amounted to Zappa's most complex compositions to date. The group recorded a three-day engagement at L.A.'s premier rock club The Roxy. Recordings from this historical event comprised most of Zappa's next release aptly entitled – *Roxy & Elsewhere*. This would also serve as the last Zappa/Mothers album Don Preston would appear on.

Don Preston reminisces about the *Roxy & Elsewhere* group. "Frank called me and said that he wanted to do a tour to celebrate ten years of the Mothers, and that he wanted to know if I would go on one tour with him. The girl on the cover of the *Roxy & Elsewhere* album was this girl that we knew – her name was Brenda Underwood, and she was a stripper at the time. She was living at my house then and is still a dear friend.

"It was a good band and a memorable tour. I got to show George Duke how to play a synthesiser, and a few other interesting things. I loved George – he was a very sweet guy and still is. He was a very strong keyboard player – he had tremen-dous chops. I was sorry to see him get into that funk stuff, but I'm sure he made a lot of money doing it.

"Napolean Murphy Brock, I didn't really know him hardly at all – he was a very good singer. I think for some reason some of the members of the band felt Napolean was holding the group back – but I thought he was great.

"Chester Thompson, he was such a great player during that time. Afterwards, I also played with him and the Fowler brothers. I was always struck by how really good he was – especially in the time department. He really held it together – his time was fantastic. Also Ralph Humphrey was great – the both of them really played well together."

Other early seventies LPs to have the Mothers monicker were variable. *One Size Fits All* (1975), an excellent album, was generally a return to form as was *Bongo Fury*, recorded with Captain Beefheart. However, it was becoming increasingly difficult to distinguish whether these were actually just Frank Zappa solo LPs which featured a backing band he happened to continue to call the Mothers, or really a band effort. As a result, in the same way he had chided the original Mothers, he continually complained that musicians were unable to do his music justice. (Whole Philharmonic orchestras were accused of being sloppy and unprofessional.)

In 1976 Zappa not only sued ex-manager Herb Cohen and Warner Brothers to gain full control of the early LPs which appeared on MGM/Verve, but also dropped the name the Mothers of Invention for good. Much comment has been passed about the conceptual watershed this represented. Up until that time, even though versions of the Mothers continued to change again and again, it still had some kind of band identity and spirit. After 1976, Zappa would tour under his name alone – the Mothers were no more.

However, what wasn't allowed to falter was the availability of early Mothers material. In 1981 Zappa set up his own Barking Pumpkin label. With the advent of CD, all the early Mothers LPs became available on that format (and remain so) and have been recently reissued and remastered by Rykodisc. Also in 1985, he released a 7-LP box set of remixed versions of the five Verve LPs.

So while all this was going on, what did the rest of the original Mothers do? First of all, in the early '70s Jimmy Carl Black put together a group with Bunk Gardner, Tjay Cantrelli from Love, and Denny Walley (who went on to record with Frank Zappa for a few years). This new group was called Geronimo Black after Jimmy's youngest son who was called Geronimo.

Jimmy Carl Black recalls: "We did our first record in 1972 with Uni Records which is part of MCA. I thought it was an excellent album but the reason it didn't happen was that three weeks after the record was released, they fired the president of Uni, Russ Reagan. He was the guy that signed Geronimo Black and was actually in charge of us – it was too bad, because we could have gone a long way had he not been fired. The second album, *Welcome Back Geronimo Black*, I put out in 1980 – it was lifted from tapes that we had done in the studio prior to signing to MCA, actually it was the tapes that had got us the deal with the record company and I always thought that they were even better produced and played than the record that we did in the studio. Plus, part of that album is recordings that Denny Walley did of me on vocals, three songs that we did before I left California and moved back to Texas."

Bunk Gardner concurs: "That's right, we had got a recording contract with Universal to make our first album, but they wouldn't subsidize us to go out on the road – so we had to do it ourselves, and it was very difficult. It only lasted a couple of years, and we all went in different directions again. I do remember a birthday party that we played in Malibu during the early afternoon of October 1972. Jimmy came in and announced, 'The Maestro is fucked up!' Needless to say I have no idea how we managed to play music and remain upright for the birthday party. Who knows what the other people thought of the band and oddly enough nobody remembers how the party ended." (In 1994 the *Geronimo Black* album was re-issued on CD by One-Way Records, USA.)

After Geronimo Black disbanded in 1972, Bunk Gardner went on to record with various artists. Unfortunately for Jimmy Carl Black, after moving back to his hometown of Anthony, Texas in 1973, in order to support himself he made donuts for Winebel's Donuts. This was truly a low point in Jimmy Carl Black's career – but it would not last for long!

After the original Mothers broke up, Motorhead joined the band Ruben and the Jets and recorded with them on their first LP. As Motorhead himself remembers, "After the Mothers broke up we were kind of in limbo. Frank had this kid called Ruben come up and say he wanted to use the name Ruben and the Jets, and play this old rock 'n' roll music. Frank figured that since I was this old rock 'n' roll horn player that I'd like to get in the band. So I did and we played a bunch of concerts. Basically they were free benefits in the park or at the school because the guys in the band were younger and mainly Mexicans. So we played benefits in East L.A. for their relatives. We did cut an album, but we never went on tour. What happened there was the guys wanted to go out and do the concerts and an album and wanted to sign up with Herb Cohen. I said, 'Hey, don't do that, I've already dealt with this guy.' But they said, 'Well, you've already been there, you can't tell us what to do.' So they signed with Herbie and got stuck. I told them I can't live like that, playing free benefits all the time, so I quit the band. I don't know what happened after that. They never played anywhere and nothing ever came of it that I know of." (The band did actually cut a second album entitled *Con Safos*).

Meanwhile Bunk Gardner had formed a band called Menage A Trois with his brother Buzz and Don Preston. (Hopefully some of these recordings will surface on Bunk's yet to be released solo CD). For a while he also played with Eartha Kitt and a guitarist called Domenic Troiano.

"Ah, Domenic," Bunk recalls. "Domenic was a very fine guitar player from Canada who I met while I was recording the Geronimo Black album here in Los Angeles. He was at that time recording his own album. We played together quite a bit, and he asked me to get a horn section together and write the arrangements for his album, which I did. I got my brother on trumpet, Tjay Cantrelli and a few other friends and we recorded his album, which I liked very much. Domenic later went on to become the lead guitarist of the James Gang [replacing Joe Walsh], but I think he liked having his own group most of the time. He certainly was a great guitar player."

Bunk then played on an album by the seminal and highly influential Tim Buckley. "I had a friend, John Balkin, who had been playing bass with Tim Buckley. We had our own band, Menage A Trois, that Tim had heard tapes of and he liked what we were doing – so we started playing with Tim. It lasted couple of years and was really enjoyable. Tim had a tremendous voice I thought. He'd always loved jazz, admired Miles Davis, and he wanted to get a little more jazz into his folksy approach but at the same time remain contemporary and maybe even a little avant-garde. I thought we filled that very well, and it was a great shame that Tim died at such an early age."

In 1973 Tim Buckley had appeared on Zappa's *Straight Label Sampler* and subsequently signed with Frank Zappa and Herb Cohen's Discreet label. However, Buckley died in June 1975 from an overdose of heroin and morphine believing it to be cocaine, tragically cutting short a promising career. Not surprisingly he was a completely different character to Frank Zappa.

"Working with Frank and working with Tim was like night and day," says Bunk Gardner. "I could relate on a personal level with Tim Buckley, I have a very soft spot in my heart for Tim, but with Frank it was a completely different story. He was never interested in you personally, everything focussed on him. He was a difficult taskmaster – nobody's perfect, so it was difficult for some people to meet his demands."

Buzz Gardner also played on some of Tim Buckley's records, as he recalls. "I did some studio work when I got back into town, one thing for Frank Sinatra. After the Mothers I started to work for Tim Buckley. I don't remember too much about the recording I did for him. One album I do remember is *Star Sailor*, I believe it was one of his best. [Indeed it was, featuring the memorable 'Song For The Siren'.]

When the original Mothers broke up, Roy Estrada had teamed up with ex-Mother Lowell George's new band Little Feat for a while, as he recalls. "I did two albums with them. (*Little Feat* and *Sailin' Shoes*). It was a tremendously popular group, although I thought I fit better with the Mothers than Lowell George and Little Feat – personality wise, but I still liked it. When I played with Little Feat we used to rehearse in a sound studio in the movie lots where they filmed *Bonanza* and all these big movies they used to make in Burbank. There was one big theatre – a sound stage – there was a huge one where they had casting set up. We were rehearsing there."

Once Estrada had left Little Feat in 1971 he moved on to playing with Captain Beefheart on his two classic LPs *Clear Spot* and *Spotlight Kid*. As Estrada recalls, "Art (Artie Tripp) was the one who got us the gig with Captain Beefheart. What I liked about that also at that time was I had to move up North in Eureka, Humbolt County. It's right by the ocean, Redwoods, it was nice clean air. I wanted to get away from the smog and hassle of L.A.. Up there you hear the ocean. It was nice. We were on a health thing." No doubt, this was good for Roy's breathing given that he has been a lifelong asthmatic.

"Beefheart was fun – I fit more," Estrada continues. "But the only thing, he was out there man. At rehearsals those poor guys he would yell at (imitates Beefheart growling). Me and Art would think, 'What the fuck's going on?' – and we would just sit back and think, this guy's out of it. He wasn't reserved like Frank – this guy was out there."

For a while Roy became a member of the Magic Band (christened Orejon) and played on a tour of England. He remembers, "We did concerts in a bunch of cities in England. Some of our fans there were Led Zeppelin. They must not have been working at the time because they would follow us and come back stage and hang out. I liked those shows – we were pushing *Clear Spot*. I think Beefheart was playing soprano sax mostly. And then he played harmonica for a set. I liked the different rhythms that we were doing. He liked a backwards drum beat – it was odd – it was nice..."

Jimmy Carl Black also teamed up a few years later to tour briefly with Captain Beefheart, as he recalls. "In 1975 Frank Zappa was on tour. One of the people on the tour was Captain Beefheart, Don Van Vliet, who I've known since I met him in 1964 with Frank. They passed though El Paso on tour and I went and sat in with them. I got to talking to Don and he mentioned that he was going to Europe later that summer and asked if I would play drums for him. So officially I joined the Magic Band in the summer of 1975. We played the Knebworth festival in England [July 1975, supporting Pink Floyd] and several other gigs, the last of which was the Roxy in Los Angeles and that's when I left. I couldn't really handle it. I loved playing with him, I learned how to play the drums backwards and he was a fun guy to play with but he didn't have that much work and I wasn't about to move back to California. There were a couple of albums that came out of that, both bootlegs, but nothing official. I still think he is the most avant-garde player in the world, and always will be. He's also a dear friend of mine and a heck of an artist."

Meanwhile Roy Estrada teamed up with Zappa again on a number of occasions. In 1975 he rejoined Zappa and both toured and recorded. (He's featured on the under-rated *Zoot Allures* from this period.)

"We played a two month tour on the East Coast (1975)," Estrada remembers. "And then another month and a half in Australia, New Zealand, and straight from there we went to Japan. The last part of 1975 I did a two month tour with Frank. This was when Terry Bozzio was playing the drums.

"When I did that tour with them, I used to go, 'AAAYYYY' [imitating his falsetto vocal style he used on 'I Come From Nowhere']. There is a guy who does that who's still popular today, my kid knows the name. [Roy tries to remember the name. Eventually he gives up and goes and asks his son.] Morrissey. Yeh, back then I think he just started too. [Morrissey didn't actually form The Smiths until the early eighties]. He's popular now. (Still mimicking the style) That's when you delve into the in-between notes. (laughs) That was a trip, we'd do it on stage and even on the buses – me and Terry would mess around. After that I did that European tour with Frank, I guess the first part of 1976. Then I moved to Colorado."

In 1978 Roy made a guest appearance on stage at the New York palladium for the shooting of the film *Baby Snakes* – he appears as the Mexican Pope character. In 1981 he once again rejoined Zappa for the recording of *Ship Arriving Too Late*

To Save A Drowning Witch. "I remember I came up one time and my van blew up – caught on fire. We were recording there at Frank's house in the studio. That's when we did Kingfish [*Thingfish*]. I think I'm on some of the sounds in there – or at least on the album with 'Valley Girls' [*Ship Arriving Too Late To Save A Drowning Witch*]."

Roy also appeared on *Them Or Us* (1981), and Mark Pinske, recording engineer extraordinaire who worked with Zappa throughout the '80s, recalls a session with Roy Estrada and Bob Harris (vocalist and keyboardist for Zappa 1980-2). "Bob did a lot of songs with Roy. The one I remember the most is on *Drowning Witch*. That is when Frank told me that Roy Estrada had such a nasaly falsetto that it sounded like 'he ate clothespins for breakfast'. We put Roy and Bob out in the yard, way out in the yard, further than the yard went... no, we had them sing up into the back walls and I mic'd them off of the walls which was the best thing I ever did.

"I would have to think a while about which songs we all did but I know that one was called 'No Not Now' because Warren Cucurillo said, 'No Not Now, hey that's Won Ton On backwards.' What a weird mind don't you think? So you know what happened after that, that gave Frank a whole new set of ideas. Then we had to do a backwards version, so there you go – Roy and Bob singing backwards on 'Won Ton On'" [from the *Them Or Us* album].

Bob Harris, who is currently vocalist/keyboardist in the band Axe (in 1997 there was talk of Bob Harris joining the Grandmothers but unfortunately nothing ever transpired) had this to say about Roy Estrada. "First of all, Roy was a very kind and immediately likeable person. When he sang he would twist and raise his face to put different timbre in his voice. He could put the sound further up in his nose than any human before or since. We were first in the control room with Frank, rehearsing and learning parts, and every time Roy opened his mouth and sang, Frank just lost it. There were different levels of humor for Frank, and some things would take him over the edge bigtime, where he was laughing uncontrollably, slapping the chair and rocking back and forth. Roy had a clear channel to Frank's funnybone, the same as Ike Willis and Ray White. With Roy came the term 'weasle vocals' like on 'No Not Now', and the backwards version. I don't know if Frank had coined that term before in the Mothers days or it was new. It was such a beautifully sick sound. I think that Frank enjoyed anyone who was not afraid to make a weird, different, strange, or even stupid sound, because the less you took/take yourself seriously, the deeper you could go into what Frank was all about. Roy could do this easily, and even during recording, Frank would still lose it every now and then. Elvis may be the 'King', Sinatra 'the Voice' – but Roy Estrada is 'the Sinus'!"

Meanwhile, both Bunk and Buzz Gardner continued to remain active musically throughout the 1970s and '80s, as Bunk Gardner explains. "Don Preston and I did a lot of parties and gigs as the Don and Bunk show (the duo have recently gotten back together in the late 90s to record and gig). When we weren't doing that we played contemporary avant-garde jazz at local theatres and art galleries as well as a bit of recording for movie soundtracks. There was also a kids TV series that Flo & Eddie wrote called *Strawberry Shortcake* – I did most of the woodwinds for that. I'm still involved with a woodwind jazz and chamber quartet that has two albums out called *The Four Winds And Rhythm* and *Blowing In The Wind*. We have been giving concerts in the L.A. school system for the last thirteen years, plus playing most of the jazz rooms in town. I've also given both my daughters piano lessons which I do hope they continue, and stay in music and have some fun with it. I played with Little Richard, did the Dick Clark Show with him for a 20th anniversary show. And Del Shannon, and Van Morrison in New York. In the late '80s I decided to go to culinary school at L.A. Trade Tech to become a chef. Soon after that I began working at the Beverly Hills Inn on Wilshire Boulevard, the Planet Hollywood and finally Anastasia restaurant in Laguna Beach. There I became head chef and continued my schooling by taking some baking classes at Orange Coast College. It was fun and really for me it was therapy to reduce stress! Meanwhile I was playing and being featured for two years with Juliette and the Torch Ensemble in L.A."

As already mentioned, in the early '90s Bunk played in a jazz band with his brother Buzz called The Hollywood Allstars at a club called Legends Of Hollywood. Don Preston was also part of the band for a while, as Buzz Gardner explains. "I was working two nights a week in a Mexican ballroom for $100. That's when I organized the quartet. The band worked one, and sometimes two nights a week at the Legends of Hollywood club. My primary interest is jazz and classical music. This was satisfying playing jazz one night a week. We played for tips and after a while the other members didn't want to work for free. So the playing stopped."

Don Preston stayed on good terms with Frank Zappa up until the late seventies. Don remembers, "I remained friends with Frank for a number of years after the *Roxy* tour. I can remember going to a screening of the *Baby Snakes* film of his. We went to this big soundstage that had this huge screen. The film was shown on a film projector that was so powerful that it had to be water cooled – it was this huge thing! The picture was mind boggling too! I had been very busy during that time recording projects like *Escalator Over The Hill* with Carla Bley."

Don Preston continued to be musically prolific as ever throughout the 1970s and '80s, as Preston himself relates. "After working with Zappa, I formed a number of bands which were all kind of jazz rock groups: Raw Milk, Loose Connection and Ogo Moto, for example. I still had ties with Zappa in those bands, they were all sort of offshoots of what Zappa was into. Eventually, I finally got it all out of my system and went back to my own roots which were jazz of course, and started recording with John Carter, Carla Bley, Gil Evans, Flora Purim and a whole bunch of people. I also toured with Al Jarreau and Lou Rawls."

Don Preston was featured on the innovative debut album by the legendary Carla Bley, as he recalls. "Carla is a phenomenal musician, and to me one of the all time great composers. I've just been so fortunate in my life to have been surrounded by all these musicians/artists that are the best in the world! But Carla, at that time we did *Escalator Over The Hill*, was about 23 or so and totally gorgeous. They decided to make her first album a three record set with a huge book and all these singers like Linda Ronstadt, Jack Bruce, all these opera singers and me! I had been a friend of hers since she lived out in L.A. around 1967. So when I was in town visiting, I used to go over to their house and visit. My wife's daughter and her daughter used to hang out and play together. Anyway, I was just so amazed that on this album there was also a collection of twenty fucking hardcore New York jazz musicians, and she controlled the whole scene. It was just unbelievable, and that's because she is such a great musician and knows exactly what she wants. She knew exactly how to tell them what to do and everybody respected her tremendously!"

Also on this seminal recording date was rock legend Jack Bruce, with whom Preston has collaborated on other musical projects. Don says of the former Cream member, "Even though Jack Bruce and I sing a duet on *Escalator Over The Hill* we never saw each other at that time (separate overdubs) although I had met Jack at a concert we did in Chicago where the Mothers opened up for Cream. I remember they had to carry Ginger Baker out to his drums because he was so out of it he couldn't walk. Jack told me this story once about Ginger, where Cream were playing in this pub somewhere. Ginger stood up from his drums, which were right next to this upright piano, and he opened the top of the piano and barfed inside it! Really terrible! (laughs) Then he sat back down at the drums and without missing a beat played the rest of the show. But, Jack says now Ginger is totally cleaned-up and is into health foods, etc. He's also a volunteer fireman somewhere in Colorado, where he now resides."

In the mid-1970s, Don Preston toured for three years and became the musical director for English pop star Leo Sayer. Preston remembers: "It was an odd gig, I guess, but it paid real well. I was the musical director for him for about three years, though I'm not on any of his albums at all. He had these producers, and they got all the top studio musicians of the day to play on his albums. To them, I wasn't a top studio musician, even though I was doing quite well with the live band. We toured the States and Europe a couple of times, and we toured Australia, New Zealand, UK, Ireland and Scotland as well. I was also on several TV shows he appeared on at the time. He's now got a big house north of London and a real nice midi studio there. I think he's toured a little bit with just midi stuff. I guess he's not real well known now, although when I first started with him years ago he had four or five hits on one record. And then the next album he had three hits, and the next one hit and so on. Finally, we'd go to a huge venue where the stage rotated, and they had to stop the stage from turning because there was only enough people there to sit in one place."

Don Preston in the mid-seventies was also featured on the pioneering album by the Residents called *Eskimo*. Preston remembers the recording session. "Well, not to break down their mystique, which I couldn't anyway, but I was playing in San Francisco with Carla Bley around 1977. The Residents came to the gig and introduced themselves. Carla had already heard of their music, but I had not. The Residents loved the show and I sort of befriended them. Then, not long after that I got the job doing the score for *Apocalypse Now*, and had to go to San Francisco to record it. So while I was there, I contacted the Residents and we hung out a lot. They said, "We're working on a new album." And I said, "Well, I have my modular synthesiser here – how about I come down and do some stuff for you guys." And they said, "Sure, come on down to the studio." So most of the stuff I played on Eskimo was sound effects, and a solo at the end of the album. Their studio blew my mind when I went there for the first time! They had this huge incredible old brick building. When you went inside you saw their incredible artwork all over the place. And then they had offices on the second floor, which was a platform that went all around the building – so you could see everybody up there working from the ground floor. Then on the ground floor there was this door, and you walked through that and it took you way into the back – it looked like this subterranean cave – and that was where their studio was. At that time it was a 16-track recorder and board of some sort. They had some basic things, like a few guitars, a bass and a mellotron – but they utilized anything that would make a sound. Then you went through another door on the right, and there was this huge soundstage that they had built. That was where they shot their films."

Of the various musical projects Don Preston was involved in throughout the seventies and eighties, the one that he is most proud of is his work with jazz great John Carter. Preston relates, "That was the most exciting for me. I recorded four albums with him and he was one of the most phenomenal musicians I've worked for – a totally brilliant and great person. I also enjoyed performing with my own jazz groups, either a trio or quartet, mostly playing the West Coast, but I did play a jazz festival in Finland."

Don Preston has also scored the music for various movie soundtracks throughout the '70s and '80s. One of the most notable movies being the critically acclaimed *Apocalypse Now*.

"Well, they called me up wanting to rent my synthesizer," Preston recalls. "I had a Modular Moog synthesizer at that time. I was talking to the guy, David Rubinson, who's no longer with us, and he was the producer for the picture. So we got to talking and he asks me, 'Oh by the way, what's your name?' So I told him my name and he said, 'Oh, why the hell are we renting this from you? We should have you come and play it on the soundtrack.' So I said, 'That sounds good to me!' He then says, 'Yeh, we can save some money on the rent too!' So I got my shit together – I rented a car and drove my stuff up there (northern California) and started working on the film. It was really fun. The highlight I think of the whole thing was at the end. I wasn't completely done yet but almost, and Coppola had a party up at his winery and we were invited. So we got up there and parked and we came down to this little clearing. There was this German band playing and they were serving hotdogs and sauerkraut – it was very nice. Later on in the evening, in one of the winery places, they had a rock band playing and a stripper, and that went on for hours. So we woke up the next morning and walked around the grounds. We came to this place where there was this long open pit and about 50 goats roasting in it – getting ready for the afternoon festivities. Then these bands started playing; first there was these Japanese drummers, and then some psychedelic band, and then the folk singers from San Francisco, and then the Italian band from *The Godfather*, and it just kept going on and on. Finally I thought, 'It's got to be over by now,' and start getting ready to leave. Then all of a sudden everybody starts pointing up at the sky and this guy jumps out of this plane. He skydives as far as he can, and the chute opens and he lands right in front of Coppola! He then pulls out a bottle of champagne and a glass and pours him some. I said, 'This has got to be the climax of the evening!' Then the Gay Liberation Marching Band comes marching out around the back of the house and then marches up to Coppola and plays Happy Birthday for him! That was quite a weekend – celebrating Easter, his birthday and the end of the movie. It was quite amazing. So that was my experience – also meeting Coppola was quite amazing as well!"

In 1980, as fate would have it, some of the original Mothers decided to join together as a group and create music once again. Thus the Grandmothers were born! Incorporating all the zaniness we had come to expect from our Mothers, the Grandmothers would continue in some respects where the original Mothers of Invention left off ten years previously.

seven

Frank Zappa ended the seventies with the conceptual *Joe's Garage* series of LPs which were generally well received. In 1980 Zappa released the album *You Are What You Is* which featured cameo appearances by both Motorhead and Jimmy Carl Black. Throughout the 1980s Zappa and his original band grew further and further apart and he became less and less inclined to use any of his old musical partners and more inclined to work with orchestras as well as the synclavier. In the eighties and early nineties Zappa continued to release some very fine and innovative albums, right up until his untimely death.

When CD became the favoured format in the late eighties Frank Zappa started releasing a long string of live and unreleased material. With the increased time available on compact discs, some of these CDs, often compilations of guitar solos, tended toward marathon listening experiences. Every year new CD compilations started appearing as Zappa began releasing various pieces from the massive archive of material that he had in his possession. (Most notably the *You Can't Do That On Stage Anymore* series – some of which featured material from the original Mothers line-ups.) He still often mixed live and studio work together, and much of this material was musically invigorating. Another recent release from 1993 *Ahead Of Their Time* features an early classic Mothers performance at the Festival Hall in London, 28 October, 1968.

Zappa's last major tour was undertaken in 1988. In the nineties the news broke that he was seriously ill with prostate cancer. After that, he concentrated on repackaging, remastering and re-evaluating his back catalogue, not to mention the never-ending stream of old live tapes that kept on coming from his vaults. Still, there were also new releases, his last being *The Yellow Shark*. In the setting of a modern classical ensemble he found musicians capable of interpreting his music as well as those rock musicians of the late sixties and seventies had done.

Unfortunately, in the early nineties a lawsuit between Zappa and some of the ex-Mothers members arose concerning a dispute over back royalties due over a period of of 25 years. When asked about the situation a few years back, Jimmy Carl Black commented, "I can't really talk about that. As far as my feelings about Frank, I loved Frank Zappa and I always will. He was like a brother to me. I learned a lot from him and I think he learned a lot from the original Mothers. Frank was a real friend of mine. I don't know how he felt, but that's the way I feel about it."

By the time the lawsuit was settled, Bunk Gardner was asked what his feelings were. "They are the same I had at the end of our association in October 1969, which is sadness and disappointment. I'm not at liberty to discuss any aspect of the lawsuit. In closing, all I can say is that in spite of some of the difficulties, I have a lot of great memories and lifetime friendships as a result of my years with the Mothers of Invention."

After the sad news of his death in December 1993, the obituaries rightly concentrated on the huge contribution Frank Zappa has made to the course of modern rock, jazz and experimental music. As one of the truly individual geniuses of his time, his influence is immeasurable. The fusion of rock, jazz, classical, r&b, *musique concrete*, improvisation and satire that he created was the inspirational springboard for scores of groups. Not least he was responsible for championing the merits of his friend Captain Beefheart (Don Van Vliet), who sadly gave up music in favour of painting in the mid-eighties, but whose own contribution to music is consistently being re-evaluated. Suffice to say for those wishing to find out more about Frank Zappa there are plenty of books available about the great man and his music, many of which are worth investigating.

In an attempt to recapture some of the spirit of the original Mothers, Don Preston had assembled the first incarnation of the Grandmothers in 1980. Initially intended as a touring band, they were intent on reviving the legacy and musical anarchy of those early Mothers LPs. Their first release was *The Grandmothers* (a collection of material by ex-Mothers of Invention members). Released in 1980 on Rhino Records (re-issued on CD in 1993 on One-Way Records, USA minus Don Preston's material) to coincide with the formation of the Grandmothers, this was a collection of late sixties/seventies unreleased material. It brought together various solo recordings from Don Preston's Raw Milk, Jimmy and Bunk's Geronimo Black, Bunk and Buzz's group Menage A Trois, as well as recordings from Elliot Ingber (the original Mothers guitarist) and Motorhead Sherwood.

Jimmy Carl Black recalls that, "The first album was the anthology of the Grandmothers. Cal Schenkel did the cover, and that was actually just each member contributing a couple of songs. My two songs were recorded by the band Geronimo Black. Don Preston had two songs; Bunk and Elliot Ingber both had two songs. That was how that album worked out. It was not us playing together."

Rumour has it that Motorhead briefly joined the Grandmothers about this time. In fact he only played once at the Roxy, the first and only gig of that Grandmothers line-up in L.A. as Motorhead explains. "Actually, Jimmy Carl Black had his band Geronimo Black, and they had a keyboard player, Andy Cahan. I don't know who originally thought of it, but to me it was Andy's idea to start the Grandmothers, to get all the old Mothers together to do an album. They gave me a call and said, 'Why don't you write a song or do something on the album?' I was married at the time and was just about to move up to Idaho to do some ranching, so I did a little song called 'Going To Idaho' and put it on the album. They did a concert at the Roxy, so I went down and did that. That was my little stint with the Grandmothers. I never really kept up with that, so I don't know what happened with it. I guess Jim Black and a few others were touring around with it, but I didn't do any more with them. I just let that go."

Bunk Gardner relates that, "The natural progression from the Mothers of Invention to the Grandmothers was brought about in 1980 by Don, myself and Jim deciding to play some of Frank Zappa's music. But mostly we wanted to record and play our own music, have everyone write, have input and contribute musically to the new group. We toured California and Europe playing contemporary and avant-garde music, plus satire and humor very much in the spirit of the Mothers. I don't think Frank liked what we were doing. We invited him once to join in with us at one of our shows, which he declined. In the beginning we enjoyed the new challenge of recording and traveling."

There followed a number of tours including the States and Europe in summer 1981 featuring Jimmy Carl Black on drums and vocals, Don Preston on keyboards and vocals, Bunk Gardner on woodwinds, Tom Fowler on bass and vocals, Walt Fowler on trumpet and keyboards and Tony Duran on guitar – the only time the Grandmothers consisted of all ex-Mothers.

Don Preston states that, "We formed the Grandmothers in 1980. Unfortunately, I think this upset Zappa quite a bit. One reason was, we had this doll – many years ago I had made Moon Zappa this Raggedy-Anne type doll of myself, complete with tongue and teeth and everything. So at the time of the Grandmothers, in 1980, I thought, "Hey what a great idea to make a doll of Frank." So I did. We took it on the road with us in Europe, and the only thing we did was this little skit where it looked like we were giving birth to this doll head. I got a call from Frank, after we got back from the tour, and he adamantly said, "Get rid of the doll!" So we of course did. I tried to tell him we weren't doing anything derogatory towards him with it – I mean we all had (and still do) the highest respect for him and his music. Anyway, we did several tours of Europe and I don't know if it was successful or not, but we sure had a lot of fun and was really good to see that there were still fans over in Europe who wanted to see that band. I thought we played some good music. We also toured the States a little bit and played the Roxy in L.A.. Then we quit. There was a problem with one of the band members who kept trying to destroy the band. Every contact we had he would just completely destroy it – I don't want to mention names. So the band had to give it up."

For a while the Grandmothers were expanded to include the guitarist Tony Duran who was later replaced by Denny Walley (Walley actually never gigged with the group, he only rehearsed with them). However, as Bunk puts it, "Soon too many problems plagued that band, economically and socially, to keep it going. It ended just short of two years after it started. It wasn't meant to be at that time."

Before they split up in 1982 they released *Looking Up Granny's Dress*, again on Rhino records. Side one featured a live sixteen-track recording of the band in Ribe, Denmark, taken from the Grandmothers tour of the previous year. Side two starts with a track recorded in 1962 by Ray Collins at Studio Z in Cucamonga. The other five tracks were again individual tracks which featured the last studio recorded vocal by Ray Collins so far released. A song he wrote entitled "Mayonnaise Mountain", which contained those golden vocals of Collins that harken back to the glory days of the original Mothers Of Invention. (This track was originally recorded in 1973 and released on the album *Welcome Back Geronimo Black*.)

Ray Collins explains: "On 'Mayonnaise Mountain', Jim Black created the Geronimo Black band after he left the Mothers, and I ran into them at the Ashgrove (nightclub) one night, when I had just walked out of an apartment that I had to vacate because I couldn't afford it, and had absolutely no place to go. So I walked up there, and they were playing, and Jim said, 'So why don't you join our band?' I said, 'All right! Great!' So I joined Geronimo Black there. They were making a demo – and this 'Mayonnaise Mountain' is really just a demo tape, actually. And so they recorded what songs they were going to put on the demo, and they asked me for one, so we actually created that song in the studio. I suppose, when you don't get the opportunity to put on the recording, or be able to record all the ideas that you have in the world, you sort of throw them out any way you can. What 'Mayonnaise Mountain' really is, is a shopping cart in a market, you know, which is piled with all the different things that people try to sell people, and are successful at it – you know, goo-goos and craggels and boggles, and Cokes, whatever. All the junk of the world, piled on top of the shopping cart. That's what 'Mayonnaise Mountain' really is. Otherwise, it's a semi-nice ballad. I don't really like the record too well. Like I say, it's a demo. I think it was around '73, somewhere around there."

When radio DJ David Porter asked Ray Collins in August '89 if he still wished to perform and if he did, would anyone still recognize him, this was Ray's response. "It wouldn't be actually correct to say I've done a lot, because I really haven't. I haven't done a lot of things in my life. I don't know why, I don't know what tends to designate me the non-doer on the planet, one of the non-doers, I don't know. I still have plans to do things, you know, I still want to record, and sing. I love to perform, but um – sometimes I wonder, when you're sitting around thinking, 'Why are you sitting around thinking?' – I've done that a lot – and wondered why it is that I've actually done very little recording and performing in my lifetime. I do love doing it, but something somehow has put a stop to it. But I know that I'm good at what I do, and know that I'll do some more again. It's really great to perform before people. Well, now the only time I would sing with a band would be if someone says, 'Here's Ray Collins, former Mother of Invention,' it's obvious who I am. People rarely recognize me. As a matter of fact, more people think that Don Preston is me, or I'm Don Preston."

In the early nineties, to the excitement of his fans, Ray Collins did release a self-made cassette of demos he recorded called *Love Songs*. Although recorded on basic equipment, Ray delivers some of his most beautiful and inspiring compositions and performances. Although, probably extremely rare to find these days, it is a must for all Ray Collins/Mothers fans.

For the rest of the eighties the various Grandmothers went their separate ways. In the late eighties Jimmy Carl Black would continue to use the name Grandmothers with musicians from his home town of Austin, Texas. As previously mentioned, Jimmy also had a temporary reconciliation with Frank Zappa, recording on his album *You Are What You Is*. He sang lead vocal on "Harder Than Your Husband" and a *200 Motels* rap on "Teenage Wind" plus some classic Jimmy Carl Black noises and sayings (along with Motorhead snorking) on the end section of "Goblin Girl".

In the late 1970s Jimmy Carl Black formed a blues group called Big Sonny & the Lowboys and recorded one album with them called *In Heat*. In 1980 Jimmy moved to Albequerque, NM and released a very rare album of songs from the '50s called *Clearly Classic*. Now a collectors item, it was initially released as a clear plastic blobbed shape LP of which only 500 were pressed. That same year the album *Welcome Back Geronimo Black* was released. In the late '80s, Jimmy Carl Black moved to Austin, Texas where he recorded with Arthur Brown, formerly of the Crazy World Of Arthur Brown (a sort of sixties UK answer to the Mothers of Invention) and later Kingdom Come.

Jimmy Carl Black explains. "When I first moved to Austin, an old friend of mine Arthur Brown was already living there – back in the '60s we had done several gigs with the Mothers with the Crazy World of Arthur Brown supporting. Arthur and I formed a painting company, painting houses for a living, for probably six years together, and in 1989 I put together some musicians and went into the studio to do ten r&b classics which were Arthur Brown's interpretation of songs like 'Unchain My Heart', 'Smokestack Lightening' and 'Hound Dog'. We put out an album together called *Brown, Black & Blue* which is now kind of a collectors item, a very good record on Blue Wave Records in the USA. By the way, there's a picture CD around of that." (This CD has recently been re-issued in 1999 on Voiceprint Records, UK.)

After that, Jimmy Carl Black formed a present day Grandmothers in 1989, with Roland St Germain on guitar, keyboards and vocals. "Actually he was the musical director of the band, did all the arranging and what-not," says Black. At the time Roland St Germain obviously felt he gained quite a lot from being in the Grandmothers. "It's a challenge for five people to sit there on stage and make it interesting," he commented. "I have never belonged to a band for longer than nine months, and for me to be in the fourth year of this has been an experience and a serious education. I've definitely grown quite a bit as a result and people seem to like what we do."

However, on the summer 1993 tour with the Grandmothers, St Germain quit when the group wouldn't perform his songs and Sandro Oliva took his place as guitarist. Along with this shuffling of guitarists it also saw Bunk and Don return to the fold to form the present day incarnation of the Grandmothers as a five piece band.

Jimmy Carl Black explains. "This new Grandmothers plays about thirty of the old Mothers of Invention songs, at least two songs from each of the original Mothers albums, and then about 60% of our show is original material which I would have to say sounds an awful lot like how the original Mothers sounded! Highly arranged, witty, a lot of social comment. It's always total improvisation. There's no plan. The Grandmothers are like the Mothers of Invention. We're a highly structured band. We know what we're doing, on everything, but yet we have the freedom, on solo spots, to take care of that part of it. No two shows are the same. That's why Don calls them that way. We don't want to get bored."

Don Preston takes up the story. "In the late '80s Jimmy Carl Black started an Austin, Texas version of the Grandmothers band. Even though he was the only original Grandmother in the new group he still called it the Grandmothers.

Anyway, they released an album (*Dreams On Long Play*) that I really didn't like. Then Jimmy moved to Europe and he called Bunk and I about reforming another Grandmothers. So in 1993, Bunk and I went over to Europe and toured with Jimmy as the Grandmothers with Ener Bladezipper on bass and an Italian guitarist named Sandro Oliva. We toured Europe for over two years. We tried getting more tours together but now there's this 25% of the gross tax in Germany which means you can't make any money touring there, so we couldn't tour Europe again. We had a promoter here in the US who said he could get us a tour here, but it would have been for so little money it wouldn't have been worth it. Jimmy, Sandro and Ener did tour in 1997 as the Grandmothers Power Trio."

Bunk Gardner remembers that most European fans were very enthusiastic about the Grandmothers. "We had to sign a lot of old Mothers albums plus the new CD and of course a lot of T-shirts. It also demonstrated to us that there really are a lot of hardcore Grandmothers and old Mothers' fans. It was interesting to see so many young fans at our concerts that presumably had first heard our music when their Mom or Dad played our music at home. The first three or four shows were a little inconsistent musically, but little things started to change and we definitely evolved over the course of the tour into a very tight, but still evolving band! With a different PA system every night it was hard to get the same overall sound and be able to hear each other like we would like to...

"If there's another tour we are going to add some new material, both original and some oldie but goodie stuff from the 1966-1969 band. This time we will also add some weirdness, maybe a transformation or two on-stage, and delve into some of our earlier humor. You can expect the unexpected. This band can boogie and still get out there in the twilight zone!"

The most recent release by the Grandmothers was *Who Could Imagine* – a mixture of live and studio recordings released in September 1994 by Brain Records in Germany (reissued on Network records). It features the Grandmothers line-up of Jimmy Carl Black, Don Preston, Bunk Gardner, Ener Bladezipper, Sandro Oliva together with an appearance by Roy Estrada. This CD was released to coincide with the Grandmothers European tour in the second half of 1994.

On returning to the US, the band found that they had been threatened with legal action by Zappa's estate for allegedly using the name the "Grandmothers of Invention". In fact, certain promotors had used the name in error instead of the correct name of the Grandmothers. The guys are adamant in stressing that the name of the band is the Grandmothers and that they have no intention of working under the name the Mothers of Invention.

Back to happier matters, in 1992 the Grandmothers contributed to the second Ant-Bee album, as Don Preston recalls. "Me, Bunk, Jimmy, Roy and Motorhead are featured on a couple new CDs with Ant-Bee called *Ant-Bee With My Favourite Vegetables And Other Bizarre Muzik* and *Lunar Muzik* [released on Divine Records, UK]. These feature material we recorded with Ant-Bee throughout the

1990s, plus some unique interview segments by each of us. Playing with Ant-Bee is very exciting and I look forward to doing more stuff, I think we do real well together, his music is very nostalgic. I haven't played that kind of material for some time now and I enjoyed it very much. Also Bunk, Jimmy and I have recorded some tracks for Ant-Bee's newest (4th) CD *Electronic Church Muzik* which features a version of my song 'Eye of Agamoto'."

"In 1992 I got a call from Bunk Gardner," says Jimmy Carl Black, "saying that a guy called Billy James was interested in me doing a little recording on one of his songs for an upcoming album that he's working on. I of course said that I'd do it, and Billy sent me a tape that he wanted me to do a talking part on a song called 'Lunar Egg Clips Runs Amuck'. I did the recording and sent it back to him, and I was very, very impressed with the type of music that he was doing. It was very Mothers-oriented, and the fact that he uses some of the best musicians that I've ever heard and that the material is definitely avant-garde. I enjoyed doing this very much and I'm looking forward to doing several other recording projects with him, possibly playing on tour with him and the Grandmothers."

1996 saw Bunk, Don, Jimmy, Motorhead and Roy all being featured on the third Ant-Bee CD *Lunar Muzik* (also featured guest appearances by members of the original Alice Cooper group and Daevid Allen of Gong). The results were grand Mother-esque tributes entitled "Snorks & Wheezes" and "Son Of Snorks & Wheezes". As Don Preston puts it, "Ant-Bee's music sometimes sounds so close to the original Mothers material it's scary! Also included is a version of my composition "Silicone Hump" arranged in the fashion of *Uncle Meat*."

"My recent musical connection with Ant-Bee has been fun", confirms Bunk Gardner. "Recording some tracks has reminded me of earlier times in my career. I've always liked the challenge of doing something different and at the same time interesting musically. So, I found in talking with Billy that we have a lot in common, and he knows where he wants to go and how to get there. I've recorded on three of the Ant-Bee albums. Also Billy is helping me put together a CD of some of my solo material I've recorded throughout the years."

Jimmy Carl Black and Don Preston also worked with Eugene Chadbourne, or as Jimmy puts it, "He's another weirdo." Jimmy recorded two albums with Chadbourne, *Locked In A Dutch Coffee House* and *Pachuco Cadaver* (a tribute to Captain Beefheart).

In 1994 the Grandmothers were back touring Europe including a date in Budapest called Euro Woodstock as part of the 25th anniversary celebrations for the famous festival. In general the group were still in high spirits. Don Preston recalls: "We toured around Europe, which was quite successful. We had designed a completely new stage show for that tour with some new original songs like 'New Age Mumbo Jumbo' and 'The Great Generic Side Show' along with some FZ hits like 'Brown Shoes Don't Make It' and 'Hungry Freaks Daddy' combined with the bizarre humor people have come to expect from the Grandmothers.

"We came back from Hungary after having played Euro-Woodstock. It was very exciting playing to an audience that stretched as far as the eye could see – all screaming their heads off. The band was tighter than it ever had been and we were playing those songs with more wit and expertise than ever before."

Bunk Gardner recalls a specific incident. "Here's a recent tour story you'll like – the Indian fell asleep on the tour bus and his false teeth fell out on the floor while he was sleeping. The customs agents came in to check things out... Obviously, we'd been partying a bit, but when they saw the false teeth on the floor they walked back out again. Obviously they were thinking, 'These guys aren't going to hurt nobody – OK let em go.' Well, the Indian got up like Gabby Hayes (imitates) just gumming everything to death. He cracked up when he found out."

In the late 1990s Bunk, Don and Jimmy continued to be active musically. Jimmy Carl Black has toured and recorded with various artists such as the Muffin Men, Behind the Mirror, and the Farrell & Black Band. In 1997, a CD of rare unreleased material by Jimmy was released on Divine Records UK called inevitably *When Do We Get Paid?* He's currently compiling a sequel entitled *Do You Got Any Beer?*

Bunk Gardner taught at various institutions in L.A. as well as performing with Don Preston as a duo called The Don & Bunk show, as Don explained at the time. "The thing Bunk and I are doing is going over real well – I'm real excited about the Don & Bunk show. I'd like to think there's a possibility of us doing a tour. I think we could do a small tour and then come back and do a bigger one, because we have a really great show. The thing is that when we were doing the Grandmothers in Europe, I was primarily the leader of the group as well as lead vocalist, although Jimmy sang some songs. Most of the show's ideas were mine and a quarter of the songs we played were mine. So I'm utilizing all that with mine and Bunk's new act. We still play some of the old Mothers material as well as new stuff I wrote. We were doing this gig in L.A. at the aptly titled Lumpy Gravy club and it was going over really well, at times it felt like the Garrick all over again!"

Although the shows were deemed a success, Preston still had some reservations, as he explains. "I didn't feel like I had it completely together for that. I mean parts of it were great, we had fans that were coming down there and checking it out. They were really getting into the show we were doing, which was partially visual with a lot of Zappa's more difficult music. So we were putting on a fairly good show. I think the main problem I had with it was that I was playing electronic equipment, and I found later on that if I didn't play on electronic equipment, but acoustic equipment, then the show went off much better. When using the electronic gear, I just wasn't getting the sound I wanted to hear – the sound wasn't right. I've been playing nothing but acoustic piano for the last six years. So when I went into the Lumpy Gravy club with the electronic gear I had, the music suffered in quality, because none of that stuff sounds like a real piano. Later on, Bunk and

I did several shows around L.A. on just acoustic instruments and those gigs came off great."

Don Preston possibly has stayed the most busy of all the Grandmothers these past few years with the release in 1993 of his first solo CD, *Vile Foamy Ectoplasm,* as he explains. "My first solo CD was released on Muffin records in Germany. It contains vintage material from throughout my career and features guest appearances by Bunk, Jimmy Carl, Howard Kaylan, Merridith Monk and Emil Richards. I put together the CD here in L.A., I reorganized it and de-noised a lot of it. I also redid a lot of the edits in it. The artwork was done by me as well, which was a piece I did prior to the album. Through the years I have been active doing artwork. So that was a piece I had done that I was proud of – it was kind of Mothers/ Cal Schenkel orientated. The album also contained interesting noise collages I used for the interludes between tracks. In the late sixties I'd walk around with a UHR tape recorder and a couple of mics, especially in New York City. I would record various things as I came across them. So that was added into the album. It should still be available through Muffin Records here in the US. Also I have a cheesy video released on the Electrik Yak label called *Ogo Moto* – a cheap sci-fi thing I filmed in 1968 plus other rare footage including a version of *Dracula* featuring Leo Sayer."

In 1997 Preston released his second solo CD *Hear Me Out.* "It got pretty good airplay all over the country", Preston explains. "It's a solo piano album – they're mostly recent songs I've written over the past 5 years. There's a couple old ones in there as well – actually there is a song on it that my dad wrote, so it's a tribute to him. The CD was released on Echograph Records in L.A.."

Don Preston describes the circumstances surrounding the release of his second solo CD. "There was a friend of mine, who lived downtown in Los Angeles in a loft, who decided to put on a small festival of downtown artists. I had lived downtown for ten years so I guess I was considered one of the artists. So there was a group of eclectic people of different genres of music to put on this concert. There were about eight or nine people – I played with a duo guitar group called the Oil Junkies. So it was mostly new music. I also contributed with a solo piano piece, in which in the middle of, I pulled my fake hand out of the piano and shot it with a gun – that helped to lighten up the evening a little bit, because it was all very serious music.

During the event one of the Oil Junkies, James Mckisick, told me he was starting a record company and asked if I was interested in doing an album for them – to which I said, "Yes." Because of financial restrictions, they decided a solo piano album would be the best. I had originally put together a solo CD of previously recorded pieces and presented it to them, which they liked but it had too much noise on the tracks. So we went into Mad Hatter studios, which at the time was owned by Chick Corea, and recorded the album. Even though the CD recieved good airplay and sold fairly well, the label never really took off. They couldn't afford to finance my next CD so, after two and a half years, I left the label."

Don Preston travelled to Berlin in November 1997 and sang in Michael Mantler's opera *The School Of Understanding* which also featured Jack Bruce and John Greaves. Preston also began working with acclaimed percussionist Amy Knoles, performing at various theatres in L.A.. In the same year Don began working with the California Ear Unit, as he explains. "In 1997 I was commissioned by the California Ear Unit, a Los Angeles chamber ensemble, to write a piece for them, which I did. It was performed on May 28, 1997 at the Bing Theatre in the L.A. County Museum."

Preston continues: "The piece that I wrote was entitled 'The Bride Stripped Bare', which refers to that famous art piece by Marcel Duchamp. I had a replica of this piece – this quite large painting done on glass that stands in the Philadelphia Museum. So, my daughter made a replica of it, and I took it to the L.A. County Museum, when we did the gig. We used it as a percussion piece, and hung it up with a device so one of the percussionists could play on it. We mic'd it and everything, and it came out really good. It was very effective because it had such an unusual sound."

In 1998 Preston composed the music for *Faust* by Goethe, which was adapted to contemporary times by John Steppling (who also directed). The play opened at the Los Angeles Theater Center on 5 October, 1998 to rave reviews. The *L.A. Weekly* reported: "Much of Faust's appeal comes from Don Preston's reverbing sound design of pipe-organ motifs and dripping water." The *L.A. Times* said: "This is *Faust* for the millinnial moment with an evocative sound landscape by venerable Don Preston. The sum is both archetypal and utterly '90s."

Most recently the *L.A. Weekly* has awarded Don Preston "Eminent Jazz Musician of 1999". Preston is currently working on two new solo CDs: "Recently, someone called me about doing an album with the trio I have been gigging around town with, who are excellent. The trio features Alex Cline on drums, and Joel Hamilton of bass. We're going into the studio to record in June 2000, and the album will be called *Transformation*.

I am also working on another CD of unreleased archival stuff, like the piece I did with the California Ear Unit. A European label has recently approached me about releasing this album in the near future. Then the Knitting Factory in New York want me to play there sometime this year, and hopefully I can get some more gigs on the East Coast at that point as well."

Beginning in August 2000, the Grandmothers embarked on a three month tour of the USA. It is the first time that they have performed in America in almost twenty years.

Who knows what else the new millenium will bring for our ex-Mothers (most of whom are now hitting retirement age). What is certain is that Bunk, Don, Jimmy, Motorhead, Ian, Art, Buzz, Ray and Roy have been entertaining people for over a quarter of a century – whether it be with vegetables, transformations, improvisations, snorks or asthmatic wheezing. One thing is for sure, we will never forget our Mothers!

where are they now?

DICK BARBER: The group's original road manager, creator of the snork, and immortalised in *200 Motels* as a vacuum cleaner, is believed now to own his own restaurant in Claremont, CA. As Bunk puts it, "Dick was a great road manager. We had fun with him."

JIMMY CARL BLACK: Currently lives in Germany. At the moment he is still in the Grandmothers and is compiling a solo CD of material. Jimmy also tours Europe with various groups such as the Muffin Men and the Farrell & Black band.

RAY COLLINS: Now lives in Claremont, CA and is still playing music, selling some of his demos mail order. In 1993 he released a cassette entitled *Love Songs* which displays he still has a very soulful voice. Unfortunately his experiences with Zappa and the Mothers left him cold. He has completely disassociated himself from the Mothers and refuses to have anything to do with them.

ROY ESTRADA: Having played with Little Feat, Leo Kotke and on various Zappa LPs, Roy has recently retired from music and started driving a truck for a living. He still keeps in touch with other former Mothers. As Bunk puts it, "Every now and then he telephones or comes over to hang out and lets me know what's been going on in his life."

ELLIOT INGBER: Became Winged Eel Fingerling in the Captain Beefheart Band. He now lives in L.A. where he has his own studio.

BUNK GARDNER: Currently still a member of the Grandmothers, Bunk lives with his wife and two daughters in Glendale, CA. Bunk also teaches at Laguna Hills Music Store and has taught music at both the Annaheim School of Music, and for two years at St. George Acadamy in Orange County. He is currently compiling a solo CD due for release soon. Bunk teaches at various music schools in L.A. and still gigs with Don Preston.

BUZZ GARDNER: After the Hollywood Allstars broke-up, Buzz retired from music.

LOWELL GEORGE: Died in 1977 after years of alcohol and drug abuse. For close to a decade he had been the frontman and leader of Little Feat. Most of the original Little Feat recordings are available on CD and well worth checking out. Little Feat reformed in the late '80s with a new singer.

BILLY JAMES: Working under the pdeudonym Ant-Bee, James has recorded with many of the ex-members of the Mothers. He is currently working on a new CD entitled *Electronic Church Muzik* featuring Bunk, Don as well as Michael Bruce (Alice Cooper group), Zoot Horn Rollo (Captain Beefheart), Daevid Allen & Gilli Smyth (Gong), Jan Akkerman (Focus), Peter Banks (Yes) and hopefully Flo & Eddie (if he can pay their fee!).

BILLY MUNDI: Jimmy says, "I haven't seen Billy since probably 1972 or 1973. That's a mystery to all of us. I don't know where Billy's at. I've heard rumours that he was in New York, I've heard rumours that he was in Dallas; I've heard rumours that he was in a lot of places."

DON PRESTON: Don has always considered himself a jazz musician having worked with the likes of Herbie Mann, Elvin Jones, Jack Bruce, Carla Bley, John Carter and Michael Mantler – and the list goes on. Widely acclaimed as an electronics genius, he became one of Frank Zappa's longer serving musicians. Throughout the '70s he did several gigs with the likes of Flo & Eddie, Leo Sayer and The Residents. Don has scored a number of film soundtracks, most notably *Apocalypse Now*. He was instrumental in the formation of the original Grandmothers in 1980 and rejoined in 1993. Don sums up: "For many years, I thought of myself as a jazz musician, but most people recognised me as a rock musician. Now people are starting to see that I am a jazz musician from my recent efforts, and I feel real good about that. I think you have to push the limits of any artform and music is one of the major elements that progresses humanity. Art is the impetus for all the other technologies of life." Still a member of The Grandmothers, he currently lives in L.A. where he is still very busy playing and composing music.

MOTORHEAD SHERWOOD: Currently lives in San Jose, CA where he is still an avid blues collector. Motorhead was one of the few original Mothers that remained on good terms with Zappa until the time of his death. He also featured on Zappa's *You Are What You Is* LP and appeared in the BBC's *Late Show* special on Frank Zappa. He said at the time: "They invited some of the ex-Mothers down. It was actually me and Ruth Underwood. They had a bunch of video stuff that I did on tour that they added in, plus a picture of the old school I took. Later on, they were supposed to be doing a longer show. When I went down to see Frank, Johnny Guitar Watson was down. I hadn't seen him in years. Frank always loved his guitar playing."

"I just feel honoured to have spent time with Frank and the other guys in the early group. As far as the fans go, I wish them well, and I really appreciate the support. I hope they love Frank as much as I do, because he was an incredible person, and his music is just something I enjoy listening to all the time. It was always new and different and incredible, and I sure hope our fans stick around for a long time. I'll close on that. Wish everybody well. Bye bye."

ARTIE TRIPP: Played in Captain Beefheart's band as Ed Marimba and then joined ex-Magic Band members in Mallard. Mallard produced two LPs (recently re-issued on one CD) and could be described as half way between the Magic Band and Little Feat. After giving up music, Tripp graduated from chiropractic school and has his own practice in Northern California near Eureka. He recently commented to *Mojo* magazine: "What I always tell people is anybody who plays the xylophone ought to be able to work on a spine." Tripp reportedly tried to alleviate some back pain for Don Van Vliet, but when the rather unpredictable man wasn't instantly cured Tripp was sent packing.

IAN UNDERWOOD: Still remains one of today's top session players and is featured on dozens of albums. He also has recorded several film soundtracks.

FRANK ZAPPA: There is probably very little to say about the great man that hasn't been said before. Often a difficult and tough taskmaster, he produced body of work which was breathtaking in its scope and diversity. He was truly a musical genius, the like of which will never be seen again. What cannot be denied is that his music continues to enthral new generations of fans. The entire Frank Zappa, Mothers of Invention and Mothers catalogues have recently been re-issued on CD by Rykodisc.

appendices

Original illustration: Joel Levicke

material sources

Most of the interview material from Don Preston, Bunk Gardner, Jimmy Carl Black, Roy Estrada, Motorhead Sherwood, Buzz Gardner, and Richard Kunc was conducted by Billy James from the years 1993 to 2000.
Ray Collins Interview – excerpts were taken from 3 sources:
A) a radio program called *Genesis Of Music* with David Porter on KPFK, 8/12/89
B) off-air tapes made by David Porter in KPFK's master control room, a coffee shop, and Ray Collins' car
C) A radio program called *Rock-and-Roll and Rhythm-and-Blues* with Steve Propes on KLON, 8/13/89
Flo & Eddie Interview – Producer and MC: Co de Kloet – Dutch Radio Show *4FM* (www.nps.nl/4fm) Oct. 30, 1990
Reprinted in *Society Pages* magazine #10 (Aug. 24, 1992) & #11 (Feb. 28, 1993)
Musician Magazine – Feb. 1994
Creem Magazine – Dec. 1974 – 'Frank Zappa VS. The Tooth Fairy' -Ed Naha
Mother! The Story Of Frank Zappa (book) – Michael Gray – 1985 – Proteus Books (UK)
The Rolling Stone Interviews (book) – copyright © 1971 by Straight Arrow Publishers, Inc. Interview conducted by Jerry Hopkins – copyright © 1968 by Straight Arrow Publishers, Inc.
No Commercial Potential – David Walley – 1972 – Dutton-Sunrise, Inc.
The Torchum Never Stops – Reinhard Preuss – 1992 – Independently Published
Zappalog – Norbert Obermans
Mojo Magazine
Mark Volman Interview – Alan Vorda – 1986 – reprinted in *Psychedelic Psounds* – Bordeline productions
Trouser Press Magazine – April 1979 – 'Bad Taste Is Timeless – Cruising Down Memory Lane With Frank Zappa – David Fricke
Goldmine Magazine – May 19, 2000 – The Alice Cooper Group – The Quintessential American Rock 'n Roll Band – Russell Hall
Tangents Magazine – 1997 – Daniel Coston
Beyond The Velvet Underground (book) – Dave Thompson – 1989 – Omnibus Press
The Vault – written by Don Preston – c p 2000 Don Preston
the electrik yak interview tapes:
motorhead speaks - 1993 interview (1992, tape, usa, electrik yak 004)
bunk speaks - 1992 interview (1992, tape, usa, electrik yak 005; = interview for ptolemaic terrascope vol.4 no.1)
dom de wilde speaks - 1992 interview (1992, tape, usa, electrik yak 006; = interview for ptolemaic terrascope)
geronimo black speaks - 1992 interview (1992, tape, usa, electrik yak 007; = interview for ptolemaic terrascope vol.3 no.4)
geronimo black speaks again - 1992 interview (1992, tape, usa, electrik yak 008; = interview for t'mershi duween)
don preston speaks! - 1992 interview (1993, tape, usa, electrik yak letc 1; = a reissue + part of a grandmothers concert)
bunk gardner speaks! - 1992 interview (1993, tape, usa, electrik yak letc 2; = a reissue + part of a grandmothers concert)
jimmy carl black speak'n at ya! - 1992 interview (1993, tape, usa, electrik yak letc 3; = a reissue + part of a grandmothers concert)

Discographies:
Patrick Neve Website
The Turtles Website
Gig List: Charles Ulrich
the big nOte files (Soon On A Web Near You)

Musician's Websites

The Real Frank Zappa Website – www.frankzappa.com
Don Preston – www.jps.net/dwpreston/
Jimmy Carl Black – www.jimmycarlblack.com
Cal Schenkel – www.ralf.com
The Turtles/Flo&Eddie – www.theturtles.com
Ant-Bee Web Bizarre - ourworld.compuserve.com/homepages/antbee/
Essra Mohawk - rockersusa/EssraMohawk
Zoot Horn Rollo – www.zoothornrollo.com
Michael Bruce – www.michaelbruceofalicecooper.com
Neal Smith – www.nealsmith.com
Bob & Suzannah Harris – www.thanaharris.com
Jack Bruce - www.jackbruce.com
Sandro Oliva - www.geocities.com/sandroliva/
Co de Kloet - www.nps.nl/4fm

Frank Zappa/Mothers Related Websites

Splat's Zappa Page (Patrick Neve) – darkwing.uoregon.edu/~splat/zappapage.html
Arf Society – ourworld.compuserve.com/homepages/arf_tr
Debra Kedabra – www.pd.nettuno.it/lama/dk/stata.htm
Home Page Replica (Capt. Beefheart) – www.shiningsilence.com/hpr/
Electricity (Capt. Beefheart) – people.a2000nl/tieman/

A Very Large Gig List – home.istar.ca/~culrich/zappa/glglist/index.htmlDavid Walley – walleyswitzend.com
Rykodisc's FZ Page – www.rykodisc.com/Rykointernal/features/195/default.htm
Black Page Website - http://www.geocites.com/SouthBeach/jetty/3640/bignoteindex.html
Idlot Bastard Website - http://www.idiotbastard.supanet.com/index.htm

The Mothers of Invention 'live' repertoire

1) The Duke – parts I, II, III
2) Mr. Green Genes
3) Holiday In Berlin
4) Cruising For Burgers
5) You're Probably Wondering Why I'm Here
6) I Ain't Got No Heart
7) Blues/Corrido/Pachuco/Behind The Sun (instrumental song titles that changed with words)
8) Lonely Nights
9) You Didn't Try To Call Me
10) Here Lies Love
11) WPJL
12) Absolutely Free
13) A Pound For A Brown
14) Take Your Clothes Off When You Dance
15) Bacon Fat
16) Kung Fu
17) Igor's Boogie
18) In The Sky
19) King Kong
20) Orange County Lumber Truck
21) Hungry Freaks Daddy
22) Status Back Baby
23) String Quartet
24) Charles Ives (the unanswered question)
25) Valerie
26) Uncle Meat
27) I'm Not Satisfied
28) Call Any Vegetable
29) My Guitar Wants To Kill Your Mama
30) Motherly Love
31) Big Boy/ Pete & O.K.Dookie
32) Mom & Dad
33) Idiot Bastard Son
34) Little Evil & Tenga
35) Dog Breath
36) Hound Dog
37) Baby Love
38) My Boyfriend's Back
39) Gee
40) Petroushka
41) Eye Of Agamoto (Don Preston composition)
42) Let's Make The Water Turn Black
43) Oh No
44) Bristol Stomp
45) Big Leg Emma
46) It Can't Happen Here
47) No Matter What You Do
48) Blue Suede Shoes
49) Sleeping In A Jar
50) Trouble Coming Every Day
51) Aegospotomus (Don Preston composition)

Discography

Frank Zappa
Solo Albums & Projects

The Mothers Of Invention: Freak Out! (1) (1966, 2LP, USA, Verve)
The Mothers Of Invention: Absolutely Free (2) (1967, LP, USA, Verve)
The Mothers Of Invention: We're Only In It For The Money (3) (1967, LP, USA, Verve)
Frank Zappa: Lumpy Gravy (4) (1967, LP, USA, Verve)
The Mothers Of Invention: Cruising With Ruben & The Jets (5) (1968, LP, USA, Verve)
The Mothers Of Invention: Mothermania (6) (1969, LP, USA, Verve)
The Mothers Of Invention: Uncle Meat (7) (1969, 2LP, USA, Bizarre)
Frank Zappa: Hot Rats (8) (1969, LP, USA, Bizarre)
The Mothers Of Invention: Burnt Weeny Sandwich (9) (1970, LP, USA, Bizarre)
The Mothers Of Invention: Weasels Ripped My Flesh (10) (1970, LP, USA, Bizarre)
Frank Zappa: Chunga's Revenge (11) (1970, LP, USA, Bizarre)
The Mothers: Fillmore East, June 1971 (12) (1971, LP, USA, Bizarre)
Frank Zappa: 200 Motels (13) (1971, 2LP, USA, United Artists)
The Mothers: Just Another Band From L.A. (14) (1972, LP, USA, Bizarre)
Frank Zappa: Waka/Jawaka (15) (1972, LP, USA, Bizarre)
The Mothers: The Grand Wazoo (16) (1972, LP, USA, Bizarre)
The Mothers: Over-Nite Sensation (17) (1973, LP, USA, Discreet)
Frank Zappa: Apostrophe (') (18) (1974, LP, USA, Discreet)
Frank Zappa: Roxy & Elsewhere (19) (1974, 2LP, USA, Discreet)
Frank Zappa And The Mothers Of Invention: One Size Fits All (20) (1975, LP, USA, Discreet)
Zappa / Beefheart / Mothers: Bongo Fury (21) (1975, LP, USA, Discreet)
Frank Zappa: Zoot Allures (22) (1976, LP, USA, Warner Brothers)
Frank Zappa: Zappa In New York (23) (1978, 2LP, USA, Discreet)
Frank Zappa: Studio Tan (24) (1978, LP, USA, Discreet)
Frank Zappa: Sleep Dirt (25) (1979, LP, USA, Discreet)
Frank Zappa: Sheik Yerbouti (26) (1979, 2LP, USA, Zappa Records)
Frank Zappa: Orchestral Favorites (27) (1979, LP, USA, Discreet)
Frank Zappa: Joe's Garage Act 1 (28) (1979, LP, USA, Zappa Records)
Frank Zappa: Joe's Garage Acts 2 & 3 (29) (1979, 2LP, USA, Zappa Records)
Frank Zappa: Tinseltown Rebellion (30) (1981, 2LP, USA, Barking Pumpkin)
Frank Zappa: Shut Up'n Play Yer Guitar (31) (1981, LP, USA, Barking Pumpkin)
Frank Zappa: Shut Up 'N Play Yer Guitar Some More (32) (1981, LP, USA, Barking Pumpkin)
Frank Zappa: Return Of The Son Of Shut Up 'N Play Yer Guitar (33) (1981, LP, USA, Barking Pumpkin)
Frank Zappa: You Are What You Is (34) (1981, 2LP, USA, Barking Pumpkin)
Frank Zappa: Ship Arriving Too Late Too Save A Drowning Witch (35) (1982, LP, USA, Barking Pumpkin)
Frank Zappa: The Man From Utopia (36) (1983, LP, USA, Barking Pumpkin)
Frank Zappa: Baby Snakes (37) (1983, LP Pict.Disc, USA, Barking Pumpkin)
The London Symphony Orchestra: Zappa Vol.1 (38) (1983, LP, USA, Barking Pumpkin)
Frank Zappa: Boulez Conducts Zappa, The Perfect Stranger (39) (1984, LP, USA, Angel)
Frank Zappa: Them Or Us (40) (1984, 2LP, USA, Barking Pumpkin)
Frank Zappa: Thing-Fish (41) (1984, 3LP, USA, Barking Pumpkin)
Frank Zappa: Francesco Zappa (42) (1984, LP, USA, Barking Pumpkin)
Frank Zappa: The Old Masters, Box 1 (43) Freak Out / Absolutely Free / We're Only In It For The Money / Lumpy Gravy / Cruising With Ruben & The Jets / Mystery Disc Box 1 (1985, 7LP, USA, Barking Pumpkin)
Frank Zappa: Frank Zappa Meets The Mothers Of Prevention (44) (1985, LP, USA, Barking Pumpkin) - American Version (1985, LP, Eur, EMI) - European Version
Frank Zappa: Does Humour Belong In Music? (45)(1986, CD, Ger, EMI)
Frank Zappa: The Old Masters, Box 2 (46)Uncle Meat / Hot Rats / Burnt Weeny Sandwich / Weasels Ripped My Flesh /Chunga's Revenge / Fillmore East, June 1971 / Just Another Band From L.A. / Mystery Disc Box 2 (1986, 9LP, USA, Barking Pumpkin)
Frank Zappa: Jazz From Hell (47) (1986, LP, USA, Barking Pumpkin)
The London Symphony Orchestra: Zappa Vol.2 (48) (1987, LP, USA, Barking Pumpkin)
Frank Zappa: The Old Masters, Box 3 (49) Waka/Jawaka / Grand Wazoo / Over-Nite Sensation / Apostrophe (') /Roxy & Elsewhere / One Size Fits All / Bongo Fury / Zoot Allures (1987, 9LP, USA, Barking Pumpkin)
Frank Zappa: Guitar (50) (1988, 2CD, USA, Ryko)
Frank Zappa: You Can't Do That On Stage Anymore Vol.1 (51) (1988, 2CD, USA, Ryko)
Frank Zappa: Broadway The Hard Way (52) (1988, 2LP, USA, Barking Pumpkin)
Frank Zappa: You Can't Do That On Stage Anymore Vol.2 (53) (1988, 2CD, USA, Ryko)
Frank Zappa: You Can't Do That On Stage Anymore Vol.3 (54) (1989, 2CD, USA, Ryko)
Frank Zappa: The Best Band You Never Heard In Your Life (55) (1991, 2CD, USA, Barking Pumpkin)
Frank Zappa: Make A Jazz Noise Here (56) (1991, 2CD, USA, Barking Pumpkin)
Frank Zappa: You Can't Do That On Stage Anymore Vol.4 (57) (1991, 2CD, USA, Ryko)
Frank Zappa: You Can't Do That On Stage Anymore Vol.5 (58) (1992, 2CD, USA, Ryko)
Frank Zappa: You Can't Do That On Stage Anymore Vol.6 (59) (1992, 2CD, USA, Ryko)
Frank Zappa: Playground Psychotics (60) (1992, 2CD, USA, Ryko)

Zappa / Mothers: Ahead Of Their Time (61) (1993, CD, USA, Ryko)
Frank Zappa: The Yellow Shark (62) (1993, CD, USA, Ryko)
Frank Zappa: Civilization Phaze III (63) (1994, 2CD, USA, Barking Pumpkin)
Frank Zappa: The Lost Episodes (64) (1996, CD, USA, Ryko)
Frank Zappa: Lather (65) (1996, 3CD, USA, Ryko)
Frank Zappa: Frank Zappa Plays The Music Of Frank Zappa (66) (1996, CD, USA, Barking Pumpkin)
Frank Zappa: Mystery Disc (67) (1998, CD, USA, Ryko)
Frank Zappa: Everything Is Healing Nicely (68) (1999, CD, USA, Barking Pumpkin)

The Beat The Boots Boxes
Beat The Boots: As An Am / The Ark / Freaks & Mother*** / Unmitigated Audacity /Anyway The Wind Blows / 'Tis The Season To Be Jelly / Saarbrucken 1978 / Piquantique (1991, 9LP, USA, Rhino)
Beat The Boots #2: Disconnected Synapses / Tengo Na' Minchia Tanta / Electric Aunt Jemima / At The Circus / Swiss Cheese / Fire! / Our Man In Nirvana / Conceptual Continuity (1992, 8CD, USA, Rhino)

Contributions, Etc... - Part 1: "Studio Z"
The Masters: 16 Tons / Breaktime (1962, 7", USA, Emmy) The B-Side was written by Ronnie Williams, Paul Buff & Frank Zappa
The Penguins: Memories Of El Monte / Be Mine (1962, 7", USA, Original Sound) The A-Side was written by Frank Zappa and Ray Collins; produced by Frank Zappa
Ron Roman: Love Of My Life / Tell Me (1963, 7", USA, Daani) The A-side was co-written by Frank Zappa; Frank Zappa also plays on this track
Baby Ray And The Ferns: How's Your Bird / The World's Greatest Sinner (1963, 7", USA, Donna) A- and B-side written by Frank Zappa; Frank Zappa plays most of the instruments
Bob Guy: Deer Jeepers / Letter From Jeepers (1963, 7", USA, Donna) A- and B-side written by Frank Zappa
The Heartbreakers: Everytime I See You / Cradle Rock (1963, 7", USA, Donna) A-Side written by Frank Zappa & Ray Collins; both sides feature Zappa on guitar
Brian Lord And The Midnighters: The Big Surfer / Not Another One (1963, 7", USA, Vigah) A-side written by Frank Zappa
Ned & Nelda: Hey Nelda / Surf Along (1963, 7", USA, Vigah) A- and B-side written by Frank Zappa and Ray Collins
Hollywood Persuaders: Tijuana Surf / Grunion Run (1963, 7", USA, Original Sound) B-side written by Frank Zappa, feat. Frank Zappa on guitar
Jim Musil Combo: Grunion Run / North Beach (1963, 7", USA, Jay Emm) A-Side written by Frank Zappa
Mr.Clean: Mr.Clean / Jessie Lee (1963, 7", USA, Original Sound) both sides written and produced by Frank Zappa
Rotations: Heavies / The Cruncher (1963, 7", USA, Original Sound) produced by Frank Zappa
Conrad & The Hurricane Strings: Hurricane / Sweet Love (1963, 7", USA, Daytone) Recorded at Studio Z; Produced by Frank Zappa (?)
The Grandmothers: Lookin' Up Granny's Dress (3) (1982, LP, USA, Rhino) Feat. Frank Zappa on one track, recorded in 1962 in studio Z

Samplers
The following samplers present material from this period:
Var.Art.: 10c Rare Meat (1983, 12", USA, Rhino)
Var.Art.: Cucamonga Years - The Early Works Of Frank Zappa (1991, CD, Jpn, MSI)
Var.Art.: Rare Beefheart - Vintage Zappa (1992, CD, NI, Disky)
Var.Art.: Frank Zappa - Early Works 1963 - 1964 (1992, CD, Jpn, Del-Fi / Tecx)
Var.Art.: Rare Meat - Early Works Of Frank Zappa (1994, CD, USA, Del-Fi)

Contributions, Etc. - Part 2: Post-"Studio Z"
Bobby Jameson: Gotta Find My Roogalator (1966, 7", USA, Penthouse) The A-side was written by Frank Zappa
Burt Ward: Boy Wonder I Love You / Orange Coloured Sky (1967, 7", USA, MGM) Produced by Tom Wilson, arranged & conducted by Frank Zappa; A-side written by Frank Zappa
Eric Burdon & The Animals: It's All Meat / He Other Side Of This Life (1967, 7", USA, MGM) A-side arranged by Zappa
The Animals: Animalism (5) (1966, LP, USA, MGM) Frank Zappa arranged two tracks
Lenny Bruce: The Berkeley Concert (1968, 2LP, USA, Reprise) produced by Frank Zappa and Herb Cohen
Wild Man Fischer: The Circle / Merry-Go-Round (1968, 7", USA, Bizarre) Produced by Zappa; Zappa played overdubs
Wild Man Fischer: An Evening With Wild Man Fischer (1) (1968, LP, USA, Bizarre) Produced by Zappa; Zappa played overdubs
Captain Beefheart: Trout Mask Replica (3) (1969, 2LP, USA, Reprise) Produced by Frank Zappa; feat. Frank Zappa on guitar & vocal
Lord Buckley: A Most Immaculately Hip Aristocrat (1969, LP, USA, Straight) Edited by Frank Zappa
G.T.O.'S: Circular Circulation / Mercy's Tune (1969, 7", USA, Straight) Produced by Frank Zappa
G.T.O.'S: Permanent Damage (1) (1969, LP, USA, Straight) Produced by Frank Zappa; feat. Frank Zappa on guitar
Jeff Simmons: Lucille Has Messed My Mind Up (2) (1969, LP, USA, Straight) Produced by Lamarr Bruister (Frank Zappa); feat.Frank Zappa on guitar
Jean-Luc Ponty: King Kong (5) (1970, LP, USA, Pacific Jazz) Arranged/produced by Frank Zappa; feat. Frank Zappa on guitar
John Lennon & Yoko Ono: Some Time In New York City (1972, 2LP, UK, Apple) feat. Mothers Of Invention 1971 band
Ruben And The Jets: If I Could Be Your Love Again / Wedding Bells (1973, 7", USA, Mercury) Produced by Frank Zappa; A-side written and arranged by Frank Zappa
Ruben And The Jets: All Nite Long / Spider Woman (1973, 7", USA, Mercury) Produced by Frank Zappa
Ruben And The Jets: Charlena / Mah Man Flash (1973, 7", USA, Mercury) Produced By Frank Zappa; B-side arranged by Frank Zappa
Ruben & The Jets: For Real (1) (1973, LP, USA, Mercury) Produced by Frank Zappa; couple of tracks written & arranged by Frank Zappa; one track features Frank Zappa on guitar
George Duke: Feel (5) (1974, LP, Ger, MPS) feat. Obdewl'x (Frank Zappa) on guitar

Grand Funk Railroad: Can You Do It / 1976 (1976, 7", USA MCA) Produced By Frank Zappa
Grand Funk Railroad: Just Couldn't Wait / Out To Get You (1976, 7", USA MCA) Produced by Frank Zappa; B-Side features Frank Zappa on guitar
Grand Funk Railroad: Pass It Around "Circula" / Don't Let 'Em Take Your Gun (1977, 7", USA MCA) Produced by Frank Zappa
Grand Funk Railroad: Good Singin, Good Playin' (13) (1976, LP, USA, MCA) Produced By Frank Zappa; feat. Frank Zappa on guitar (1999, CD, USA, MCA) has one extra track from the same sessions
Black Sabbath: Archangel Rides Again (Bootleg CD) Zappa introduces the band at a 1976/12/06 concert
Robert Charlebois: Petroleum (1977, 7", Fr, RCA) features Zappa on guitar
Robert Charlebois: Swing Charlebois Swing (1977, LP, Fr, RCA) feat. Frank Zappa on guitar (on 1 track)
Flint: Flint (1978, LP, USA, CBS) Feat.Frank Zappa on guitar
Captain Beefheart: Bat Chain Puller (1978, Unreleased Album) Produced by Frank Zappa
L.Shankar: Dead Girls Of London (1979, 7", USA, Zappa) Produced by Frank Zappa, written by Frank Zappa / L.Shankar; features Frank Zappa on vocals
L.Shankar: Touch Me There (1) (1979, LP, USA, Zappa Records) Produced by Frank Zappa, feat. Stucco Homes (Frank Zappa); couple of tracks co-written by Frank Zappa
Var.Art.: The Nova Convention (1979, LP, Giorno Poetry Systems) Frank Zappa reads 'The Talking Asshole'
Var.Art.: Music From The 21st Century (1981, LP USA, GNP) Features Frank Zappa on one track
Dweezil Zappa: Havin' A Bad Day (1) (1986, LP, USA, Barking Pumpkin) Produced by Frank Zappa & Bob Stone
Dweezil Zappa: Let's Talk About It / Electric Hoedown (1986, 7", USA, Barking Pumpkin) produced by Frank Zappa
Frank Zappa: The Guitar World According To Frank Zappa (1987, K7, USA, Guitar World) guitar solos by Frank Zappa
Frank Zappa: The Supplement Tape (1990, K7, Nl, Stemra) compilation tape from the Dutch radio special, incl. int. & music
Prazsky Vyber: Adieu C.A. (1991, CD, CSFR, AP) Feat.Frank Zappa Playing A Guitar Solo On One Track
Jefferson Airplane: Loves You (1992, 3CD, USA, RCA) One track written by Frank Zappa & Grace Slick, recorded June 5, 1968; feat. Frank Zappa
Lowell George & The Factory: Lightning-Rod Man (1) (1993, CD, Fr, Edsel Records)- including 2 tracks from fall 1966; produced by Zappa; feat.Frank Zappa on piano and vocals
Var.Art.: Mediamix Interaktiv Volume 1 - Issue 1 (1993, CDR, Ger) = a digital magazine; feat.an interview with Frank Zappa
Var.Art.: Funny - The Movie (1993, CDR, USA) = A movie; feat. a joke told by Frank Zappa
Var.Art.: A Chance Operation - The John Cage Tribute (1993, 2CD, USA, Koch) Feat. one track by Frank Zappa
The Monkees: Head (1994, CD, USA, Rhino) feat. a spoken Frank Zappa contribution from the 1968 Monkees movie
Frank Zappa: The Interview (1999, CDr, Ger, Arf-Society) 1990/07/30 Interview with Frank Zappa
Urban Gwerder: Im Zeichen Des Magischen Affen (1999, book + CD, Suisse) includes fragment from Frank Zappa & The Mothers, Live in Basel 1974
Captain Beefheart: Grow Fins - Rarities (1965-1982) (1999, 5CD, USA, Revenant) Features Zappa on one track
Frank Zappa Films & Videos
200 Motels – 1971
Baby Snakes – 1979 film/ 1987 video
Dub Room Special – 1982
Does Humor Belong In Music? – 1985
Uncle Meat – 1987
The Amazing Mr. Bickford – 1987
Video From Hell – 1987
True Story of 200 Motels – 1989

The Grandmothers
The Grandmothers: Grandmothers (1) (1981, LP, USA, Panda)
The Grandmothers: The Official Fan Club Talk Album (2) (1981, LP, USA, Panda) 3 different editions
The Grandmothers: Lookin' Up Granny's Dress (3) (1982, LP, USA, Rhino)
The Grandmothers: Dreams On Long Play (4) (1993, CD, Ger, Muffin)
The Grandmothers: A Mother Of An Anthology (5) (1993, CD, USA, One Way)
The Grandmothers: Who Could Imagine (6) (1994, CD, Nl, Munich)
The Grandmothers: Eating The Astoria (7) (2000, CD, It, Obvious Music)

The Turtles
Out Of Control (as the Crossfires) – 1963
It Ain't Me Babe – 1965
You Baby – 1966
Happy Together – 1967
Golden Hits Vol. I – 1967
Battle Of The Bands – 1968
Turtle Soup – 1969
Golden Hits Vol. II – 1970
Wooden Head – 1970

Flo & Eddie
The Phlorescent Leech & Eddie – 1972
Flo & Eddie – 1973
Illegal, Immoral and Fattening – 1975
Moving Targets – 1976
Rock Steady With Flo & Eddie – 1981

Necessity Is...

The Best Of Flo & Eddie – 1987
The History Of Flo & Eddie and The Turtles – 1988
The Turtles Featuring Flo & Eddie – Captured Live! – 1992
For Kid Stuff Records
The World Of Strawberry Shortcake – 1980
Strawberry Shortcake In Big Apple City – 1981
Strawberry Shortcake's Pet Parade – 1982
Let's Dance With Strawberry Shortcake – 1983
Introducing The Care Bears – 1983
The Care Bears Care For You – 1983
Adventures in Care-a-lot – 1983
The Care Bears Christmas – 1983

Jimmy Carl Black

1962 Keys - Stretch Pants / Just A Matter Of Time (45 rpm 7")
1966 Mothers Of Invention- Freak Out! (percussion, drums, also sings in some foreign language)
1967 Mothers Of Invention- Absolutely Free (drums)
1967 Frank Zappa- Lumpy Gravy (chorus)
1968 Mothers Of Invention- We're Only in It for the Money (Indian of the group, drums, trumpet, vocals)
1968 Mothers Of Invention- Cruising with Ruben and the Jets (drums & lewd pulsating rhythm)
1969 GTO's- Permanent Damage (drums)
1969 Mothers Of Invention- Uncle Meat (drums, droll humor, poverty)
1969 Mothers Of Invention- Mothermania: The Best of the Mothers (drums)
1969 Mothers Of Invention- Burnt Weeny Sandwich (drums, percussion)
1970 Mothers Of Invention- Weasels Ripped My Flesh (drums)
1971 Frank Zappa- 200 Motels (soundtrack) vocals, dialogue
1972 Geronomo Black- Geronimo Black (drums, vocals)
1979 Big Sonny and the Lo Boys- In Heat
1979 Big Sonny & The Lo Boys - Love Me Two Times / Love Potion no.9 (45 rpm 7", non-album track)
1980 Geronomo Black- Welcome Back (drums)
1981 Jimmy Carl Black- Clearly Classic
1981 Grandmothers- Official Grandmothers Fan Club Talk Album
1981 Grandmothers- An Anthology of a Grandmother (s/t)
1981 Frank Zappa- You Are What You Is (vocals)
1982 The Grandmothers- Looking Up Granny's Dress
1986 Mothers Of Invention- We're Only in It for the Money/Lumpy Gravy (Indian of the group, drums, trumpet, vocals)
1987 Jimmy Carl Black & The Mannish Boys- Lil' Dab'l Do Ya (label: Amazing)
1988 Frank Zappa- You Can't Do That on Stage Anymore (Sampler) (Percussion, Drums)
1988 Frank Zappa- You Can't Do That on Stage Anymore vol. 1 (drums)
1988 Austin Lounge Lizards- Highway Cafe of the Damned (drums)
1988 Arthur Brown- Brown, Black & Blue (drums)
1990 Eugene Chadbourne- Chadbourne Baptist Church
1991 Frank Zappa- The Ark (drums)
1991 Frank Zappa- Tis the Season to Be Jelly (drums)
1991 Frank Zappa- You Can't Do That on Stage Anymore, vol. 4 (drums)
1991 Henry Vestine - Guitar Gangster
1992 Frank Zappa- Electric Aunt Jemima (drums)
1992 Frank Zappa- Our Man in Nirvana (drums)
1992 Frank Zappa- You Can't Do That on Stage Anymore, vol. 5(drums)
1992 Frank Zappa- You Can't Do That on Stage Anymore, vol. 6 (drums, vocals)
1993 Frank Zappa- Ahead of Their Time (drums)
1993 Grandmothers- A Mother of an Anthology
1993 The Muffin Men- Say Cheese And Thank You
1993 Eugene Chadbourne and Jimmy Carl Black- Locked In A Dutch Coffeeshop
1994 Preston, Don- Vile Foamy Ectoplasm (percussion, vocals)
1994 Grandmothers- Who Could Imagine?
1994 Ant Bee- With My Favorite "Vegetables" & Other Bizarre Muzik (with Don Preston, Bunk Gardner, Roy Estrada and Motorhead!
1994 Muffin Men - Mülm
1995 Various Artists: Wavelength Infinity: A Sun Ra Tribute
1995 Grandmothers- Dreams on Long Play (drums, vocals)
1995 Eugene Chadbourne and Jimmy Carl Black- Pachuco Cadaver
1996 Frank Zappa- The Lost Episodes (drums)
1996 Tom Shaka with Jimmy Carl Black and Lars-Luis Linek- Blues Magic
1996 Andy Cahan - Snarfel
1997 Ant Bee- Lunar Muzik (with Bunk Gardner, Don Preston, Roy Estrada, Bob Harris, and Motorhead Sherwood)
1997 Muffin Men- Frankincense
1997 Jimmy Carl Black- When Do We Get Paid
1997 Eugene Chadbourne- Chadbourne Barber Shop
1997 Eugene Chadbourne - Psychad
1998 Frank Zappa- Mystery Disc

1998 Behind The Mirror & Jimmy Carl Black- Cockroach Albert
1998 Muffin Men- MufFinz
1999 Farrell & Black- Black Limosine
1999 Muffin Men- God Shave the Queen
2000 Thana Harris- Thanatopsis
2000 Grandmothers- Eating The Astoria
2000 Jimmy Carl Black- Secrets of Crater 6 "Albuquerque Bound" Sound Warehouse '45 single
Jimmy Carl Black Filmography:
1967 Mondo Hollywood (as himself)
1971 Frank Zappa's 200 Motels (as Lonesome Cowboy Burt)
1987 Uncle Meat (as himself)
1989 The True Story of 200 Motels

Don Preston
1967 Mothers of Invention- Absolutely Free
1968 Mothers of Invention- We're Only in It for the Money
1968 Mothers of Invention- Cruising with Ruben and the Jets
1969 GTO's- Permanent Damage
1969 Mothers of Invention- Uncle Meat
1969 Mothers of Invention- Mothermania: The Best of the Mothers
1969 Mothers of Invention- Burnt Weeny Sandwich
1970 Mothers of Invention- Weasels Ripped My Flesh
1971 Smith, Bob- The Visit
1971 Mothers of Invention- Fillmore East: June 1971
1971 Carla Bley / Paul Hains- Escalator over the Hill
1972 Flo & Eddie- Phlorescent Leech and Eddie
1972 Lennon, John- Sometime in New York City
1972 Mothers of Invention- Just Another Band From L.A.
1972 Frank Zappa- Waka/Jawaka
1973 Frank Zappa- The Grand Wazoo
1974 Frank Zappa- Roxy & Elsewhere
1974 Bobbi Humphrey - Satin' Doll
1974 Frank Zappa- Apostrophe'
1979 Apocalypse Now
1970 Still Rock
1980 Geronimo Black- Welcome Back
1980 Residents- Commercial Album
1981 Grandmothers- Official Grandmothers Fan Club Talk Album
1982 The Grandmothers- Looking Up Granny's Dress
1983 Krieger, Robby- Versions
1985 Michael Mantler - Alien
1986 Carter, John- Dance of the Love Ghosts
1987 Flo & Eddie- Best of Flo & Eddle
1987 Michael Mantler - Live
1988 Carter, John- Fields
1988 Frank Zappa- You Can't Do That on Stage Anymore (Sampler)
1988 Frank Zappa- You Can't Do That on Stage Anymore, vol. 1
1989 Carter, John- Shadows on a Wall
1989 Frank Zappa- You Can't Do That on Stage Anymore, vol. 3
1989 Ivo Perelman - Ivo
1989 Aurora - s/t
1989 Bobby Bradford / John Carter Quintet - Comin' On
1989 Gil Evans - Where Flamingos Fly
1990 Gramavision 10th Anniversary Sampler
1991 Frank Zappa- The Ark
1991 Frank Zappa- Tis the Season to Be Jelly
1991 Frank Zappa- Unmitigated Audacity
1991 Frank Zappa- You Can't Do That on Stage Anymore, vol. 4
1992 Frank Zappa- Electric Aunt Jemima
1992 Frank Zappa- Our Man in Nirvana
1992 Frank Zappa- Swiss Cheese/Fire
1992 Jefferson Airplane- Jefferson Airplane Loves You
1992 Frank Zappa- You Can't Do That on Stage Anymore, vol. 5
1992 Frank Zappa- You Can't Do That on Stage Anymore, vol. 6
1992 Frank Zappa- Playground Psychotics
1992 Ono, Yoko Ono Box
1993 Frank Zappa- Ahead Of Their Time
1993 Chadbourne/Black- Locked In A Dutch Coffeeshop
1994 Music from the 21st Century- Krieger, Robby
1994 Don Preston- Vile Foamy Ectoplasm (Efa)
1994 Grandmothers- Who Could Imagine?

1994 Ant Bee- With My Favorite "Vegetables" & Other Bizarre Muzik (with Bunk Gardner, Jimmy Carl Black, Roy Estrada and Motorhead!
1996 Don Preston- Hear Me Out
1996 Frank Zappa- The Lost Episodes
1997 Ant Bee- Lunar Muzik (with Bunk Gardner, Jimmy Carl Black, Roy Estrada, Bob Harris, and Motorhead Sherwood)
1998 Frank Zappa- Mystery Disc
1999 Strange World Carnival -S/T
Don Preston Filmography: (Sometimes Credited As: Don W. Preston)
1968 Ogo Moto
1971 Take The A Train
1971 Frank Zappa's 200 Motels (as member of Mothers of Invention)
1971 Miami Vendetta
1976 Dracula
1976 Apocalypse Now
1982 Android (composer)
1983 The Being (aka Easter Sunday, Freak, Pottsville Horror) (composer)
1983 Pucker Up And Act Like A Dog
1984 Night Patrol (composer)
1986 Eye of the Tiger (composer)
1987 Video From Hell
1987 Uncle Meat (as himself, Dom DeWilde, Biff Debris, Uncle Meat)
1987 Blood Diner (composer)
1987 The Underachievers (composer)
1987 Believe In Eve
1989 The True Story of 200 Motels
1991 Aircraft Carriers
1991 Chopper Wars
1991 Paratroopers
1991 Was Black
1995 Sawbones (aka Prescription for Murder) (composer for TV movie)
Don Preston Awards
Siver Award for Beleive In Eve - Best Film In Philedelphia 1993
Award Of Excellence - from Mayor Tom Bradley - Los Angeles - 1975
Three seperate awards from L.A. Weekly Magazine
Two seperate awards from Dramalog Magazine

Bunk Gardner
1962 Joanna And The Playboys
196? Themes From The Hip
1967 Mothers of Invention- Absolutely Free (woodwinds)
1968 Mothers of Invention- Lumpy Gravy (woodwinds)
1968 Mothers of Invention- We're Only in It for the Money (all woodwinds, mumbled weirdness)
1968 Mothers of Invention- Cruising with Ruben and the Jets (tenor sax)
1969 Mothers of Invention- Uncle Meat (piccolo, flute, clarinet, bass clarinet, soprano sax, alto sax, tenor sax, bassoon (all of these electric and/or non-electric depending))
1969 Mothers of Invention- Mothermania: The Best of the Mothers (woodwinds)
1969 Mothers of Invention- Burnt Weeny Sandwich (woodwinds)
1970 Buckley, Tim- Starsailor (horn)
1970 Mothers of Invention- Weasels Ripped My Flesh (tenor sax)
1972 Troiano, Domenic- Domenic Troiano
1972 Geronimo Black- Geronimo Black (Flute, Bassoon, Sax (Tenor), Wind, Tenor (Vocal))
1972 Nicholas Greenwood - Cold Cuts
1980 Geronimo Black- Welcome Back (wind)
1981 Grandmothers- Official Grandmothers Fan Club Talk Album
1982 The Grandmothers- Looking Up Granny's Dress
1986 Mothers of Invention- We're Only in It for the Money/Lumpy Gravy (all woodwinds, mumbled weirdness)
1988 Frank Zappa- You Can't Do That on Stage (Sampler) (woodwinds)
1988 Frank Zappa- You Can't Do That on Stage Anymore, vol. 1 (tenor sax)
1991 Frank Zappa- You Can't Do That on Stage Anymore, vol. 4 (tenor sax)
1991 Frank Zappa- The Ark (tenor sax)
1992 Frank Zappa- Electric Aunt Jemima (tenor sax)
1992 Frank Zappa- Our Man in Nirvana (tenor sax)
1992 Frank Zappa- You Can't Do That on Stage Anymore, vol. 5 (tenor sax, vocals)
1993 Frank Zappa- Ahead of Their Time (tenor saxophone, clarinet)
1993 Grandmothers- A Mother of an Anthology (Bassoon, Horn, Recorder, Saxophone, Producer)
1994 Preston, Don- Vile Foamy Ectoplasm (flute, tenor sax)
1994 Grandmothers- Who Could Imagine?
1994 Ant Bee- With My Favorite "Vegetables" & Other Bizarre Muzik (with Don Preston, Jimmy Carl Black, Roy Estrada and Motorhead!)
1994 Caged 3000 OST
1996 Andy Cahan - Snarfel

1997 Ant Bee- Lunar Muzik (with Don Preston, Jimmy Carl Black, Roy Estrada, Bob Harris, and Motorhead Sherwood)
1998 Frank Zappa- Mystery Disc
1999 Bruce Cameron - Midnight Daydream
2000 Grandmothers- Eating The Astoria
Bunk Gardner Filmography:
1987 Uncle Meat (as himself)

Elliott Ingber
1966 Mothers Of Invention- Freak Out (guitar)
1968 Fraternity of Man- Fraternity of Man (guitar)
1969 Canned Heat- Hallelujah (vocals)
1969 Mothers Of Invention- Mothermania- The Best of the Mothers (guitar)
1969 Fraternity of Man- Get It on (guitar)
1971 Little Feat- Little Feat (guitar)
1972 Captain Beefheart & The Magic Band- Spotlight Kid
1972 Shakey Jake Harris- The Devil's Harmonica (guitar)
1974 Captain Beefheart- Bluejeans & Moonbeams (guitar)
1974 Peter Ivers Band - Terminal Love
1978 Juicy Groove- First Taste
1978 Little Feat- Waiting for Columbus (guitar)
1981 Grandmothers- Official Grandmothers Fan Club Talk Album
1981 Little Feat- Hoy Hoy (guitar)
1982 The Grandmothers- Looking Up Granny's Dress
1992 Frank Zappa- You Can't Do That on Stage Anymore, vol. 5 (guitar)
1993 Grandmothers- A Mother of an Anthology (guitar)
1993 George, Lowell- Lightning-Rod Man (guitar)
1996 Frank Zappa- The Lost Episodes (slide guitar)
1998 Frank Zappa- Mystery Disc
1999 Captain Beefheart- Grow Fins: Rarities 1965-1982
1999 Fraternity Of Man - X
2000 Little Feat- Hotcakes & Outtakes: 30 Years Of Little Feat
Sessions for Shakey Jake Harris' "The Devil's Harmonica" were September 1971, and included Ron Selico, John Mayall, and Elliot Ingber. (source: John Mayall Sessionography)
Elliot Ingber Filmography:
1987 Uncle Meat- Himself
1987 Video From Hell- Himself

Ray Collins
Solo Albums:
1981? Album of demos on Polar (?) records
1982 Of Blues, Myself & I (KRC)
1984 Magnolia (Montclair)
1993 Love Songs (cassette)
Appearances:
1966 Frank Zappa- Freak Out! (lead vocals, harmonica, tambourine, finger cymbals,
 bobby pin, tweezers)
1967 Frank Zappa- Absolutely Free (vocals)
1968 Frank Zappa- Cruising with Ruben and the Jets (lead vocals)
1969 Frank Zappa- Uncle Meat (swell vocals)
1969 Frank Zappa- Mothermania- The Best Of The Mothers
1970 Mothers of Invention- Burnt Weeny Sandwich
1970 Frank Zappa- Weasels Ripped My Flesh (Vocal on "Oh No")
1974 Frank Zappa- Apostrophe (') (background vocals)
1980 Geronimo Black- Welcome Back (Vocals)
1982 The Grandmothers- Looking Up Granny's Dress
1983 Frank Zappa- Rare Meat
1986 Frank Zappa- Apostrophe/Over-nite Sensation (background vocals)
1992 Frank Zappa- You Can't Do That on Stage Anymore, volume 5 (tambourine, vocals)
1991 Frank Zappa- 'Tis the Season to Be Jelly
1993 Grandmothers- A Mother of an Anthology (Vocals)
1995 Frank Zappa- Cucamonga Years- The Early Works of FZ (MSI)
1996 Frank Zappa- The Lost Episodes (Vocals)
1998 Frank Zappa- Cucamonga- Frank's Wild Years (Del-Fi)
1998 Frank Zappa- Mystery Disc
Ray Collins Filmography:
1971 Frank Zappa's 200 Motels (as himself, Bill Yards)
1987 Uncle Meat (as himself)

Billy Mundi
1966 Buckley, Tim- Tim Buckley
1967 Stone Poneys- Stone Poneys Featuring Linda Ronstadt

1967 Neil, Fred- Fred Neil
1967 Mothers Of Invention- Absolutely Free
1968 Earth Opera- Earth Opera
1968 Rhinoceros- Rhinoceros
1968 Mothers Of Invention- We're Only in It for the Money
1969 Rhinoceros- Satin Chickens
1969 Mothers Of Invention- Mothermania: The Best of the Mothers
1969 Mothers Of Invention- Uncle Meat
1970 Martyn, John- Stormbringer
1970 Dylan, Bob- New Morning
1971 McGuire, Barry- Barry McGuire & the Doctor
1971 Pearls Before Swine- Beautiful Lies You Could Live
1971 Stewart, John- Sunstorm
1972 Battin, Skip- Skip
1972 Borderline- Sweet Dreams & Quiet Desires
1972 Fogerty, Tom- Tom Fogerty
1972 Muldaur, Geoff- Sweet Potatoes
1972 Peter, Paul and Mary- Peter
1972 Rundgren, Todd- Something/Anything?
1972 Razmataz- For The First Time
1973 Brewer & Shipley- Rural Space
1973 Simon, John- Journey
1975 Beth, Karen- New Moon Rising
1975 Fabulous Rhinestones- Rhinestones
1975 Ronstadt, Linda- Stone Poneys Featuring Linda Ronstadt
1978 McCaslin, Mary- Bramble & the Rose
1981 Average Band- Some People
1986 Mothers Of Invention- We're Only in It for the Money/Lumpy Gravy
1987 Muldaur, Geoff- Pottery Pie
1991 Frank Zappa- Tis the Season to Be Jelly
1992 Frank Zappa- You Can't Do That on Stage Anymore, vol. 5
1992 McCaslin, Mary- Things We Said Today: The Best of M
1996 Ringer, Jim- Best of Jim Ringer: Band of Jesse J
1997 Dylan, Bob- Nashville Skyline/New Morning/John
1998 Frank Zappa- Mystery Disc (LP only)
Akstens, Tom- Original and Traditional Music
Billy Mundi Filmography:
1987 Uncle Meat (as Rollo)

Roy Estrada
1966 Mothers Of Invention- Freak Out (bass, boy soprano)
1967 Mothers Of Invention- Absolutely Free (bass)
1968 Frank Zappa- Lumpy Gravy (chorus)
1968 Mothers Of Invention- We're Only in It for the Money (electric bass, vocals, asthma)
1968 Mothers Of Invention- Cruising with Ruben and the Jets (high weazlings, dwaedy-doop & electric bass)
1969 GTO's- Permanent Damage (bass)
1969 Mothers Of Invention- Uncle Meat (electric bass, cheeseburgers, Pachuco falsetto)
1969 Mothers Of Invention- Mothermania: The Best of the Mothers (bass, vocals)
1969 Mothers Of Invention- Burnt Weeny Sandwich (bass, vocals)
1970 Ulz, Ivan- Ivan the Ice Cream Man (bass)
1970 Cooder, Ry- Ry Cooder (bass)
1970 Mothers Of Invention- Weasels Ripped My Flesh (bass, vocals)
1971 Little Feat- Little Feat (bass, vocals)
1971 Kottke, Leo- Mudlark (bass)
1972 Captain Beefheart- Clear Spot (bass)
1972 Captain Beefheart & The Magic Band- Spotlight Kid (bass)
1972 Various Artists- The Whole Burbank Catalog
1972 Various Artists- The Days of Wine and Vinyl
1972 Little Feat- Sailin' Shoes (bass, vocals)
1972 Van Dyke Parks- Discover America (bass)
1974 Howdy Moon- Howdy Moon Guitar (bass)
1976 Frank Zappa- Zoot Allures (bass, vocals)
1981 Little Feat- Hoy Hoy (bass, vocals, liner notes)
1981 Frank Zappa- Shut Up 'N Play Yer Guitar (bass, vocals)
1982 Frank Zappa- Ship Arriving Too Late to Save a Drowning Witch (vocals)
1983 Frank Zappa- The Man from Utopia (vocals)
1983 Frank Zappa- Baby Snakes
1984 Frank Zappa- Them or Us (vocals)
1986 Mothers Of Invention- We're Only in It for the Money/Lumpy Gravy (electric bass, vocals, asthma)
1988 Frank Zappa- You Can't Do That on Stage Anymore (Sampler) (bass, vocals)
1988 Frank Zappa- You Can't Do That on Stage Anymore, vol 1 (bass, vocals)

1989 Frank Zappa- You Can't Do That on Stage Anymore, vol. 3 (bass, vocals)
1991 Frank Zappa- The Ark (bass, vocals)
1991 Frank Zappa- Tis the Season to Be Jelly (bass, vocals)
1991 Frank Zappa- You Can't Do That on Stage Anymore, vol. 5(bass, vocals)
1992 Frank Zappa- Electric Aunt Jemima (bass, vocals)
1992 Frank Zappa- Our Man in Nirvana (bass, vocals)
1992 Frank Zappa- You Can't Do That on Stage Anymore, vol. 6 (bass, vocals)
1993 Frank Zappa- Ahead of Their Time (bass, vocals)
1994 Preston, Don- Vile Foamy Ectoplasm (violin)
1994 Grandmothers- Who Could Imagine?
1994 Ant Bee- With My Favorite "Vegetables" & Other Bizarre Muzik (with Don Preston, Jimmy Carl Black, Bunk Gardner and Motorhead!
1994 Frank Zappa- Civilization Phaze III
1995 Frank Zappa- Strictly Commercial
1996 Frank Zappa- The Lost Episodes (bass)
1996 Frank Zappa- Läther
1996 Frank Zappa- Frank Zappa Plays The Music Of Frank Zappa
1997 Frank Zappa- Have I Offended Someone?
1997 Ant Bee- Lunar Muzik (with Bunk Gardner, Don Preston, Jimmy Carl Black, Bob Harris, and Motorhead Sherwood)
1998 Frank Zappa- Mystery Disc
1999 Captain Beefheart- Grow Fins: Rarities 1965-1982
1999 Captain Beefheart- The Dust Blows Forward
1999 Various Artists- '80s New Wave - Millenium Party
2000 Little Feat- Hotcakes & Outtakes: 30 Years Of Little Feat
Roy Estrada Filmography:
1979 Baby Snakes
1987 Uncle Meat (as himself)

Motorhead Sherwood

1966 Mothers Of Invention- Freak Out (sound effects, uncredited)
1967 Mothers of Invention- Absolutely Free (soprano, baritone saxophone)
1967 Frank Zappa- Lumpy Gravy
1968 Mothers of Invention- We're Only In It For The Money (road manager, soprano & baritone saxophone, all purpose weirdness & teen appeal (we need it desperately)
1968 Mothers of Invention- Cruising with Ruben and the Jets (baritone sax & tambourine)
1969 Mothers of Invention- Uncle Meat (pop star, frenetic tenor)
1969 Mothers of Invention- Mothermania: The Best of the Mothers
1969 Mothers of Invention- Burnt Weeny Sandwich (woodwinds, vocals)
1970 Mothers of Invention- Weasels Ripped My Flesh (Baritone Sax and Snorks)
1973 Ruben and the Jets- For Real!
1980 The Grandmothers
1981 Grandmothers- Official Grandmothers Fan Club Talk Album
1981 Frank Zappa- You Are What You Is (tenor saxophone, vocals)
1982 The Grandmothers- Looking Up Granny's Dress
1988 Frank Zappa- You Can't Do That on Stage (Sampler) (tenor saxophone, vocals)
1988 Frank Zappa- You Can't Do That on Stage Anymore, vol. 1
1991 Frank Zappa- You Can't Do That on Stage Anymore, vol. 4
1991 Frank Zappa- The Ark
1991 Frank Zappa- 'Tis the Season to Be Jelly
1992 Frank Zappa- Electric Aunt Jemima
1992 Frank Zappa- Our Man in Nirvana
1991 Frank Zappa- You Can't Do That on Stage Anymore, vol. 5
1993 Grandmothers- A Mother of an Anthology
1994 Frank Zappa- Civilization Phaze III
1994 Ant Bee- With My Favorite "Vegetables" & Other Bizarre Muzik (with Don Preston, Jimmy Carl Black, Roy Estrada and Bunk Gardner!)
1997 Frank Zappa- Have I Offended Someone?
1997 Ant Bee- Lunar Muzik (with Bunk Gardner, Don Preston, Jimmy Carl Black, Roy Estrada, and Bob Harris.)
1998 Frank Zappa- Mystery Disc
Filmography:
1968 BBC live in the studio
1971 Frank Zappa's 200 Motels
1987 Uncle Meat- (as himself)
1989 The True Story of 200 Motels

Art Tripp

1968 Mothers of Invention- Cruising with Ruben and the Jets (drums)
1969 Mothers of Invention- Uncle Meat
1969 Mothers of Invention- Mothermania
1969 Mothers of Invention- Burnt Weeny Sandwich

1969 Jean-Luc Ponty- King Kong: JLP Plays the Music of FZ (drums)
1969 Mothers of Invention- Weasles Ripped My Flesh
1969 Captain Beefheart & The Magic Band- Trout Mask Replica (uncredited)
1970 Captain Beefheart & The Magic Band- Lick My Decals Off, Baby
1972 Captain Beefheart & The Magic Band- Clear Spot
1972 Captain Beefheart & The Magic Band- The Spotlight Kid
1972 Various Artists- The Whole Burbank Catalog
1972 Various Artists- The Days of Wine and Vinyl
1975 Mallard- Mallard
1978 Captain Beefheart- Shiny Beast (Bat Chain Puller)
1978 Stewart, Al- Time Passages (percussion)
1979 Various Artists- Pumping Vinyl
1988 Frank Zappa- You Can't Do That On Stage Anymore, Volume 1
1991 Frank Zappa- You Can't Do That On Stage Anymore, Volume 4
1991 Frank Zappa- The Ark
1992 Frank Zappa- You Can't Do That On Stage Anymore, Volume 5
1992 Jefferson Airplane- Jefferson Airplane Loves You (percussion, drums, xylophone)
1993 Frank Zappa- Ahead of Their Time (percussion, drums)
1994 Buckley, Tim- Live at the Troubadour 1969 (drums)
1996 Frank Zappa- The Lost Episodes
1998 Frank Zappa- Mystery Disc
1999 Captain Beefheart- Grow Fins: Rarities 1965-1982
Art Tripp Filmography:
1971 Frank Zappa's 200 Motels
1987 Uncle Meat- (as himself)
1989 The True Story of 200 Motels

Ian Underwood

1968 Mothers of Invention- We're Only in It for the Money (piano, woodwinds, wholesome)
1968 Mothers of Invention- Cruising with Ruben and the Jets (redundant piano triplets)
1969 GTO's- Permanent Damage (keyboards)
1969 Hurvitz, Sandy- Sandy's Album Is Here at Last! (arranged and produced)
1969 Mothers of Invention- Uncle Meat (electric organ, piano, harpsichord, celeste, flute, clarinet, alto sax, baritone sax, special assistance, copyist, industrial relations & teen appeal)
1969 Mothers of Invention- Mothermania: The Best of the Mothers (piano, woodwinds)
1969 Ponty, Jean-Luc- King Kong (conductor, tenor sax)
1969 Frank Zappa- Hot Rats (Piano, Organus Maximus, All Clarinets, All Saxes)
1969 Various Artists- October 10, 1969
1969 Mothers of Invention- Burnt Weeny Sandwich (keyboards, woodwinds)
1970 Simmons, Jeff- Lucille Has Messed up My Mind (Saxophone)
1970 Mothers of Invention- Weasels Ripped My Flesh (Alto Sax)
1970 Mothers of Invention- Chunga's Revenge (piano, electric piano, organ, pipe organ, electric alto sax with wah-wah pedal, tenor sax, rhythm guitar)
1971 Mothers of Invention- Fillmore East: June 1971 (woodwinds, keyboards, vocals)
1971 Frank Zappa- 200 Motels (soundtrack and movie) (keyboards & winds)
1972 Lennon, John- Sometime in New York City (keyboards, alto saxophone)
1972 Mothers of Invention- Just Another Band from L.A. (woodwinds, keyboards, vocals)
1973 Frank Zappa- Over-Nite Sensation (flute, clarinet, alto and tenor sax)
1973 Various Artists- All Singing - All Talking - All Rocking
1974 Hubbard, Freddie- High Energy
1974 Flo & Eddie- Illegal, Immoral and Fattening (keyboards)
1974 Frank Zappa- Apostrophe (saxophone)
1974 Various Artists- Hard Goods
1975 Ambrosia- Ambrosia (saxophone)
1975 Hubbard, Freddie- Liquid Love (synthesizer)
1975 Jones, Quincy- Mellow Madness (synthesizer)
1975 McRae, Carmen- I Am Music (programming)
1975 Mouzon, Alphonse- Man Incognito (synthesizer)
1976 Ambrosia- Somewhere I've Never Travelled (saxophone)
1976 Spirit- Farther Along
1976 Chunky Novi & Ernie- Chunky Novi & Ernie (synthesizer, wind)
1976 Seawind- Seawind (synthesizer, programming)
1976 Parton, Dolly- Say Forever You'll Be Mine (synthesizer)
1976 Johnson, Alphonso- Moonshadows (synthesizer)
1976 Lee, John [1]- Still Can't Say Enough (synthesizer)
1976 Brothers Johnson- Look Out for #1 (synthesizer, programming)
1976 McRae, Carmen- Can't Hide Love (synthesizer)
1976 Ritenour, Lee- First Course (synthesizer, programming)
1977 Angelle- Angelle (Moog synthesizer)
1977 Coltrane, Chi- Road to Tomorrow (synthesizer)
1977 Mason, Harvey- Funk in a Mason Jar

1977 Quateman, Bill- Night After Night (synthesizer)
1977 Seawind- Window of a Child (synthesizer)
1977 Johnson, Alphonso- Yesterday's Dreams (synthesizer)
1977 Mendes, Sergio- Sergio Mendes and the New Brasil '77 (synthesizer)
1977 Grusin, Dave- Discovered Again (synthesizer)
1977 Sidran, Ben- Cat and the Hat (synthesizer)
1977 Brothers Johnson- Right on Time (synthesizer)
1977 Connors, Norman- Romantic Journey (synthesizer)
1977 Pointer, Noel- Phantazia (synthesizer)
1977 Jones, Quincy- Roots (keyboards)
1977 Ritenour, Lee- Captain Fingers (synthesizer, keyboards)
1978 Alpert, Herb- Herb Alpert/Hugh Masekela (synthesizer)
1978 Roberts, Bruce- Bruce Roberts (keyboards)
1978 Handy, John- Where Go the Boats (synthesizer)
1978 Hodges James & Smith- What Have You Done for Love
1978 Robertson, Carter- Shoot the Moon (synthesizer)
1978 Streisand, Barbra- Songbird (synthesizer)
1978 Dolly Parton- Heartbreaker (synthesizer)
1978 Barbieri, Gato- Ruby, Ruby (synthesizer)
1978 Ritenour, Lee- Captain's Journey (synthesizer)
1978 Jackson, Milt- Milt Jackson Sings and Plays Soul (synthesizer)
1979 Manilow, Barry- One Voice (synthesizer)
1979 Springfield, Dusty- Living without Your Love (synthesizer)
1979 Alessi Brothers- Words & Music (synthesizer)
1979 Cornwall, Hugh- Nosferatu (synthesizer, sax)
1979 Sweetbottom- Turn Me Loose (synthesizer)
1979 Franklin, Rodney- In the Center (synthesizer)
1979 Jones, Quincy- Superdisc (synthesizer)
1979 Dunson, Van- Van Dunson (synthesizer)
1979 Schifrin, Lalo- No One Home (synthesizer)
1979 Lee, Peggy- Close Enough for Love (keyboards)
1979 Streisand, Barbra- Wet (synthesizer)
1979 Manhattan Transfer- Extensions (synthesizer)
1979 Ritenour, Lee- Feel the Night (synthesizer)
1980 Franklin, Rodney- You'll Never Know (synthesizer)
1980 Russell, Brenda- Brenda Russell (synthesizer)
1980 Jones, Quincy- Dude (synthesizer)
1980 Grusin, Dave- Mountain Dance (synthesizer)
1981 Bayer Sager, Carol- Sometimes Late at Night (synthesizer)
1981 Scarbury, Joey- America's Greatest Hero (synthesizer)
1982 Eye to Eye- Eye to Eye (synthesizer)
1982 LaBounty, Bill- Bill La Bounty (synthesizer)
1982 Watts, Ernie- Chariots of Fire (synthesizer)
1982 Post, Mike- Television Theme Songs
1982 New American Orchestra- Blade Runner (Not O.S.T.) (synthesizer)
1982 Knight, Jerry- Love's on Our Side
1982 Blade Runner- Blade Runner (synthesizer)
1983 Jordan, Marc- Hole in the Wall (synthesizer)
1983 Nielson/Pearson Band- Blind Luck (synthesizer)
1983 Oxo- Oxo (engineer)
1983 Ingram, James- It's Your Night (synthesizer)
1984 Springfield, Rick- Hard to Hold (synthesizer)
1985 USA for Africa: We Are We Are the World (synthesizer arrangements)
1985 Witness [MST]- Witness
1986 The Boston Pops- Holst's "The Planets" (synthesizer)
1986 Frank Zappa- We're Only in It for the Money/Lumpy Gravy (piano, woodwinds, wholesome)
1986 Frank Zappa- Apostrophe/Over-nite Sensation (flute, clarinet, alto saxophone, tenor saxophone)
1987 Flo & Eddie- Best of Flo & Eddie (keyboards)
1988 Willow- Willow [O.S.T.] (guitar)
1988 Frank Zappa- You Can't Do That on Stage Anymore (Sampler) (keyboards, alto saxophone)
1988 Frank Zappa- You Can't Do That on Stage Anymore, vol. 1 (keyboards, alto saxophone)
1988 Grusin, Dave- Collection (synthesizer)
1989 Frank Zappa- You Can't Do That on Stage Anymore, vol. 3 (keyboards, alto saxophone)
1990 Frank Zappa- Supplement Tape (Keyboards, Wind)
1990 Jones, Quincy- Back on Block (synthesizer, programming, handclapping)
1991 Ingram, James- Power of Great Music: The Best of J (synthesizer)
1991 Frank Zappa- Freaks & Motherfu*%!!@
1991 Frank Zappa- The Ark
1991 Frank Zappa- 'Tis the Season to Be Jelly
1991 Frank Zappa- You Can't Do That on Stage Anymore, vol. 4 (clarinet, alto sax)
1991 Isley Brothers- Tracks of Life (synthesizer)

147

1992 Frank Zappa- At the Circus
1992 Frank Zappa- Disconnected Synapses
1992 Frank Zappa- Tengo Na Minchia Tanta
1992 Frank Zappa- Electric Aunt Jemima
1992 Frank Zappa- Swiss Cheese/Fire
1992 Frank Zappa- Our Man in Nirvana
1992 GRP- GRP 10th Anniversary Collection (synthesizer)
1992 Russell, Brenda- Greatest Hits (synthesizer)
1992 Jefferson Airplane- Jefferson Airplane Loves You
1992 Bolton, Michael- Timeless (The Classics) (piaon)
1992 Frank Zappa- You Can't Do That on Stage Anymore, vol. 5 (piano, sax, clarinet)
1992 Frank Zappa- You Can't Do That on Stage Anymore, vol. 6 (keyboards, sax)
1992 Ono, Yoko- Ono Box (Keyboards, Vocals, Wind)
1992 Frank Zappa- Playground Psychotics (keyboards, alto saxophone, dialog)
1992 Sneakers - O.S.T. (vocals)
1992 Unlawful Entry- Unlawful Entry
1992 Schuur, Diane- In Tribute (synthesizer)
1993 Feinstein, Michael- Forever (keyboards)
1993 Frank Zappa- Ahead of Their Time (alto saxophone, piano)
1993 Streisand, Barbra- Back to Broadway (synthesizer)
1994 Bishop, Stephen- On & On: Hits of Stephen Bishop (synthesizer)
1995 Jumanji- Jumanji [o.S.T.] (instrumental)
1996 Frank Zappa- The Lost Episodes (sax, woodwinds, fender rhodes)
1996 Bolton, Michael- This Is the Time: The Christmas Album (synthesizer)
1996 Hyman, Phyllis- Legacy of Phyllis Hyman (Synthesizer, Piano, Keyboards)
1996 Rene & Angela- Come My Way (Synthesizer, Piano,Keyboards, Piano (Electric), Programming)
1997 Frank Zappa- Have I Offended Someone?
1997 Devil's Own- Devil's Own
1997 Instrumental History of Jazz (synthesizer)
1997 Titanic- (Syntehsizer)
1998 Frank Zappa- Mystery Disc
1998 Various Artists- Rykodisc 15th Anniversary Sampler
2000 Little Feat- Hotcakes & Outtakes: 30 Years Of Little Feat
 GRP- Grp Digital Sampler, Vol. 1 (synthesizer)
 Garrett, Lee- Heat for the Feets (synthesizer)
 Saint Nicklaus, Dick- Magic (synthesizer)
 Mosquito Coast- Mosquito Coast
 Grusin, Dave- Cinemagic (synthesizer)
 Charles, Ray- Genius & Soul: 50th Anniversary Col- (synthesizer, programming)
 Nina Hagen- Fearless
Ian Underwood miscellaneous crew filmography (1990s) (1980s) (1970s)
 1.Braveheart (1995) (London Symphony Orchestra - synth programming)
 2.Honey, I Shrunk the Kids (1989) (synthesizer effects)
 3.*batteries not included (1987) (spaceship sounds)
 4.Aliens (1986) (synthesizer effects)
 5.Krull (1983) (synthesizer effects)
 ... aka Dragons of Krull (1983)
 ... aka Dungeons and Dragons (1983/II)
 ... aka Dungeons of Krull, The (1983)
 ... aka Krull: Invaders of the Black Fortress (1983)
 6.Blade Runner (1982) (synthesizers)
 7.Demon Seed (1977) (electronic performances)
Ian Underwood actor filmography:
 1971 Frank Zappa's 200 Motels (as a member of the Mothers Of Invention)
 1987 Uncle Meat (as himself)
 1989 The True Story of 200 Motels

Cal Schenkel
Album artwork credits:
1968 Mothers Of Invention- We're Only in It for the Money
1967 Frank Zappa- Lumpy Gravy
1967 Sandy Hurvitz- Sandy's Album Is Here At Last!
1968 Mothers Of Invention- Cruising with Ruben and the Jets
1968 Wild Man Fischer- An Evening With Wild Man Fischer
1969 Captain Beefheart & His Magic Band- Trout Mask Replica
1969 Mothers Of Invention- Uncle Meat
1969 Frank Zappa- Hot Rats
1969 Mothers Of Invention- Burnt Weenie Sandwich
1970 Lord Buckley- A Most Immaculately Hip Aristocrat
1970 Lenny Bruce- The Berkeley Concert
1970 Frank Zappa- Chunga's Revenge

1970 The Fugs- Golden Filth
1971 Mothers Of Invention- Fillmore East: June 1971
1971 Frank Zappa- 200 Motels
1972 Mothers Of Invention- Just Another Band from L.A.
1973 Tom Waits- Closing Time
1973 Tim Buckley- Sefronia
1973 Frank Zappa- The Grand Wazoo
1973 Ruben & The Jets- For Real!
1974 Tim Buckley- Look At The Fool
1974 Frank Zappa- Apostrophe (')
1974 Tom Waits- The Heart of Saturday Night
1975 Frank Zappa- One Size Fits All
1975 Zappa/ Beefheart- Bongo Fury
1975 Tom Waits- Nighthawks At The Diner
1976 Frank Zappa- Zoot Allures
1976 Tom Waits- Small Change
1981 Frank Zappa- Tinsel Town Rebellion
1986 Frank Zappa- Does Humor Belong in Music?
1991 Frank Zappa- Best Band You Never Heard In Your Life
1992 Frank Zappa- Playground Psychotics
1993 Frank Zappa- Ahead of Their Time
1994 Rig- Belly to the Ground (artwork, samples)
1997 Ant Bee- Lunar Muzik
1998 Frank Zappa- Cheap Thrills
1998 Frank Zappa- Mystery Disc
1998 Deja Voo Doo- Carpe P.M.: Honor Comes Only After Humility
1999 Captain Beefheart- Grow Fins: Rarities 1965-1982
Cal Schenkel Filmography:
1971 Frank Zappa's 200 Motels- production design
1974 Cal Schenkel's Reel
1974 Apostrophe (') promo ad TV/CM ?
1972 The Naked Ape (3 min. reel)
1974 Animation promo reel for the album, Apostrophe (')
1987 Uncle Meat- (as himself)
1987 The Amazing Mr. Bickford (cover art)
1989 The True Story of 200 Motels

Buzz Gardner
1969 Frank Zappa- Burnt Weeny Sandwich (Horn)
1970 Buckley, Tim- Starsailor (Horn)
1970 Frank Zappa- Weasels Ripped My Flesh (Trumpet, Flugelhorn)
1970 2 Originals of the Mothers of Invention
1972 Troiano, Domenic- Domenic Troiano (Trumpet)
1972 Geronimo Black- Geronimo Black (Trumpet)
1980 Geronimo Black- Welcome Back
1981 Grandmothers- Official Grandmothers Fan Club Talk Album
1982 The Grandmothers- Looking Up Granny's Dress
1988 Frank Zappa- You Can't Do That on Stage Anymore (Sampler) (Horn)
1988 Frank Zappa- You Can't Do That on Stage Anymore, vol. 1 (Trumpet)
1991 Frank Zappa- You Can't Do That on Stage Anymore, vol. 4 (Trumpet)
1992 Frank Zappa- You Can't Do That on Stage Anymore, vol. 5 (Trumpet)
1993 Grandmothers- A Mother of an Anthology (Clarinet, Trumpet, Flugelhorn, Horn)
Buzz Gardner Filmography:
1987 Uncle Meat (as himself)

Mothers Of Invention Tour Dates 1964 - 1972

Date	City	State	Country	Venue
64/	Fontana	CA	USA	Shack
64/	Los Angeles	CA	USA	Brave New World
64/	Norwalk	CA	USA	
64/	Pomona	CA	USA	Broadside
64/	Pomona	CA	USA	Broadside
64/	Torrance	CA	USA	Tom Cat
64/05/10	Pomona	CA	USA	Broadside
64/65	Pomona	CA	USA	Red Flame
65/	Los Angeles	CA	USA	The Action
65/	Los Angeles	CA	USA	Cafe Unicorn
65/	Los Angeles	CA	USA	Canter's Delicatessen
65/	Los Angeles	CA	USA	Cosmo Alley Cafe
65/	Los Angeles	CA	USA	The Trip
65/11/	Los Angeles	CA	USA	Whisky A Go-Go
65/11/06	San Francisco	CA	USA	Longshoremen's Hall
65/12/	Los Angeles	CA	USA	Whisky A-Go-Go
66/	San Francisco?	CA?	USA	Avalon Ballroom
66/02-03/		TX	USA	
66/03-04/	Los Angeles	CA	USA	
66/03/		TX	USA	
66/04/07-16	Waikiki	HI	USA	Da Swamp
66/05/	Hayward	CA	USA	Frenchie's
66/05/	San Diego	CA	USA	
66/05/	Seattle	WA	USA	
66/05/27-29	San Francisco	CA	USA	Fillmore Auditorium
66/06/03-04	San Francisco	CA	USA	Fillmore Auditorium
66/06/24-25	San Francisco	CA	USA	Fillmore Auditorium
66/07/	Bethesda	MD	USA	Kerby Scott Dance Party
66/07/	Dallas	TX	USA	TV Show
66/07/	Detroit	MI	USA	TV Show
66/07/	Washington	DC	USA	Roundtable Restaurant
66/07/	Windsor	Ontario	Canada	TV Show
66/07/12	Los Angeles?	CA?	USA	Swingin' Time
66/07/23	Los Angeles	CA	USA	Danish Center
66/07/23	Los Angeles?	CA?	USA	Dave Prince's Club 1270
66/08/13	Los Angeles	CA	USA	Shrine Exposition Hall
66/09/	Los Angeles	CA	USA	Lindy Opera House
66/09/09	San Francisco	CA	USA	Fillmore Auditorium
66/09/10	San Francisco	CA	USA	Scottish Rites Temple
66/09/17	Los Angeles	CA	USA	Shrine Exposition Hall
66/09/27	Los Angeles	CA	USA	Whisky A-Go-Go
66/10/02	Los Angeles	CA	USA	Whisky A-Go-Go
66/10/29	Santa Barbara	CA	USA	Earl Warren Showgrounds
66/11/	Detroit	MI	USA	
66/12/09	East Lansing	MI	USA	Michigan Union
66/12/16-17	New York	NY	USA	Balloon Farm
66/12/23-31	New York	NY	USA	Balloon Farm
67/	Los Angeles	CA	USA	Whisky A-Go-Go
67/01/	Los Angeles	CA	USA	
67/01/07-21	Montreal	Quebec	Canada	New Penelope
67/02/03-04	Los Angeles	CA	USA	Lindy Opera House
67/02/17-19	San Francisco	CA	USA	Fillmore Auditorium
67/03/03-05	San Francisco	CA	USA	Fillmore Auditorium
67/03/23-04/03	New York	NY	USA	Garrick Theatre (2 shows midweek, 3 shows sat/sun)
67/04/		MD	USA	University Of Maryland
67/04/	New York	NY	USA	Garrick Theatre
67/04/06-19	New York	NY	USA	Garrick Theatre
67/05/	Boston	MA	USA	Psychedelic Supermarket
67/05/	Toronto	Ontario	Canada	
67/05/02-21	New York	NY	USA	Cafe Au Gogo (2 shows midweek, 3 shows sat/sun)
67/05/24-09/05	New York	NY	USA	Garrick Theatre (2 shows Su/Tu/W/Th, 3 shows F/Sa)
67/06/28	New York	NY	USA	Village Theater
67/09/	Buffalo	NY	USA	
67/09/	Cincinnati	OH	USA	
67/09/	Detroit	MI	USA	

67/09/	Miami	FL	USA	
67/09/	New York	NY	USA	Town Hall
67/09/23	London		UK	Royal Albert Hall
67/09/24	Amsterdam		Netherlands	Concertgebouw
67/09/30	Stockholm		Sweden	Konserthuset
67/10/	Copenhagen		Denmark	Tivoli
67/10/	London		UK	The Speakeasy
67/10/	London		UK	Royal Albert Hall
67/10/	New York	NY	USA	Garrick Theatre
67/10/01	Copenhagen		Denmark	Falkoner Theatret
67/10/02	Lund		Sweden	Olympen
67/10/28	Rochester	NY	USA	War Memorial Theater
67/11/	Providence	RI	USA	
67/11/03	Baltimore	MD	USA	Eastern High School
67/12/	Chicago	Il	USA	International Amphitheater
67/12/01	Detroit	MI	USA	Ford Auditorium
67/12/02-03	Ann Arbor	MI	USA	Fifth Dimension (2 shows12/02)
67/12/09	Pasadena	CA	USA	Civic Auditorium
67/12/14	San Francisco	CA	USA	Fillmore Auditorium
67/12/15-16	San Francisco	CA	USA	Winterland
67/12/22-23	New York	NY	USA	Town Hall
67/12/26-31	Philadelphia	PA	USA	Trauma
68/	Syracuse	NY	USA	War Memorial Theater
68/01/	Louisville	KY	USA	
68/01/	Miami	FL	USA	Thee Image
68/01/	New York	NY	USA	Town Hall
68/01/28	Toronto	Ontario	Canada	Convocation Hall, University Of Toronto
68/02/	Birmingham		UK	
68/02/01	Boston	MA	USA	Boston Tea Party
68/02/01	London		UK	Royal Albert Hall
68/02/29	New York	NY	USA	Hilton Hotel
68/03/	Berkeley	CA	USA	Community Theater
68/03/04	Fullerton	CA	USA	
68/03/15-16	Miami	Fl	USA	Thee Image
68/03/22-24	Philadelphia	PA	USA	Electric Factory (2 shows 03/24)
68/04/	Philadelphia	PA	USA	Arena
68/04/09	Chicago	IL	USA	International Amphitheatre
68/04/10	Detroit	MI	USA	Grande Ballroom
68/04/19-20	New York	NY	USA	Fillmore East (2 shows)
68/04/26	Cincinnati	OH	USA	Taft Auditorium (2 shows)
68/04/27	Chicago	IL	USA	Coliseum
68/04/28	Detroit	MI	USA	Grande Ballroom (2 shows)
68/05/	Berkeley	CA	USA	Community Theater
68/05/	Louisville	KY	USA	
68/05/	Miami	FL	USA	Thee Image
68/05/03	Denver	CO	USA	The Dog
68/05/10-11	Los Angeles	CA	USA	Shrine Exposition Hall
68/05/18	Hallandale	FL	USA	Gulfstream Park
68/05/25	Fresno	CA	USA	Selland Arena
68/05/29	Farmington	UT	USA	Lagoon
68/06	Detroit	MI	USA	Grande Ballroom
68/06/	Phoenix	AZ	USA	Veterans Memorial Coliseum?
68/06/	San Bernardino	CA	USA	Swing Auditorium
68/06/	Santa Barbara	CA	USA	
68/06/	Seattle	WA	USA	
68/06/	Tucson	AZ	USA	
68/06/01	San Diego	CA?	USA	Community Concourse
68/06/03	Los Angeles	CA	USA	Shrine Exposition Hall
68/06/06	San Francisco	CA	USA	Fillmore West
68/06/07-08	San Francisco	CA	USA	Winterland
68/06/21	San Jose	CA	USA	Civic Auditorium
68/06/28-30	Los Angeles	CA	USA	Cheetah
68/07/	Chicago	IL	USA	Kinetic Playground
68/07/	Santa Monica	CA	USA	
68/07/14	Los Angeles	CA	USA	Cheetah
68/07/23	Los Angeles	CA	USA	Whisky A-Go-Go
68/08/	Joey Bishop TV Show			
68/08/	Steve Allen TV Show			
68/08/	Baltimore	MD	USA	
68/08/	Elgin	IL	USA	
68/08/	Houston	TX	USA	The Catacombs

Date	City	State	Country	Venue
68/08/	Lake Geneva	IL	USA	Playboy Club
68/08/	Miami	FL	USA	Thee Image
68/08/03	New York	NY	USA	Wollman Rink, Central Park (2 shows)
68/08/09-10	Milwaukee	WI	USA	The Scene
68/08/24	Seattle	WA	USA	Seattle Center Arena
68/08/25	Vancouver	BC	Canada	Kerrisdale Arena
68/08/30	Dallas	TX	USA	Memorial Auditorium
68/09/	Los Angeles	CA	USA	Pandora's Box
68/09/15	Pasadena	CA	USA	Rose Bowl
68/09/17	Los Angeles	CA	USA	
68/09/27	Bremen		Germany	
68/09/28	Essen		Germany	Grugahalle
68/09/30	Frankfurt		Germany	
68/10/	London		England	Colour Me Pop
68/10/	Vienna		Austria	
68/10/	Worcester		UK	
68/10/01	Stockholm		Sweden	Konserthuset
68/10/03	Copenhagen		Denmark	Tivoli Gardens
68/10/04	Hamburg		Germany	Market Hall
68/10/06	Bremen		Germany	Beat Club
68/10/09	Munich		Germany	Deutsches Museum Kongressaal
68/10/10	Paris		France	Olympia
68/10/16	Berlin		Germany	SportPalast
68/10/20	Amsterdam		Netherlands	Concertgebouw (2 shows)
68/10/23	London		England	Colour Me Pop TV Show
68/10/25	London		England	Royal Festival Hall (2 shows)
68/10/28	Paris		France	Olympia
68/11/	Toronto	Ontario	Canada	
68/11/08	Fullerton	CA	USA	Cal State Fullerton Gymnasium
68/11/30	Berkeley	CA	USA	Community Theater
68/12/	Philadelphia	PA	USA	Spectrum
68/12/06-07	Los Angeles	CA	USA	Shrine Exposition Hall
69/			Germany	
69/			Denmark	
69/			France	
69/	Los Angeles	CA	USA	Shrine Exposition Hall
69/01/24-25	Los Angeles	CA	USA	Shrine Exposition Hall (2 shows)
69/01/31	Boston	MA	USA	War Memorial Auditorium
69/02/	Boston	MA	USA	The Ark
69/02/	Stratford	CT	USA	Ballroom
69/02/07-08	Miami	FL	USA	Thee Image
69/02/11-12	Philadelphia	PA	USA	Electric Factory
69/02/13	New York	NY	USA	The Factory
69/02/14	New York	NY	USA	McMillin Theater, Columbia University (2 shows)
69/02/15	Madison	NJ	USA	Drew University
69/02/21-22	New York	NY	USA	Fillmore East (2 shows)
69/02/23	Toronto	Ontario	Canada	Rock-Pile (2 shows)
69/03/		RI	USA	
69/03/	Allentown	PA	USA	
69/03/	Baltimore	MD	USA	
69/03/	Boston	MA	USA	
69/03/	Chicago	IL	USA	
69/03/	Hartford	CT	USA	Hartford Ballroom
69/03/	Montreal	Quebec	Canada	
69/03/	Rochester	NY	USA	War Memorial Theater
69/03/	Syracuse	NY	USA	
69/03/01	Westbury	NY	USA	Westbury Music Fair
69/03/02	Philadelphia	PA	USA	Arena
69/03/15	Fullerton	CA	USA	Cal State University
69/03/31	Los Angeles	CA	USA	Aquarius Theatre
69/04/	Long Island	NY	USA	
69/04/	New York	NY	USA	Columbia University
69/04/12	San Diego	CA	USA	Convention Hall
69/04/18	Vancouver	BC	Canada	Agrodome
69/04/19	Seattle	WA	USA	Seattle Center Arena
69/04/26	Allentown	PA	USA	Muhlenberg College Memorial Hall
69/04/27	Baltimore	MD	USA	Civic Center
69/05/17	Detroit	MI	USA	Ford Auditorium
69/05/19	Toronto	Ontario	Canada	Massey Hall
69/05/23	Appleton	WI	USA	Memorial Chapel, Lawrence University
69/05/30	Birmingham		UK	Town Hall (2 shows)

69/05/31	Newcastle		UK	City Hall (2 shows)
69/06/01	Manchester		UK	Palace Theatre (2 shows)
69/06/03	Bristol		UK	Colston Hall (2 shows)
69/06/05	Portsmouth		UK	Guild Hall (2 shows)
69/06/06	London		UK	Royal Albert Hall
69/06/07	Paris		France	Olympia
69/06/13-14	New York	NY	USA	Fillmore East
69/06/27	Denver	CO	USA	Mile High Stadium
69/06/28	Charlotte	NC	USA	Coliseum
69/06/29	Miami	FL	USA	Jai Alai Fronton
69/07/	Minneapolis	MN	USA	Tyrone Guthrie Theater
69/07/05	Newport	RI	USA	Festival Field
69/07/11	Philadelphia	PA	USA	Spectrum
69/07/12	Laurel	MD	USA	Laurel Race Track
69/08/		SC	USA	
69/08/	Minneapolis	MN	USA	Tyrone Guthrie Theater
69/08/02	New York	NY	USA	Wollman Rink, Central Park
69/08/03	Atlantic City	NJ	USA	Atlantic City Race Track
69/08/06	Highland Park	IL	USA	Ravinia Outdoor Music Center
69/08/08	Framingham	MA	USA	Carousel Theater
69/08/10	Warrensville Heights	OH	USA	Musicarnival
69/08/15	Ottawa	Ontario	Canada	National Arts Center (2 shows)
69/08/16-18	Montreal	Quebec	Canada	International Bandshell, (2 shows 08/16 and 08/17)
69/08/19	Ottawa	Ontario	Canada	CJOH-TV show
70/	Appleton	WI	USA	
70/	Beloit	WI	USA	
70/	Jacksonville	FL	USA	Auditorium
70/	Lake Geneva	WI	USA	
70/02/08	San Diego	CA	USA	Sports Arena
70/03/	Los Angeles	CA	USA	USC? UCLA?
70/03/07	Los Angeles	CA	USA	Olympic Auditorium
70/03/20	Los Angeles	CA	USA	Hollywood Palladium
70/04/	El Monte	CA	USA	Legion Stadium
70/04/	Madison	WI	USA	
70/04/	Miami	FL	USA	
70/04/19	Berkeley	CA	USA	Community Theater
70/05/06	Chicago	IL	USA	Auditorium Theater (2 shows)
70/05/08-09	New York	NY	USA	Fillmore East (2 shows each night)
70/05/10	Philadelphia	PA	USA	Academy Of Music
70/05/15	Los Angeles	CA	USA	Pauley Pavilion, UCLA
70/06/	Amsterdam		Netherlands	Paradiso
70/06/12	San Antonio	TX	USA	Municipal Auditorium
70/06/13	Atlanta	GA	USA	Atlanta Stadium
70/06/18	Uddel		Netherlands	VPRO TV
70/06/28	Shepton Mallet		UK	Bath & West Showground
70/07/01	Highland Park	IL	USA	Ravinia Outdoor Music Center
70/07/03-04	Indianapolis	IN	USA	Middlearth
70/07/05	Minneapolis	MN	USA	Tyrone Guthrie Theater (2 shows)
70/08/09	Port Chester	NY	USA	Capitol Theatre
70/08/21	Santa Monica	CA	USA	Civic Auditorium
70/09/17	Calgary	Alberta	Canada	Jubilee Auditorium
70/09/18	Edmonton	Alberta	Canada	Kinsmen Field House
70/09/19	Vancouver	BC	Canada	Coliseum
70/09/22	Portland	OR	USA	Pamplin Sports Arena, Lewis & Clark College
70/09/25-26	San Rafael	CA	USA	Pepperland
70/10/04	San Diego	CA	USA	Peterson Gym, San Diego State University
70/10/08	San Antonio	TX	USA	Memorial Center, Trinity University
70/10/09	Tallahassee	FL	USA	Tully Gymnasium, Florida State University
70/10/16-17	Port Chester	NY	USA	Capitol Theatre
70/10/18	Boston	MA	USA	Boston Tea Party (2 shows)
70/10/21	Cincinnati?	OH?	USA	Music Hall
70/10/25	Minneapolis	MN	USA	Depot (2 shows)
70/11/05-07	San Francisco	CA	USA	Fillmore West
70/11/13-14	New York	NY	USA	Fillmore East (2 shows each night)
70/11/20	Columbus	OH	USA	Veterans Memorial Stadium (2 shows)
70/11/21	Chicago	IL	USA	Auditorium Theatre
70/11/26	Liverpool		UK	Mountford Hall
70/11/27	Manchester		UK	Free Trade Hall
70/11/29	London		UK	Coliseum (2 shows?)
70/12/01	Stockholm		Sweden	Konserthuset (2 shows?)
70/12/02	Copenhagen		Denmark	KB-Hallen

70/12/04	Hamburg		Germany	
70/12/05	Frankfurt		Germany	Kongresshalle
70/12/06	Amsterdam		Netherlands	Concertgebouw (2 shows)
70/12/08	Duesseldorf		Germany	Tonhalle
70/12/12	Vienna		Austria	Konzerthaus
70/12/13	Munich		Germany	
70/12/14	Rotterdam		Netherlands	De Doelen
70/12/15	Paris		France	Palais Gaumont
70/12/16	Brussels		Belgium	Paleis voor Schone Kunsten
70/12/17	Lille		France	
70/71	Eugene	OR	USA	
71/	Chicago	IL	USA	
71/	Harrisburg	PA	USA	State Farm Show Building
71/	San Francisco	CA	USA	Fillmore West
71/05/09	Los Angeles	CA	USA	Whisky A Go-Go
71/05/18	Claremont	CA	USA	Bridges Auditorium, Pomona College
71/05/21	Chicago	IL	USA	Auditorium Theatre
71/05/22	Delaware	OH	USA	Selby Field, Ohio Wesleyan University
71/05/23	Columbus	OH	USA	Ohio Theater
71/05/25	Detroit	MI	USA	
71/05/27	Madison	WI	USA	Field House, University Of Wisconsin
71/05/29	Rochester	MI	USA	Baldwin Pavilion, Oakland University
71/06/	Virginia Beach	VA	USA	
71/06/05-06	New York	NY	USA	Fillmore East (2 shows each day)
71/07/02	Quebec	Quebec	Canada	Le Colisee
71/07/03	Ottawa	Ontario	Canada	Civic Center Arena
71/07/04	Montreal	Quebec	Canada	Centre Paul Sauve
71/07/05	Montreal	Quebec	Canada	CHOM-FM
71/07/08	Winnipeg	Manitoba	Canada	Arena
71/07/09	Edmonton	Alberta	Canada	Kinsmen Field House
71/07/10	Vancouver	BC	Canada	Agrodome
71/08/07	Los Angeles	CA	USA	Pauley Pavilion, UCLA
71/08/25	Berkeley	CA	USA	Community Theater
71/08/26	Seattle	WA	USA	Convention Center
71/08/28	Portland	OR	USA	Memorial Coliseum
71/08/29	Spokane	WA	USA	Kennedy Pavillion, Gonzaga University
71/10/	Virginia Beach	VA	USA	
71/10/01	Sacramento	CA	USA	Memorial Auditorium
71/10/06	Boston	MA	USA	Music Hall (2 shows)
71/10/08	New Haven	CT	USA	Arena
71/10/09	Springfield	MA	USA	John M. Greene Hall
71/10/11	New York	NY	USA	Carnegie Hall (2 shows)
71/10/13	Toronto	Ontario	Canada	Massey Hall
71/10/15	Providence	RI	USA	Lowes State Theater
71/10/16	Stony Brook	NY	USA	SUNY (2 shows)
71/10/17	Baltimore	MD	USA	Lyric Theatre (2 shows)
71/10/19	Indianapolis	IN	USA	Coliseum
71/10/21	St. Louis	MO	USA	Fox Theatre
71/10/23	Kansas City	MO	USA	Cowtown Ballroom (2 shows)
71/10/24	Denver	CO	USA	University of Denver Arena
71/11/	ABC TV		USA	
71/11/	Louisville	KY	USA	
71/11/17			Italy	
71/11/19	Stockholm		Sweden	Folkets Hus
71/11/20	Aarhus		Denmark	
71/11/21	Copenhagen		Denmark	KB-Hallen (2 shows)
71/11/22	Odense		Denmark	
71/11/23	Duesseldorf		Germany	Rheinhalle
71/11/24	Berlin		Germany	Deutschlandhalle
71/11/26	Hamburg		Germany	
71/11/27	Rotterdam		Netherlands	The Ahoy
71/11/28	Frankfurt		Germany	Jahrhunderthalle (2 shows)
71/11/29	Munich		Germany	Zirkus Krone
71/11/30	Vienna		Austria	
71/12/03	Milan		Italy	
71/12/04	Montreux		Switzerland	Casino
71/12/10	London		UK	Rainbow Theater
72/09/10	Los Angeles		CA	Hollywood Bowl
72/09/15	Berlin		Germany	Deutschlandhalle
72/09/16	London		UK	Oval Cricket Ground
72/09/17	The Hague		Netherlands	Houtrust Hallen

Date	City	State	Country	Venue
72/09/18	Copenhagen		Denmark	
72/09/22-23	New York	NY	USA	Felt Forum
72/09/24	Boston	MA	USA	Music Hall
72/10/27	Montreal	Quebec	Canada	Forum
72/10/28	Syracuse	NY	USA	War Memorial Theater
72/10/29	Binghamton	USA	NY	Men's Gym, Harpur College
72/10/31	Passaic	NJ	USA	Capitol Theater (2 shows)
72/11/	Bloomington	IN	USA	
72/11/	Detroit	MI	USA	Cobo Hall
72/11/01	Waterbury	CT	USA	Palace Theater
72/11/03	Richmond	VA	USA	Syria Mosque
72/11/04	Charlotte	NC	USA	Park Center
72/11/05	Columbia	SC	USA	
72/11/07	Commack	NY	USA	Long Island Arena
72/11/10	Philadelphia	PA	USA	Irvine Auditorium University Of Pennsylvania (2 shows)
72/11/11	Washington	DC	USA	DAR Constitution Hall (2 shows)
72/11/12	Providence	RI	USA	Palace Theater
72/12/02	Kansas City	MO	USA	Cowtown Ballroom (2 shows)
72/12/03	Lincoln	NE	USA	Pershing Auditorium
72/12/08	Vancouver	BC	Canada	Agrodome
72/12/09	Portland	OR	USA	Paramount Northwest Theatre (2 shows)
72/12/10	Seattle	WA	USA	Paramount Theatre (2 shows)
72/12/15	San Francisco	CA	USA	Winterland

Titles available from SAF and Firefly Publishing

No More Mr Nice Guy: The Inside Story of The Alice Cooper Group
By Michael Bruce and Billy James UK Price £11.99
The dead babies, the drinking, executions and, of course, the rock 'n' roll.

Procol Harum: Beyond The Pale
by Claes Johansen UK Price £12.99
Distinctive, ground breaking and enigmatic British band from the 60s.

An American Band: The Story of Grand Funk Railroad
By Billy James UK Price £12.99
One of the biggest grossing US rock 'n' roll acts of the 70s - selling millions of records and playing sold out arenas the world over. Hype, Politics & rock 'n' roll - unbeatable!

Wish The World Away: Mark Eitzel and American Music Club
by Sean Body UK Price £12.99
Sean Body has written a fascinating biography of Eitzel which portrays an artist tortured by demons, yet redeemed by the aching beauty of his songs.

Go Ahead John! The Music of John McLaughlin
by Paul Stump UK Price £12.99
One of the greatest jazz musicians of all time. Includes his work with Miles Davis, Mahavishnu Orchestra, Shakti. Full of insights into all stages of his career.

Lunar Notes: Zoot Horn Rollo's Captain Beefheart Experience
by Bill Harkleroad and Billy James UK Price £11.95
For the first time we get the insider's story of what it was like to record and play with an eccentric genius such as Beefheart, by Bill Harkleroad - Zoot himself!

Meet The Residents: America's Most Eccentric Band
by Ian Shirley UK Price £11.95
An outsider's view of The Residents' operations, exposing a world where nothing is as it seems. It is a fascinating tale of musical anarchy and cartoon wackiness. Reprinted to coincide with the recent world tour.

Digital Gothic: A Critical Discography of Tangerine Dream
by Paul Stump UK Price £9.95
For the very first time German electronic pioneers, Tangerine Dream mammoth output is placed within an ordered perspective.

The One and Only - Homme Fatale: Peter Perrett & The Only Ones
by Nina Antonia UK Price £11.95
An extraordinary journey through crime, punishment and the decadent times of British punk band leader, Peter Perrett of The Only Ones

Plunderphonics, 'Pataphysics and Pop Mechanics
The Leading Exponents of Musique Actuelle
By Andrew Jones UK Price £12.95
Chris Cutler, Fred Frith, Henry Threadgill, John Oswald, John Zorn, etc.

Kraftwerk: Man, Machine and Music
By Pascal Bussy UK Price £11.95
The full story behind one of the most influential bands in the history of rock.

Wrong Movements: A Robert Wyatt History
by Mike King UK Price £14.95
A journey through Wyatt's 30 year career with Soft Machine, Matching Mole & solo artist.

Wire: Everybody Loves A History
by Kevin Eden UK Price £9.95
British punk's most endearing and enduring bands combining Art and Attitude

Tape Delay: A Documentary of Industrial Music
by Charles Neal
Marc Almond, Cabaret Voltaire, Nick Cave, Chris & Cosey, Coil, Foetus, Neubauten, Non, The Fall, New Order, Psychic TV, Rollins, Sonic Youth, Swans, Test Dept and many more...

Dark Entries: Bauhaus and Beyond
by Ian Shirley UK Price £11.95
The gothic rise of Bauhaus, Love & Rockets, Tones on Tail, Murphy, J, and Ash solo.

Gentle Giant – Acquiring The Taste
by Paul Stump. Price: To be confirmed.
Based around the Shulman brothers, Gentle Giant quickly acquired a large cult following the world over. Their music has endured over time and new generations are as entranced by their intricate sound as were audiences of 30 years ago.

Time of the Season: A History of The Zombies
by Claes Johansen Price: to be confirmed.
Formed in 1963, The Zombies featured Rod Argent and Colin Blunstone. Their undenied masterpiece, the album Odessey & Oracle, was recorded at Abbey Road during that famous Summer of 1967 and featured the classic "Time Of The Season" and recently made Mojo's best 100 LPs of all time.

Poison Heart: Surviving The Ramones
by Dee Dee Ramone and Veronica KofmanUK Price £11.95
Dee Dee's crushingly honest account of life as junkie and Ramone. A great rock story!

Minstrels In The Gallery: A History Of Jethro Tull
by David Rees UK Price £12.99
At Last! To coincide with their 30th anniversary, a full history of one of the most popular and inventive bands of the past three decades

DANCEMUSICSEXROMANCE: Prince - The First Decade
by Per Nilsen UK Price £12.99
A portrait of Prince's reign as the most exciting black performer to emerge since James Brown and Jimi Hendrix.

Soul Sacrifice: The Santana Story
by Simon Leng UK Price £12.99
In depth study of seventies Latin guitar legend whose career began at Woodstock through to a 1999 number one US album.

Opening The Musical Box: A Genesis Chronicle
by Alan Hewitt UK Price £12.99
Drawing on hours of new interviews and packed with insights, anecdotes and trivia, here is the ultimat compendium to one of the most successful and inventive bands of the modern rock era.

Blowin' Free: Thirty Years Of Wishbone Ash
by Gary Carter and Mark Chatterton UK Price £12.99
Packed with memorabilia, many rare photos, a definitive discography and utilising unprecedented access to band members and associates, Gary Carter and Mark Chatterton have charted the long and sometimes turbulent career of one of England's premier rock outfits.

To Hell and Back with Catatonia
by Brian Wright UK price £12.99
Fronted by the brassy, irrepressible Cerys Matthews, Catatonia exploded onto the British pop scene in 1998 with hits like 'Mulder and Scully' and 'Road Rage'. Author Brian Wright has been an ardent Catatonia supporter since their earliest days. Drawing on first hand experience, new interviews and years of research, he charts their struggle from obscure 1993 Cardiff pub gigs to the Top Ten.

The Manic Steet Preachers – Prole Art Threat
by Ben Roberts UK price £12.99
Prole Art Threat takes a fresh look at one of the most controversial and important bands of the recent rock era. Drawing on new research and hours of interviews with band insiders, the first book from 21-year-old Ben Roberts charts the Manics' progress from Blackwood misfits to rock iconoclasts.

Mail Order

All SAF and Firefly titles are available by mail order from the world famous
Helter Skelter bookshop.
You can either phone or fax your order to Helter Skelter on the following
numbers:

Telephone: +44 (0)20 7836 1151 or Fax: +44 (0)20 7240 9880
Office hours: Mon-Fri 10:00am - 7:00pm, Sat: 10:00am - 6:00pm,
Sun: closed.

Postage prices per book worldwide are as follows:

UK & Channel Islands	£1.50
Europe & Eire (air)	£2.95
USA, Canada (air)	£7.50
Australasia, Far East (air)	£9.00
Overseas (surface)	£2.50

You can also write enclosing a cheque, International Money Order, or registered
cash. Please include postage. DO NOT send cash. DO NOT send foreign cur-
rency, or cheques drawn on an overseas bank. Send to:

Helter Skelter Bookshop,
4 Denmark Street, London, WC2H 8LL, United Kingdom.
If you are in London come and visit us, and browse the titles in person!!

Email: helter@skelter.demon.co.uk
Website: http://www.skelter.demon.co.uk

For the latest on SAF and Firefly titles check the SAF website:
www.safpublishing.com

About the Author

...960 and a native of North Carolina, graduated from Berklee College of ...ved to Los Angeles in 1983 to work with guitarist Steve Vai. James ...ai's first solo album *Flex-Able*. Through Steve Vai, James met Frank Zappa ...ging various ideas on rhythm with him throughout the early 1980s (some of ...ed in James' unpublished text book on rhythmic theory). Throughout the mid-...in Los Angeles, James recorded drums, tablas and percussion for various album

...39 James unveiled his secret musical project, ANT-BEE, and subsequently signed to ...omp Records in L.A., who released the album *ANT-BEE - Pure Electric Honey* in 1990. ...album received rave reviews, especially in Europe, and ANT-BEE was catapulted to cult ...tus. In 1992 James linked up with members of the ex-Mothers Of Invention (Frank Zappa's ...rst group) and recorded the album *ANT-BEE With My Favorite Vegetables And Other Bizarre Muzik* for Divine Records UK. In 1994 James decided to return to North Carolina to work on the third ANT-BEE album.

Once on the East Coast he connected with ex-Alice Cooper Group guitarist and songwriter Michael Bruce. James recorded and toured throughout 1995 with Michael Bruce, and co-wrote a book with Bruce about his Alice Cooper days entitled *No More Mr. Nice Guy*. The book was released on SAF Publishing UK in 1996 and was a best seller in Europe. 1997 saw the release of ANT-BEE's *Lunar Muzik* CD, also on Divine Records UK, and featured guest performances by ex-Mothers Of Invention, ex-Alice Cooper Group members and Daevid Allen of Gong.

In 1998, James co-wrote a book about Captain Beefheart and the Magic Band with original guitarist Bill Harkleroad (Zoot Horn Rollo) entitled *Lunar Notes* (also on SAF). As well as the completion of *An American Band,* a book detailing the history of US legends Grand Funk Railroad (SAF), 1998 also saw James recording the fourth ANT-BEE album *Electronic Church Muzik*, which features previous guest stars, as well as Jan Akkerman, Peter Banks, Zoot Horn Rollo and Gilli Smyth. Also, James was project co-ordinator and guest artist on guitarist Bruce Cameron's *Midnight Daydream* CD, which featured Jack Bruce, Mitch Mitchell, the Band Of Gypsies and other legendary artists. James is in the process of completing books on Todd Rundgren and Peter Banks.

Contact: Glass Onyon Distribution, PO Box 207, Carolina Beach, NC28428-0207 USA.
Fax: 910 793 0650

Ant-Bee's Web Bizarre: http://ourworld.compuserve.com/homepages/antbee/

saf publishing

www.safpublishing.com